Elizabeth George

HARVEST HOUSE PUBLISHERS

EUGENE, OREGON

Harvest House Publishers has made every effort to trace the ownership of all poems and quotes. In the event of a question arising from the use of a poem or quote, we regret any error made and will be pleased to make the necessary correction in future editions of this book.

Italics in Scripture verses indicate author emphasis.

*Cover photo © Trinette Reed / Blend Images / Alamy*

*Cover by Dugan Design Group, Bloomington, Minnesota*

**WALKING WITH THE WOMEN OF THE BIBLE**
Adapted from *Women Who Loved God*

Published 2008 by Harvest House Publishers
Eugene, Oregon 97402
www.harvesthousepublishers.com

Library of Congress Cataloging-in-Publication Data

George, Elizabeth
[Women who loved God]
Walking with the women of the Bible / Elizabeth George.
p. cm.
ISBN 978-0-7369-2377-4 (pbk.)
1. Women Prayers and devotions. 2. Women in the Bible Meditations. I. Title.
BV4844.G433 2008
242.'643—dc22

2007039196



**Printed in the United States of America**

11 12 13 14 15 / VP-NI / 10 9 8 7 6 5

# A Note from Elizabeth

Do you love God and want to know more about Him? About how He helps and sustains His people...including you? Are you looking for ways to handle hard times? Guidelines for making better decisions? Or are you unsure how to live out your love for Him? Perhaps you'd like a mentor—a woman who's followed Jesus for a long time and wants to help you in your faith walk?

Through insightful readings focused on the women of the Bible you'll discover how God leads, encourages, uses, and works in the lives of people. Written just for you, these devotions are for today's woman and are practical, helpful, and hands on. The women in God's Word have shown me—and they'll show you too—how to live out the Lord's plan and will right now...today! I'll also share the wisdom He's taught me through my many years of living for Him. Together we'll explore how to follow and serve Him wholeheartedly, how to love others more thoroughly, how to strengthen our trust in Him, and how to put wings on our dreams.

May your journey to greater faith be filled with joy, delight, and adventure each step of the way. You'll never be the same after walking with the women of the Bible!

Your friend in Him,

Elizabeth George

## 1 Reflecting God's Glory

*God created man in His own image.*
GENESIS 1:27

*Do you know you were created in the image of God?* When God created woman, He created her in His image. Let this sink into your heart and mind. You are creative, intelligent, and rational because you were created in God's image!

*Do you know you are a reflection of God's glory?* That's what being created in His image means. You reflect Him to other people. Every time you reach out in love, perform a deed of kindness, soften your heart in forgiveness, show a little extra patience, and follow through in faithfulness, other people experience the character of God through you!

Do you know you are created to have fellowship and communion with God? "God is faithful, by whom you were called into the fellowship of His Son, Jesus Christ our Lord" (1 Corinthians 1:9).

As a reflection of God's glory, why not…

*Resolve* never to criticize or downgrade yourself, but instead
*Rejoice* that you are fearfully and wonderfully made.

*Resolve* to walk by faith paths you may not understand and
*Rejoice* in the promise of His nearness as He directs your way.

*Resolve* to live as a child of God through His Son, Jesus Christ, and
*Rejoice* that as God's child your name is written in heaven.

*Resolve* to commune with God daily through prayer and Bible study, and
*Rejoice* in His strength each day and hope in Him for tomorrow.

*Resolve* to reflect His glory and
*Rejoice* in His love!

## 2 *Fairest of Creation*

*Male and female He created them.*
GENESIS 1:27

God had been busy for six days creating His beautiful new world. The stage was set. The Creator's magnificent scenery was finished and in place. His sun, moon, and stars lit up His perfect planet. All creatures great and small enjoyed a perfect environment. Yet God wasn't quite finished. At last He presented His masterpieces to the rest of nature. First the man, Adam. Then—finally and dramatically—the woman, Eve.

Devised by a perfect God, Eve reflected His divine perfection in her femaleness. Created for a position of honor, woman was born to life's loveliest, most lofty throne of glory—"the glory of man" (1 Corinthians 11:7). What can you do to revel in your femaleness?

- *Accept your femininity.* There's no need to feel inferior, second-class, or second-rate. Woman was God's last creation. After God presented woman He proclaimed His creation "very good." Adam and Eve were alike, yet different. One was male and one female. Together as well as individually they reflected God's image and glory.
- *Embrace your womanhood.* Own your loveliness, your uniqueness, your beauty as a female. Delight yourself in God's handiwork—in being a woman.
- *Cultivate your femininity.* This book is about the gracious, glorious, beautiful, prized-by-God women of the Bible. As you read, allow God's truths to permeate your understanding. You are of very high value to Him!
- *Excel in your role as a woman.* As God's woman, be the best of the best. Delight in His perfect design, in His good and acceptable and perfect will for your life. He created you as a woman! As such, you join Eve's exalted position of "fairest of creation."[1]

## 3 The Mother of All Living

*Eve...was the mother of all living.*
GENESIS 3:20

"Guilty!" God pronounced after Adam's wife listened to the tempter, ate of the forbidden tree, and involved her husband in rebellion. It reverberated in Eve's heart and mind. There was no doubt about her guilt. But as darkness settled in, she heard Adam declare, "Your name shall be called 'Eve...the mother of all living.'" With these words Eve glimpsed a fresh ray of light.

Having been given a name filled with promise, Eve realized she, the guilty sinner, could still serve her gracious and forgiving God. How? By bearing Adam's children and becoming the mother of many generations (1 Corinthians 11:12). Her name reflected the role she would play in spiritual history.

"Eve." From death sprang life. From darkness, light. From the curse, a blessing. From a sentence of death, hope for the future. From the stinging despair of defeat, the strength of budding faith. Eve was the mother of all living!

Do you know your life counts too? True, you share Eve's sentence of physical death (Romans 5:12). But you also have life to give and pass on! How?

- You give life through your physical efforts to care for others.
- You share spiritual life by telling others about Jesus.
- You are the life of your home, bringing the sparkle of laughter and joy to other people.
- You pass physical life on to your children.
- You can pass the potential for eternal life on to your children by teaching them the gospel of Jesus Christ.

Feed your spiritual life by sending your roots deep into God's love. The energy of life, the purpose of life, all you have of life to pass on is from the Lord!

# 4 *All I Need*

***I have gotten a manchild with the help of the* L*ORD*.**
GENESIS 4:1 NASB

Things had begun so well. How Eve cherished her memory of Adam's delighted face when God gave her to him. They had been so happy together in the beautiful perfection of the Garden of Eden. Life had been wonderful until...No, she wouldn't think about what she'd done. About the serpent's lies. About inviting her precious husband to eat the forbidden fruit from the tree of knowledge. She shuddered, thinking of all the changes that had taken place...in her marriage...in her garden home...in her relationship with God.

Emotional pain was now part of Eve's daily life. And now she experienced physical pain like she'd never imagined possible. Childbirth was so hard. What could she do to ease the agony in her mind and her body? Where could she turn for help? God! The same Someone she'd defied. Yet He came to her rescue.

"I have gotten a manchild with the help of the LORD," Eve declared. I'm sure she went on in delight, "I've given birth to a baby—the first baby ever born!" How grateful she was to have the ever-present help of God amid her confusion and pain.

Knowledge of God's love and trustworthiness flooded and soothed Eve's sore soul. She knew she could lean on Him no matter what new challenges lie ahead. Eve was thankful.

Are you thankful? I hope so! You can be thankful that...

- you can trust God even though you've stumbled and fallen in the past
- you can trust God with any issue you face in the present
- you can trust God for whatever happens in the future

## 5 Hope When You're Hurting

*Adam knew his wife...and she bore a son.*
GENESIS 4:25

Loss tears at the heart, and Eve had suffered many. She lost...

- her perfect relationship with God (Genesis 3:8)
- the bliss of a sinless marriage (Genesis 3:12)
- her ideal home in the Garden of Eden (Genesis 3:23)
- her lack of acquaintance with evil (Genesis 3:22)
- her son Abel, murdered by his brother (Genesis 4:8)
- her son Cain, whom God sent away (Genesis 4:12)

She had little left to lose. Eve had dipped into her barrel of hope more times than she could count. How much did she have left?

But oh, the goodness of the Lord! "Adam knew his wife again, and she bore a son and named him Seth, 'For God has appointed another seed for me.'" The gift of Seth, whose name means "appointed," refilled Eve's barrel of hope. "Appointed" by God, Seth would be the one from whom God's Son would come, bringing bountiful and eternal hope to all mankind—including you!

How do you handle heartbreaking losses? Place your faith and confidence in these hope-filled realities:

*God's faithfulness.* "I know the plans I have for you... plans to prosper you and not to harm you, plans to give you hope and a future" (Jeremiah 29:11 NIV).

*God's promises.* Among the more than 8000 promises in the Bible[2] is the assurance that you can do all things through Christ who strengthens you (Philippians 4:13).

*God's goodness.* Although weeping may endure for a night, "joy comes in the morning" because the Lord is good. "His mercy is everlasting, and His truth endures to all generations" (Psalm 30:5 and 100:5).

## 6 A Boatload of Faith

*I will establish my covenant with you…and your wife.*
GENESIS 6:18 NIV

We don't know her name so let's call her "Mrs. Noah." She spent her days loving her husband, Noah, raising their three sons, and caring for their home. Daily life was simple…until "the call" came from the Lord.

Grieved over the wickedness of mankind, God decided to destroy humans, the animals of the fields, and the birds of the air. But Noah trusted and walked with God, so God chose to save him and his family. God told him to make an ark.

As Noah moved forward in obedience, Mrs. Noah may have mused, *What can I do? How can I help him fulfill God's plan?*

*Pray.* She could pray for mankind as God's judgment loomed, for her husband as he served the Lord, and for her family to also follow God.

*Encourage.* Husbands thrive on their wives' cheerful, hope-filled words of support. She could encourage Noah in his work.

*Believe.* She may have wondered about the ark and the flood possibility, but she could choose to believe.

*Help.* She could help with the animals and gather the food they'd need for their mysterious voyage of faith.

*Follow.* She could—by faith—follow her husband's leading day by day for 120 years, for 43,800 days…right into the ark of salvation that transported her family into an unknown future.

*Lord, I want to have faith that prays persistently, chooses righteousness, encourages fellow believers, helps Your kingdom, and follows You faithfully. Help me find strength for today and hope for tomorrow as I sail into the future You have for me.*

## 7 Trusting God in Your Journey

*So Noah went out, and his sons and his wife and his sons' wives with him.*
GENESIS 8:18

At last the voyage was over! All 371 days! Mrs. Noah remembered the many years her faithful husband had built the ark and the ridicule they withstood. However, trusting in God, they followed His strange instructions to the letter.

She'd gladly followed her husband into the finished ark. And she was thrilled that their sons and daughters-in-law chose to also. Regret for the people left behind, uncertainty about the future, and relief that God was with them flowed through her as God shut the door behind the Noahs, sealing them, the animals, and their cargo in the ark.

She was leaving the only home she had ever known and the people she grew up with. Where were they going? What would their new home be like? What would it be like without neighbors?

Statistics place a household move near the top of the stress scale—and no one had ever experienced a drastic move like the Noahs made! How do you handle the questions and uncertainties change brings? Like Mrs. Noah, you can choose, by faith, to believe...

- God is in control
- He knows what He's doing
- He has a plan and a purpose
- He knows what's best
- He'll take care of everything

Mrs. Noah stepped off the ark and into her new world. As a sign of encouragement, God hung a rainbow in the heavens. That beautiful object of promise shining through the clouds filled Mrs. Noah with comfort and hope...just as it does you today.

What changes are you facing? Ask your never-changing God to show you how you can grow with each step you take.

## 8 Trusting God One More Time

*Sarai was barren; she had no child.*
GENESIS 11:30

"Sarai was barren; she had no child." Seven words. A simple statement of cold, hard fact. Perhaps Sarai (whom God later called Sarah) wondered, *What's gone wrong? What have I done? Why hasn't God blessed me with children?* On and on her questioning went…and so did her pain. Nothing could relieve it, soothe it, take it away. Childlessness was a stigma that seared deeply into her soul with each childless sunrise.

Sarah was the wife of Abram (whose name was changed to Abraham) and a follower of God. She was barren for many years, but then God promised Abraham and Sarah a child in their old age. But the baby was a long time coming. With aching heart and stinging tears, Sarah trusted God one more time, for one more day, over and over. Despite a few setbacks, she learned that faith—instead of giving up, succumbing to bitterness, lashing out at others, turning her back on God, giving in to a contentious spirit, and manipulating the situation—is the best way to face the distresses of life.

For 11 years Sarah grabbed on to God's promise. That's more than 4000 "faith reaches"! Then God's promise was fulfilled and Isaac was born. Oh, how Abraham and Sarah must have rejoiced!

Faith, like physical muscle, is developed and strengthened with use. Each time you trust God as you face seemingly unbearable, unusual, unchangeable circumstances, your faith increases. Are you facing a difficult issue today? Reach out to God one more time! Turn toward the unknown, the unseen, the eternal, and watch your faith grow.

# 9 *Faith Means Moving Forward*

*[Abraham] took [Sarah] his wife...*
*to the land of Canaan.*
GENESIS 12:5

"Oh, the heartache! Will it ever go away?" Perhaps these words darkened Sarah's thoughts the day she followed her full-of-faith husband out of Haran. Leaving Haran was bad enough, but going to the land of Canaan made it even worse! Canaan was 600 miles away from her family and friends. Abraham had announced they were going to Nowhere Land, as far as Sarah was concerned.

Just when Sarah was getting used to Nowhere Land, a famine struck. They had to move to Egypt—300 miles away! *Oh, if only I were still in Haran,* Sarah may have thought.

But backward gazes can be dangerous and impede spiritual growth. But how can we look forward and faithfully follow God when circumstances are bad? Here's a great acronym!

***F****ace forward.* Real life happens in the present, and God's blessings happen now and in the future.

***A****ccept your circumstances.* God uses the difficulties of life to help you mature and grow in Him.

***I****f you're following God,* you will find Him in all your circumstances.

***T****rust in the Lord.* God will keep you in perfect peace when your mind is focused on Him.

***H****ope for the future.* God is a bright star who will light your path in the present darkness.

*Dear God of Sarai,*
*grant that such a one as I*
*may see the good in bad*
*and the faith to be had...*
*following Thee!*

# 10 You Are Beautiful

*You are a woman of beautiful countenance.*
Genesis 12:11

Every year women who desire greater physical beauty spend billions of dollars on makeup, hair treatments, dental work, cosmetic surgeries, and physical conditioning. There seems to be no price too high for beauty. Do you ever wish for greater beauty? Sarah, Abraham's wife, had just the opposite problem! God blessed her with great beauty. Even at birth it was obvious, and her proud parents appropriately named her Sarah, which means "princess." But beauty isn't always a blessing. Sarah's beauty was a blessing...and a curse.

One time when Abraham and Sarah were traveling in Egypt, people noticed her beauty...and word soon reached the Pharaoh. He sent for her and was captivated when they met. This impressive leader possessed massive military forces and great wealth, but he wanted one more thing—the beautiful Sarah.

This was exactly what Abraham predicted! In fact, when they entered Egypt he told Sarah to say she was his sister (she was a half-sister) instead of his wife. He was afraid someone would kill him to get to Sarah!

As you know, deceit always returns with a bite. We'll get to the rest of the story in the next devotion.

Why not take a quick minute right now and pray? God created you, and you are beautiful. Thank Him for that gift. His Word says you are fearfully and wonderfully made (Psalm 139:14). Look into the mirror of God's Word and adorn your heart with the wisdom found there, such as true beauty is found in a gentle and quiet spirit (1 Peter 3:4).

# 11 *A Strong and Constant Faith*

*The woman was taken to Pharaoh's house.*
GENESIS 12:15

In the last devotion Sarah was taken to Pharaoh's court because the ruler had heard of her great beauty. Although Abraham followed God in a mighty way, he was still human and imperfect. Because he feared someone would kill him to possess her, he'd asked Sarah to say she was his sister. She did as he asked, and now she was stuck in Pharaoh's harem!

Did fiery thoughts about Abraham rage in Sarah's heart? Did she think he was selfish to sacrifice her safety and well-being to preserve his life? Did she wonder with fear, *What will happen to me? Will I ever see Abraham again? What will life be like as a member of a harem? What will I do when Pharaoh calls for me?* Scripture doesn't record Sarah's thoughts or reaction. Don't you hope the silence indicates Sarah's faith remained strong and constant as she sat in her harem prison? That she steadfastly waited on the Lord for deliverance?

God's Word encourages us to trust in God in all circumstances. Whether you're facing trials today or life is going smoothly, turn to Him for wisdom and strength:

- Wait on the LORD; be of good courage, and He shall strengthen your heart (Psalm 27:14).
- Rest in the LORD, and wait patiently for Him (Psalm 37:7).
- Those who wait on the LORD shall renew their strength (Isaiah 40:31).

How can you develop stronger faith in the midst of a trial? Talk to God about your problem. Be assured of His love and care. Trust in His wisdom. Wait on His solution.

## 12 *God to the Rescue!*

*But the Lord plagued Pharaoh.*
GENESIS 12:17

We're in Egypt with…

- Sarah—Abraham's beautiful wife is currently in the Pharaoh's harem
- Abraham—the man who usually follows God, is free outside the palace walls
- Pharaoh—the powerful heathen leader of Egypt, is pleased with Sarah and lavishing Abraham with gifts on her behalf
- Pharaoh's household—They're going about their work

Sarah is in a terrible spot because of Abraham's fear. Worried abut his safety because of someone coveting his wife, he declared "She is my sister." Consequently, Pharaoh sent for her and has her in the palace. Although Scripture is silent on Sarah's state of mind, hopefully she is patiently waiting on God to deliver her.

But there is one more present! The mighty God of Abraham and Sarah watches as the human drama unfolds. At the perfect moment He makes His dramatic, miraculous move. Genesis 12:17 records, "The LORD plagued Pharaoh and his house with great plagues because of [Sarah]." God is going to make sure Sarah is released.

When the Pharaoh realizes what's going on, he confronts Abraham, "Why did you say, 'She is my sister'? I might have taken her as my wife. Now therefore, here is your wife; take her and go your way" (Genesis 12:19-20).

Sarah is safe! God took care of her, and isn't it wonderful He watches over you too? When life seems impossible and unbearable, He will come through for you. In His own time and in His own way, He will rescue you. Psalm 46:1-2 says, "God is our refuge and strength, a very present help in trouble."

## 13 An Encouragement and Blessing

*The Angel of the Lord found her.*
GENESIS 16:7

Abraham and his wife, Sarah, certainly led interesting lives. Although they both followed God, they were human and made mistakes. But God still promised them a child in their old age. Sarah, long barren, became impatient and decided to "help" God by having her maid, Hagar, bear Abraham's child.

Hagar was pregnant, but it wasn't turning out like Sarah planned. Hagar now despised Sarah and lorded it over her. Maybe she flaunted her ability to get pregnant. Maybe she ordered Sarah about because she was pregnant with Abraham's child. Sarah finally had enough. She checked with Abraham, and then treated Hagar harshly.

Hagar decided to run away, living up to the meaning of her name—"flight." She ran into the wilderness, her emotions reeling.

But God was watching over Hagar and Abraham's unborn child. He sent an angel to comfort this distraught woman. Through the angel Hagar received from God:

- *Instructions.* For her safety and well-being—and the baby's too—she was told to return to Sarah. There Hagar would receive food, water, shelter, and help.
- *Encouragement.* The angel told her she would bear a son. Even though life was bleak now, she would one day have a son, have a family.
- *A magnificent promise.* God would multiply Hagar's descendants. Although Hagar was a servant, she'd become the mother of many.

What an encouragement and blessing for Hagar!

Do you need encouragement? A fresh, shining vision of hope? Spend time with God...talking and listening. Read His "letters" to you—the Bible—for His promises, wisdom, and instructions.

## 14 God Hears Every Word!

*The Lord has heard your affliction.*
GENESIS 16:11

Hagar, tired from running through the desert, rested beside a spring of water in the wilderness, her head filled with confused thoughts. The handmaiden was pregnant with Abraham's child, which was set up by his wife, Sarah, who now mistreated her.

"Now what?" Hagar's heart cried out. God heard her affliction and responded by sending an angel to help. What love and grace! Hagar knew God had come to her aid. In fact, when her baby was born, the boy was named "Ishmael," which means "God hears."

When you're faced with life's afflictions, you can pray knowing God hears every word. Among the prayers you can rely on are...

*Arrow prayers.* On the spot and at the very second Nehemiah needed God's help, he shot his "arrow prayer" upward to heaven. God gave him the words he needed as he asked the king for permission to go to Jerusalem and rebuild the city's wall (Nehemiah 2:4).

*Liquid prayers.* The psalmist said, "You've kept track of my every toss and turn through the sleepless nights, each tear entered in your ledger, each ache written in your book" (Psalm 56:8 MSG). Saint Augustine called our tears "liquid prayers."

*Wordless prayers.* When you don't know what to pray or your heart is too heavy for words, the Holy Spirit helps (Romans 8:26).

Prayer is the answer to every problem because you're talking to the God of the universe. And He cares! Trust Him and pray believing. Rejoice with the psalmist who says, "I love the LORD, because He has heard my voice and my supplications" (Psalm 116:1).

## 15 *God Always Knows*

*You-Are-the-God-Who-Sees.*
Genesis 16:13

A curse or a blessing? Is the fact that God is omnipresent and omniscient a curse or a blessing? Ask Hagar! She encountered these two unfathomable attributes of God.

Hagar fled into the wilderness to escape her difficult home life. When she was at the end of all human hope, an "Angel of the Lord found her," giving her help and comfort. Hagar knew she'd encountered God. "Then she called the name of the Lord who spoke to her, You-Are-the-God-Who-Sees; for she said, 'Have I also here seen Him who sees me?' "

God is also immutable—He never changes. That means His ministry to you is complete, on target, and constant!

- Because God provides, you shall not want (Psalm 23:1).
- Because God leads you, you're never alone (Psalm 23:3).
- Because God is with you, you shall not fear (Psalm 23:4).
- Because God comforts, you're always encouraged (Psalm 23:4).

When no one understands your struggles, have hope because your omniscient, omnipresent, immutable God is with you! What does He see and how does He respond?

- your affliction............He is always at work
- your struggles............He is fulfilling His purposes in your life
- your mistreatment......He is providing courage and strength
- your faithfulness ........He is helping you
- your needs.................He is offering His compassion and love

What courage you gain knowing "the eyes of the Lord are on the righteous" (1 Peter 3:12)!

## 16 *Graduation!*

*You shall not call her name Sarai.*
GENESIS 17:15

In biblical times a name change essentially meant a "promotion"—a recognition of new status. And like in school, promotions had to be earned. Required courses must be successfully completed before a diploma is delivered. Genesis 17 offers a snapshot of Sarah's promotion in the school of faith. God said to Abraham, "As for Sarai...you shall not call her name Sarai, but Sarah shall be her name. And I will bless her and also give you a son by her; then I will bless her, and she shall be a mother of nations."

What courses did Sarah complete to qualify for promotion? As you read along, grade yourself in the blanks provided.

- *Sarah followed her husband.* She trusted Abraham as he followed God. Her life was filled with moves and changes, but she accepted her lifestyle as God's will and her husband as God's instrument in her life. _______
- *Sarah trusted God.* She almost failed the course, but God's love covered her mistakes. She grew in faith as she hoped...prayed...and trusted God. _______
- *Sarah waited on God.* Actually, she was still learning to wait. Sarah was getting the instruction she needed to continue her long wait for the son God promised. Waiting was never easy for Sarah. _______
- *Sarah developed a gentle and quiet spirit.* "Sarai" carried the connotation of "contention" as well as "princess." And she was certainly contentious at times. But Sarah eventually adorned herself with the kind of spirit that pleases God (1 Peter 3:4-5). _______

How'd you do? And what steps can you take to grow in these areas? Write them down and get started on them today!

## 17 Keeping Faith When Life Is Hard

*I will bless her and...give you a son by her.*
GENESIS 17:16

How many times had it happened? Sarah could count at least five times when God promised Abraham a son, a seed, an offspring—and still she wasn't pregnant! For a while they thought Ishmael, Abraham's son with Hagar, was "the son of promise." But God told Abraham, "Sarah your wife shall bear you a son." This time God mentioned Sarah specifically. No wonder Abraham fell down because he was laughing so hard. Sarah was 90 years old!

With her new name shining bright, Sarah undoubtedly wanted her deepening faith to be equally brilliant. But did she wonder, just like you and I do sometimes, how to believe in God's promises when situations seem impossible and the waiting never-ending? Scripture is full of suggestions for maintaining faith.

*By choice.* The opposite of faith is disbelief or doubt. When God presents one of His dazzling promises, He offers you the choice of accepting its dazzling brilliance or smothering it in a dark cloud of doubt.

*By faith.* Strength for today and hope for tomorrow are realized by putting your trust and faith in God's promises. Look for God's handiwork and His answers to your questions. Enjoy His strength and hope.

*By exercise.* Faith is like a muscle. Through exercise it gradually increases in strength and size. When you choose to believe God and His promises and live accordingly, your faith is exercised and you grow stronger.

Is there an area of your life that stretches your faith? Do you have a physical problem like Sarah? A family problem? A personal struggle? A financial test? Exercise your faith! Push through any uncertainty and focus on the One whose promises never fail.

## 18 Your Lasting Legacy

*She shall be a mother of nations.*
GENESIS 17:16

God said of Sarah, "She shall be a mother of nations; kings of peoples shall be from her." In time, Sarah's ancestors became "as the stars of the heaven and as the sand which is on the seashore." The roll call of Sarah's descendants includes great patriarchs of the faith, kings, and the Savior of the world, Jesus Christ—and continues right on down to you if you've been born spiritually into the line of Abraham through Christ (Romans 4:16-25). The lowly Sarah, pilgrim from Ur and stranger in Canaan, became the progenitor of all the saints through the ages!

Another woman will also be a mother of nations. Who? You! As you faithfully teach your children the life-saving, life-giving truths of Scripture, you invite your children into God's family. As you pass on the gospel to your beloved children, they can, in turn, pass it on to the next generation. Your godly influence will continue through time and through generations as innumerable as the stars and the sand!

Are you thinking, *But I don't have children. This doesn't apply to me?* Oh, but it does! By sharing the life-changing truth about Jesus with coworkers, neighbors, and family members you give people the opportunity to be born spiritually new in Him. You have so much to offer to others. Don't waste a moment of your faith stewardship. Pass it on!

## 19 The Flame of Faith

*Is anything too hard for the LORD?*
GENESIS 18:14

Is anything too hard for God? Abraham and Sarah faced this question. God sent them a message saying Abraham would father a child with Sarah. When Sarah heard this, she laughed to herself at the absurdity. She was well past the age of childbearing. She was wearing out, withering, falling apart. Having a baby would take a miracle. But God, who knows all and hears everything, heard her laugh. He asked Abraham, "Is anything too hard for the LORD?"

How would you answer that question? Search your heart for any dark corner of doubt about God's ability and willingness to accomplish His will and help you:

- Is the physical difficulty you face too hard for the Lord?
- Is the heartache you suffer too hard for the Lord?
- Is a problem in your marriage or family too hard for the Lord?
- Is your financial condition too hard for the Lord?
- Is the path you're on too hard for the Lord?

No, and a thousand more nos! Nothing you face is beyond the resources, the ability, or the love of your heavenly Father! Do you really believe this? Then cease doubting! Resolve that any issue you now face or will ever face, or any wound that has been inflicted or will ever be inflicted, is in the capable hands of an all-powerful and loving God. Nothing you will ever face is too hard for Him!

Let this knowledge fire your faith and shine brightly in every nook and cranny of your life. Not only will you grow dramatically in the Lord, but He will use the light of His presence in your life to reach out to others.

## 20 Blessings Will Come

*At the appointed time...Sarah shall have a son.*
Genesis 18:14

There is no such thing as "time wasted"...if you're waiting on the Lord. Sarah, the woman God called "a mother of nations," waited on the Lord's promise of a son for 25 years—and way past her childbearing years. Amid her strong faith Sarah experienced moments of doubt. *Is the promise real? Is God going to follow through?*

Few things are tougher than waiting on God's timing—His "appointed time." Yet we're all enrolled in God's School of Waiting. He uses this time to teach and transform us. But He also blesses us! Look for these special gifts and savor them.

*Blessing #1: Increased value.* Waiting increases the value and importance of what you're waiting for. Whether it's being delivered from suffering, discovering God's purpose, waiting for direction, clearing up confusion, affording a new home, getting married, attending a family reunion, anticipating a prodigal's return or a child's birth, waiting makes the desired object or event a greater treasure when it finally occurs.

*Blessing #2: Increased time.* While we're waiting God gives us the precious gift of time—to embrace life's circumstances, to press closer to God's loving and understanding heart, to grow in the grace of patience, to encourage others who also experience the pain of waiting.

*Blessing #3: Increased faith.* Faith grows and is strengthened through time. And when the time of waiting is done and God blesses you with fulfillment, what a time for rejoicing! And this results in even deeper faith!

## 21 A Diamond in the Rough

*Abimelech king of Gerar sent and took Sarah.*
GENESIS 20:2

When Sarah heard her husband, Abraham, say to the king of Gerar, "She is my sister," her mind undoubtedly flashed back 25 years to the time Abraham offered the same half-truth to Egypt's Pharaoh. And the result was the same! Abimelech, believing she was single, had Sarah brought to him. Can't you hear Sarah whispering, "Again, Lord?"

Isn't it encouraging to know that even the great saints of the Bible—men and women who did mighty things for God—struggled with tribulations? God uses troubles in life to hone our faith. Growing spiritually in Him is like becoming a multifaceted gem. A raw stone is cut, the gem turned, another facet incised, and the process is repeated. As God turns Sarah's life, He is grinding and polishing to bring the beauty of faith into her soul. The chisel of trial hurts, but the end result? A beautiful, radiant glow that sparkles. When you face difficult times, remember the Lord is working! His Word encourages you to...

- *Pray.* "The righteous cry and the LORD hears, and delivers them out of all their troubles" (Psalm 34:17).
- *Trust.* "Trust in the LORD with all your heart, and lean not on your own understanding" (Proverbs 3:5).
- *Believe.* "Faith is the substance of things hoped for, the evidence of things not seen" (Hebrews 11:1).
- *Wait.* "I waited patiently for the LORD; and He inclined to me, and heard my cry" (Psalm 40:1).

Is something in your life a recurring problem? Are there conflicts and troubles you constantly face? Allow God to use the difficulties and disappointments in life as polish to transform your faith into a glistening diamond that takes in and reflects His love. What beauty He will create!

## 22 *You Are Never Alone!*

*And God said…"I did not let you touch her."*
GENESIS 20:6

Sarah was separated from Abraham again. Since their marriage in Ur, they had been constantly together…except for that horrible time when she was taken by Egypt's Pharaoh. And now she was in the same predicament…except with Abimelech, the king of Gerar. Through his fear, Abraham once again put her at risk by uttering four simple words: "She is my sister."

The future looked hopeless. When God's promise seemed to be foiled and her future with Abraham finished, Sarah discovered afresh the powerful truth she experienced those decades ago in Egypt. God was with her! He…

- acted on her behalf by speaking to Abimelech in a dream
- protected her by threatening the king's life
- preserved her purity and safety
- facilitated her release by closing the wombs in Abimelech's household
- restored her to Abraham

Just like Sarah, you are in God's constant and powerful presence. No matter where you are, no matter what you encounter, no matter how alone you feel, you are never alone!

- Above you are God's overshadowing wings (Psalm 91:4).
- Beneath you are God's everlasting arms (Deuteronomy 33:27).
- All around you is the angel of the Lord, ready to save you (Psalm 34:7).
- Inside you is God's peace that passes all understanding (Philippians 4:7).

## 23 *God Keeps His Promises!*

*And the LORD did for Sarah as He had promised.*
GENESIS 21:1 NASB

Finally! After waiting 25 years for God's promise of a child to be fulfilled, Sarah was pregnant. In the quiet precision of His timing and plan, God did exactly what He said He'd do. Divine grace and miraculous power worked in Sarah's once-lifeless womb, and she and Abraham were going to have a son!

And just like He loved Abraham and Sarah, God loves and watches over you. His Word contains approximately 8000 promises to His children—and that includes you! In difficulty and disaster, trial and tragedy, trauma and testing, you can trust God's promises. You can be confident He'll always be with you.

There's an amazing story that fills me with wonder.

A French woman created a "promise box" to teach her children that the promises of God bring special comfort in times of need. The small box contained 200 promises copied from the Bible. Later, war came to France, and no food was available. The woman's children were emaciated and hungry, wearing rags and worn-out shoes. The mother turned to her promise box for encouragement and strength. In desperation she prayed, "Lord, I have such great need. Is there a promise here that is really for me? Show me, O Lord, what promise I can have in this time of famine, nakedness, peril, and sword." Blinded by tears, she reached for the box to pull out a promise and knocked it over. God's promises showered down around her—on her lap and on the floor. Not one was left in the box. Suddenly she realized *all* of God's promises were hers! Supreme joy flooded her soul as she realized He was with her in the hour of her greatest need.[3]

Hebrews 10:23 assures us, "He who promised is faithful." God is trustworthy. Believe it! You can count on Him.

## 24 *Sounds of Joy*

*God has made me laugh.*
Genesis 21:6

The tent rang with sounds of joy. Sarah and Abraham couldn't contain their glee as they held their promised son. Sarah's shameful barrenness had ended! Finally—after 25 years, after hearing the promise again and again, after a visit from God and two angels—little Isaac, soft and wrinkled, was born to the weathered and wrinkled parents. In their exultant joy they named the babe Isaac, meaning "he laughs."

"Who would have said to Abraham that Sarah would nurse children? For I have borne him a son in his old age," Sarah marveled. God, who is always fully able, provided a miracle. Now instead of her being scorned, people would join her in rejoicing. Isaac was the child of her own body, the child of her old age, the child of God's promise, the fruit of tested faith, the gift of God's grace, and the heaven-appointed heir to Abraham. Can you imagine Sarah's jubilant heart song?

Why not join her in a chorus of praise? Even if life is difficult right now, lift your voice in joy because of the hope you have in Christ. Rejoice that either here or in heaven, depending on God's appointed time, you'll experience the full, unimaginable blessing of His wonderful promises completely fulfilled. Sing with the psalmist in wonderful anticipation:

> Weeping may remain for a night, but rejoicing comes in the morning...You turned my wailing into dancing; you removed my sackcloth and clothed me with joy (Psalm 30:5, 11 NIV).

Spiritual joy is not an emotion. It's a response to a Spirit-filled life (Galatians 5:22). Can you "count it all joy when you fall into various trials" (James 1:2)? By an act of faith, resolve to be joyous in your present difficulty. That's walking by the Spirit!

## 25 "Fear Not" Power

*Fear not.*
Genesis 21:17

After Isaac, Abraham and Sarah's son, was born, there was great rejoicing. But Hagar refused to join in. Because of her ever-present negative attitude, Sarah asked Abraham to send Hagar and Ishmael away. Upset, Abraham consulted God, who told him to do as Sarah asked. But He also assured Abraham that He would watch over Ishmael. So Abraham told Hagar she and her son had to leave (Genesis 21).

In the desert their water supply ran out, and Hagar and Ishmael were dying of dehydration. The best Hagar could do was thrust her son under the scant shade of a desert scrub, drag herself away from his pathetic sobs, and weep while she waited for death to come. Suddenly, booming out of the heavens, came the voice of an angel: "Fear not, for God has heard the voice of the lad." How encouraged Hagar must have been!

What are your favorite "fear nots" in the Bible? Does your list include these from the King James Version?

> "Fear not…I am thy shield" (Genesis 15:1).
>
> "Fear not…for I am with thee" (Genesis 26:24).
>
> "Fear ye not, stand still, and see the salvation of the LORD" (Exodus 14:13).

Any conflict is won up front when you "fear not." So don the armor of the biblical "fear nots." They'll form an effective, protective covering against fear. Memorize or write them down and keep them handy so they'll always be ready to use. "God has not given us a spirit of fear, but of power and of love and of a sound mind" (2 Timothy 1:7)! Praise His wonderful name!

## 26 Do Something!

*Arise, lift up the lad.*
GENESIS 21:18

In the life story of Hagar, God presents a powerful, two-step plan for successfully enduring distresses and overcoming the obstacles of life:

*Step 1—a negative command:* Fear not!

*Step 2—a positive command:* Do something!

Hagar's energy was spent and so was her faith when God issued His Step 1 order. Calling out to Hagar as she and her son awaited death in the desert, the angel of the Lord commanded, "Fear not!"

Next God delivered Step 2: "Arise!" In other words, "Do something! Put feet on your faith." God's message was, "Don't give up—get up! Continue. Move. Muster your energy. Take action!"

Why a call to action? Because action—continuing to do what you can—conquers depression, staves off defeat, shakes off despair, and vanquishes discouragement.

Are there challenges in your path today? Do you face a hopeless situation? Insurmountable odds? A disaster? Tune your ear and your heart and your strength to God's voice of wisdom. He says, "Arise... move...do something!" Ask Him for wisdom and guidance and then plan your day. Make a to-do list. Get off the couch or out of bed. Commit to life. To reaching forward. To attaining the "prize of the high calling of God in Christ Jesus" (Philippians 3:14). Tap into the strength promised to you in Christ.

Take on a "go get 'em" attitude and posture. Act! A law of physics states, "A body at rest tends to remain at rest, and a body in motion tends to remain in motion." So move!

Doing something is great advice, but there is one caution to heed. Make sure your movement is in God's direction. Read God's Word. Seek godly counsel. Then with God's leading, move out.

# 27 And God Took Action

*I will make him a great nation.*
GENESIS 21:18

Picture Hagar and her son, Ishmael. In a stark, barren wilderness without water, these two destitute people lay down to die. The end of life seemed near and inevitable.

As the utter darkness of faithlessness and futility overtook Hagar, God acted. Truly, His mercies and compassion fail not. Through the blur of hopelessness, Hagar found fresh, rising hope. An angel's voice sounded forth God's assurance: "I will make him a great nation." Yes, there was hope for tomorrow!

Are you enjoying the blazing glory of the many promises God gives you in Scripture? Thank God for these too!

- *His constant presence to cheer and guide you.* "I am with you always" (Matthew 28:20).
- *A new body.* He "will transform our lowly body that it may be conformed to His glorious body" (Philippians 3:21).
- *A life without sorrow or pain.* "God will wipe away every tear from their eyes; there shall be no more death, nor sorrow, nor crying. There shall be no more pain" (Revelation 21:4).
- *Eternal life in His gracious presence.* "I give them eternal life, and they shall never perish" (John 10:28).
- *Rest for your soul.* "Come to Me, all you who labor and are heavy laden, and I will give you rest" (Matthew 11:28).

Just as God promised, Hagar lived to see Ishmael grow up, marry, and become the ruler of a great nation. God keeps His promises!

## 28 Pause, Pray, and Praise

*And she saw a well of water.*
GENESIS 21:19

One of God's many marvelous names is "Jehovah-jireh," meaning "God provides." Hagar came to appreciate that glorious truth when God graciously provided for her and Ishmael's needs. As you consider what God supplied for Hagar, remember He provides these very resources for you in your troubles.

> *Comfort*—Hagar and her son were dying when God made His presence known. He saw the distressed mother and child, heard their cries of despair, rescued them, and comforted them physically and emotionally.

When do you most need the comfort of God's presence and provision? Take heart! God sees your distresses, hears your cries, and comforts you in your troubles.

> *Encouragement*—Left alone to raise her son, Hagar was failing at the task. Stranded in the desert, their water was gone and no one was around to help. But God called out encouragement. "Fear not!" He proclaimed.

Do you ever feel the despair of failure? Do you struggle with hopelessness? Fear not! The Lord knows your needs.

> *Instruction*—God's instruction accompanied His encouragement. "Arise, lift up the lad and hold him with your hand." She wasn't to give up on life, on her son, or on God. She was to get up, grab the lad, and go on!

Need resources? God's Word is full of instruction and counsel. Jehovah-jireh gladly pours out His wisdom to you in any situation. All you need to do is open your Bible, read, believe, and talk to Him!

# 29 *God's Plentiful Provision*

*And she saw a well of water.*
GENESIS 21:19

The God who provides reached out and helped Hagar. God heard their cries and met their needs through comfort, encouragement, and instruction. But He didn't stop there!

> *Promise*—Indicating all was not lost for her son, God promised Hagar, "I will make him a great nation." When no ray of hope was evident, God gave the mother a promise to cling to.

Whatever your life situation, you've been promised "all things that pertain to life" (2 Peter 1:3). You can go through life fueled by God's promise of faithfulness.

> *Guidance*—Whether Hagar looked to God or not, God looked to her—and looked out for her. "God opened her eyes" and directed her to a nearby spring. He led Hagar, blinded by fear and exhaustion, safely to water.

God delights in leading you. He is constantly available to guide you through the events and circumstances of your life. He is the Good Shepherd who leads His sheep (Psalm 23).

> *Provision*—When God opened Hagar's eyes, she saw a well. In her frightening plight, God provided a spring, a fountain, a source of life!

Your promise for today—and every day—is God's guidance and His plentiful provision if you continually walk in His ways.

## 30 *Seasons of Life*

*Sarah lived one hundred and twenty-seven years.*
GENESIS 23:1

Sarah is the only woman in the Bible whose actual age is given. She lived 127 years. And in those years, what seasons did she go through?

*First, a season of leaving.* How hard it was for Sarah to leave the prosperous, culturally advanced metropolis of Ur, along the lush Euphrates River valley, to go to Haran (Genesis 11)! And then God, through her husband, Abraham, asked her to leave Haran to go into the arid desert.

*Second, a season of learning.* Sarah's lessons included following her husband. For 60 long years they never settled down for long. And there was also Sarah's often-repeated assignment of trusting God in His promise of a son. During 25 years of waiting, her faith surged and waned. The agony of passing time was especially difficult for Sarah.

*Third, a season of leaning.* Sarah was taken into harems twice. Out of fear, Abraham told the Egyptian Pharaoh, "She is my sister," so Pharaoh took her to the palace. Later Abraham repeated this deceit to King Abimelech, who also took Sarah home. Cut off from her husband, Sarah leaned on God. She discovered, as the psalmist did, that "God is our refuge and strength, a very present help in trouble" (Psalm 46:1).

*Finally, a season of loving.* In His goodness and at His appointed time, God gifted 90-year-old Sarah with Isaac, her very own baby! How she must have cherished every second of the 37 years she was privileged to be a loving mother.

Did you notice Sarah's "seasons" had nothing to do with her age? They had to do with her situation and attitude. What season are you in today? Trust God for His perfect plan.

# 31 Making Time Count

*So Sarah died.*
GENESIS 23:2

As one wedding ceremony puts it, marriage lasts "until death parts the partners." The day arrived when Sarah, faithful wife to Abraham, slipped away. But death is the doorway to eternal life for God's saints!

Have you thought about death? And does your perspective match what God says about death? Note these truths.

*Truth #1.* How you die is as important as how you live. "For if we live, we live to the Lord; and if we die, we die to the Lord" (Romans 14:8). Face death boldly with unfailing courage. Your goal is to glorify and exalt Christ by your life and through your death.

*Truth #2.* How you view death is important. The world views it as the end, as the entrance into something unknown, as something awful, something to be feared. But for God's people, "to die is gain" (Philippians 1:21). As someone pointed out, "God strips me of everything to give me everything!"

*Truth #3.* How you define death is important. In Philippians 1:23 Paul describes death as departing and being with Christ. The imagery used is one of loosening the ropes on a tent, pulling up the tent stakes, and moving on. Each day brings you closer to the exchange of this imperfect life for residence in a world of glory.

Do you know the hour of your death? No. But death is certain. So what are you doing to ensure your life has been meaningful? Model Christ. Share Him with family and friends. Be faithful to God. Make time count!

## 32 *A Remarkable Name and Legacy*

*Milcah, the wife of Nahor...*
GENESIS 24:15

Her name is listed in God's Word, but there is very little detail about the life of Milcah. What can we piece together?

- Her name means queen.
- Her father was Haran, the father of Abraham.
- Her brother was Abraham, friend of God.
- Her sister-in-law was Sarah, a beautiful woman of faith.
- Her husband was Nahor, brother to Abraham.
- Her children included eight sons.
- Her lovely granddaughter was Rebekah, who later married Isaac.

How can you follow in Milcah's steps?

*Be faithful to God.* When Abraham needed a godly wife for his Isaac—the son from whom the entire Jewish race would arise—he knew she would be among the offspring of Milcah.

*Be faithful to your husband.* Over the years Milcah must have steadfastly loved and served her husband through thick and thin.

*Be faithful to raise your children God's way.* Eight sons are listed to Milcah's credit. Her son Bethuel fathered Rebekah, who married the patriarch Isaac.

Milcah lived up to her regal name in bearing and dignity. She helped establish a godly seed in a godless world.

Faithfulness is the training ground for greater service. Where can you show faithfulness today?

## 33 *Dedicated to God*

*The daughter of Bethuel...*
Genesis 24:24

We meet only a handful of single women in Scripture. In Genesis 24 God presents Rebekah, a woman of stunning faith and service. What qualities make her one of God's special servants?

- *Purity*—She was chaste until marriage.
- *Industriousness*—Rather than looking for a husband or moping and mourning over the lack of one, Rebekah served her family and others.
- *Hospitality*—Her home was open to those who needed care.
- *Energy*—Abundant activity is a sign of happiness, and Rebekah had energy to spare as she went extra miles to serve people.

If you're a single woman, God has a beautiful plan for you. He encourages you to remain "holy both in body and in spirit." You also have more time to serve God because you're not distracted by a husband or children. As you use the same qualities Rebekah had to fully engage in "the things of the Lord" (1 Corinthians 7:34), you'll be given glorious opportunities to help others.

Is singleness a reality for you today? Although you may desire to be married, while you wait for God's leading in that area, give yourself wholeheartedly to His service and His cause.

## 34 Risking All for God

*[God] will send His angel before you.*
GENESIS 24:7

How does a man find a wife? This was the predicament Abraham was in. But the wife he needed to find was not for himself. She was for his only son, 37-year-old Isaac. "Who?" and "How?" were questions that probably plagued Abraham.

Realizing that the continuation of his family line and the fulfillment of God's promise to make his family a great nation were at stake, Abraham called in his oldest servant, the faithful Eliezer. After receiving a solemn oath from Eliezer, Abraham sent this 85-year-old servant on a 500-mile journey to find a wife for Isaac. This woman would have to be willing to follow Eliezer back to an unfamiliar land and marry a man she'd never met! What requirements did God and Abraham have for Isaac's future wife?

- *She must not be a Canaanite.* A wife from godless people might influence Isaac and his offspring away from the true God.
- *She must be from Abraham's family.* He instructed Eliezer, "You shall go to my country and to my family."
- *She must be willing to follow Eliezer back to the land of Abraham and Isaac.* A woman who would do this would be a woman willing to forsake all—in faith—for the glorious future God had ordained.

Are you actively following the God of the Bible and embracing His standards? You have a tremendous influence on your world, your friends, your husband, your children, and your extended family. Let God's light shine!

# 35 The Woman God Wants You to Be

*Let her be the one You have appointed.*
GENESIS 24:14

After his 500-mile journey to find Abraham's son a wife, Eliezer and his camels were tired and thirsty. They stood at a well by Nahor. Eliezer reviewed the qualities he was searching for:

*Wanted: The Ideal Wife*

Must be physically strong and healthy,
energetic, able to work hard.
Must be friendly, industrious, kind, compassionate,
generous, love to serve, and devoted to God.

Then Eliezer did one more thing. He lifted his "want list" before God. He knew God would lead him to such a woman. Have you considered what's on and not on Eliezer's list?

- Eliezer didn't mention appearance or wealth.
- He asked for godly character qualities.
- He sought physical attributes important for living in that time and place.

And the New Testament confirms Eliezer's list for you today—

> Do not let your adornment be merely outward—arranging the hair, wearing gold, or putting on fine apparel—rather let it be the hidden person of the heart, with the incorruptible beauty of a gentle and quiet spirit, which is very precious in the sight of God (1 Peter 3:3-4).

Do you focus on godly character rather than beauty? Is being kind and loving more important than being assertive and successful? Are adjustments needed to be who God wants you to be?

## 36 Willing to Work

*Rebekah...came out with her pitcher.*
Genesis 24:15

We tend to evaluate a person's character based on our first meeting. First impressions make such an impact. It was no different when Abraham's servant first saw Rebekah. Tired from the long journey, Eliezer waited by the town well in Nahor for the young women to come draw water. He prayed, asking God to bring the right woman for Isaac and have her offer him a drink of water. Before he'd finished speaking, "Behold, Rebekah...came out with her pitcher on her shoulder."

Eliezer saw right away that Rebekah was a working woman. Probably twice a day she took a heavy clay pitcher to the town's water source to draw precious water and carry it home. What can we surmise about her?

See her beautiful qualities of diligence and faithfulness. Watch carefully her tireless industry and humble willingness to engage in menial work. Observe her ability to do demanding work. Marvel at her servant heart that placed the needs of her family above any concern about what others might think.

Do you view menial work as degrading? Do you think physical work is done by other people and not you? Do you dread rolling up your sleeves and working on "necessary but thankless" tasks? In His Word God praises the enchanting-but-industrious Rebekah. So if you're tempted to put off or disdain difficult work, look to this beautiful woman for courage and example. Also read about the woman of Proverbs 31, "She girds herself with strength, and strengthens her arms...Strength and honor are her clothing" (Proverbs 31:17, 25).

What about you? Are you helping and influencing the people God puts in your life? Does your church need your energy working with children or in Sunday school or in the office? Be willing to work, and see where you can serve today.

# 37 An Old Man and 10 Camels

*I will draw water for your camels also.*
GENESIS 24:19

Jesus told people, "Whoever compels you to go one mile, go with him two. Give to him who asks you" (Matthew 5:41-42). Thousands of years before God's Son uttered these words, Rebekah was putting the principle into practice.

Picture an old man and 10 thirsty camels lingering around a well in a dusty, arid city of Mesopotamia. The man traveled 500 miles to find a wife for his master's son. "O LORD God...please give me success this day," the tired servant prayed. Before he added an "amen" to his request, a beautiful young woman came to the well to draw water.

Eliezer hurried to meet the woman and said, "Please let down your pitcher that I may drink." How did the beautiful Rebekah respond? Gracious and helpful, she said, "Drink, my lord." And then she volunteered to take care of the 10 camels!

I wonder how many draws of water from the well Rebekah had to make to satisfy those thirsty camels? A camel can drink as much as 25 gallons after a long journey! The generous, energetic Rebekah probably hastened back and forth from the well to the trough many times to satiate the weary animals. Rebekah went "many extra miles" on that extraordinary day.

No price can be put on the sterling qualities Rebekah exhibited in her attitudes and actions that day by the well. Her servant spirit shone like the sun, revealing her sincere and good heart. She was respectful, aware of those in need, willing to help, generous, and tireless. Giving drink to the tired old man met one of his needs, so Rebekah expanded her care to include his animals.

Today why not follow beautiful Rebekah's footsteps and be on the lookout for a needy person you can help? And then do more than is needed.

# 38 Open Your Heart and Home

*We have...room to lodge.*
GENESIS 24:25

Abraham's servant Eliezer traveled hundreds of miles in the desert climate. As he prayed beside a town well, the lovely Rebekah appeared. After first drawing water from the cistern to satisfy his thirst—and even taking care of the camels' thirst—Rebekah respectfully answered the man's questions regarding who she was and whether her family had a place for him to stay. In her welcoming way, Rebekah replied with her name and an invitation for food, lodging, and fodder for the animals. Inside Rebekah's family home, Eliezer would be the recipient of assistance, refreshment, shelter, and rest.

Do you see your home as a gift from God to be used for the comfort and well-being of others? A Christian home is earth's sweetest picture of heaven and a welcome relief in our stressed and weary society. Won't you open your arms and your heart to those in pain? Consider the teens you know who live where parents are seldom home, where few meals are served, and where apathy reigns. Think about the little ones next door who could rest a moment in your warm, peaceful kitchen, a welcome respite from the angry shouting under their own roof. Ponder the needs of a widow or widower who has no one to talk to. Count the singles you know who are on their own.

Why not serve a meal to a neighbor who is searching for answers? Or have tea with a brokenhearted mother struggling over her child. Offer a listening ear, an encouraging word, and a heartfelt prayer to those in need. Hospitality is a matter of the heart—your heart. All who enter your door offer you opportunities to minister. Welcome them into your home sweet home—a home where Jesus lives in the heart of the hostess.

# 39 "I Will Go"

*And she said, "I will go."*
Genesis 24:58

Talk is one thing. Action is another. And action has always been a measure of true faith. Rebekah added her name to God's roll call of the truly faithful when she took a gigantic leap in trusting Him.

The progression of events that led to that giant step of faith began when Abraham told his servant Eliezer to go to his relatives and find a wife for his son Isaac. When Eliezer reached his destination, the beautiful Rebekah, daughter of Abraham's distant relative Bethuel, invited him to stay in her family's home. While there, her father and brother agreed that Rebekah would marry Isaac.

However, when talk turned to a departure date for their cherished Rebekah, her mother and brother said, "Let the young woman stay with us a few days, at least ten; after that she may go." When Eliezer said he needed to return home, they said, "We will call the young woman and ask her personally." When they asked her, "Will you go with this man?" the question really was "Will you go now or wait?"

Rebekah's remarkable faith was evident as she stated, "I will go." She was basically saying, "I will go...with a stranger...to live in an unknown land...to be the wife of an unknown man. I will go...even though I will probably never see my family again...even though I have no time to prepare...even though the nomadic life of Abraham's family will be strenuous. I will go!"

Take a quick inventory of your life. Is there any act of faith you're postponing—even for a few days? Any decision you're putting off? Waiting may be easier, but the harder path of faith in action promises greater blessings. Delayed obedience is really disobedience, and delayed action puts off God's blessings. Step out in faith today.

# 40 *Industrious and Joyful*

*So they sent away Rebekah...and her nurse.*
GENESIS 24:59

The Christian life is one of selfless service to others, and one picture in particular is worth a thousand words when it comes to understanding what this looks like in God's eyes. Deborah, Rebekah's lifelong servant, offers a beautiful portrait of devoted service.

As a bond servant, Deborah was obligated to perform—without question or delay—her mistress' will. Whatever the order, Deborah was to do it quickly, quietly, without question. That job description meant leaving the house of Bethuel to journey 500 miles with Rebekah to her new home—and doing so immediately! While Bethuel's family talked about this surprising turn of events, I'm sure Deborah was trying to adjust to the idea that in the morning she was leaving forever. And she was probably busily packing for both of them!

Deborah is a study in diligence as well as service. Her name, in fact, means "bee," suggesting industry and usefulness. We can imagine she was constantly active and ever caring.

You too are called to serve people. How can you be industrious and willing like Deborah? Try these tactics.

- *Tackle your work energetically.* Whatever chore you face, do it with all your might and with a mind to work. Do your work heartily and for the Lord, not to individuals.
- *Tackle your work joyfully.* Choose to work with a joyful heart as well as a servant heart. You'll find more satisfaction when you approach work as a labor of love.

Since you're ultimately serving God in your work, develop a positive attitude and do the best you can. And how is your energy level and attitude when you're home? That's where your greatest industry and joy needs to be focused.

## 41 *A Legacy of Faith*

*And they blessed Rebekah.*
GENESIS 24:60

Twenty-four hours ago life had been so different for Rebekah and her family. An ordinary trip to the well changed the course of their history and, in fact, the history of the world! Rebekah had simply gone, as she did every day, to draw water for the household. Yet on that God-appointed day, a stranger was waiting, a foreigner sent by their kinsman Abraham to get a bride for his son Isaac.

Dear, kind Rebekah gave the servant water and invited him to her family home for the night. Over dinner her father and brother agreed that Rebekah was the woman God had chosen to marry Abraham's heir. As the sun rose the next morning, Rebekah mounted one of the stranger's camels and left for the mysterious, faraway land of Canaan.

Weeping and waving as the caravan carrying their precious Rebekah headed out, the family prayed and blessed the daughter and sister they would probably never see again—

> Our sister, may you become the mother of
> thousands of ten thousands; and may your
> descendants possess the gates of those
> who hate them (Genesis 24:60).

If you're a mother, consider your impact. Your children are a blessing and a heritage from God, a source of joy to be brought up in the training and instruction of the Lord. When their time to leave home comes, you'll be sad...but you can also rejoice in what their future holds. If they're willing, God will use them through the ages to affect millions as they pass the baton of faith to yet another generation.

So your mission is clear. It's never too early to start your children's spiritual education. What are you doing today to train and prepare them to be that "legacy of faith" tomorrow?

## 42 The ABCs of Living God's Will

*And [Rebekah] followed the man.*
GENESIS 24:61

Knowing God's will is our greatest treasure. As you pray, seek godly counsel, and live according to what is revealed in God's Word, you'll discover His specific will for you. Learn more from the following ABCs based on God's will for Rebekah.

***A****sk God.* Through prayer and by reading God's Word, you can access the heart and mind of the Lord.

***B****e faithful.* The need to make a decision is never a reason to neglect your duties. God leads you as you remain obedient in everyday life.

***C****onsult others.* "Where there is no counsel, the people fall; but in the multitude of counselors there is safety."[4]

***D****ecide for yourself.* You can be seeking, obedient, and asking, but ultimately you must decide to heed God's will.

***E****xecute your decision.* Once you know God's will, take action! Move out. Go full speed ahead.

***A****sk God.* Abraham's servant prayed fervently and specifically about finding the right wife for Isaac.

***B****e faithful.* Rebekah was led to the next phase of God's will for her life while she was faithfully serving her family in the details of daily life.

***C****onsult others.* Rebekah's father and brother were involved in counseling her and agreed to her marriage to Isaac.

***D****ecide for yourself.* Family members agreed, God's will was evident, but Rebekah had to choose to follow God's plan.

***E****xecute your decision.* Rather than lingering, Rebekah acted immediately and began her journey of faith...by faith!

Ask God to open your eyes and heart to His will for you. And don't be surprised when you discover it's right in front of you!

## 43 To Be a Wife

*She became his wife.*
GENESIS 24:67

What a romantic and dramatic moment when Rebekah and Isaac were at last united! After a long journey through the desert Rebekah finally caught her first glimpse of her husband-to-be. He was in the fields meditating. Can you picture him walking and praying and waiting? When he saw the caravan he probably wondered, *Can it be Eliezer? Did the old servant find a bride for me?* The answer was yes.

Isaac "took Rebekah and she became his wife, and he loved her."

Rebekah then took the next step in God's divine design for her. She endeavored to be a godly wife. What does that mean?

- *Leave your family and cleave to your husband.* When you marry, you're freed from the authority of your parents to be joyfully bound to your husband. He is now the most important person in your life (Genesis 2:24).
- *Help your husband.* God has ordained your role as assisting your husband with his responsibilities, his tasks, his goals (Genesis 2:18).
- *Follow your husband.* God has given the difficult role of leadership to your husband. Your role is to follow (Genesis 3:16; Ephesians 5:22).
- *Respect your husband.* How lovely to be in the presence of a wife who respects her husband. She treats him as she would respond to Christ. This is God's lovely, high calling for you (Ephesians 5:33).

How well are you following God's guidelines? Do any areas need improvement?

## 44 *Prayer with Contentment*

*She was barren.*
Genesis 25:21

God's ways are not our ways, and His timing is not always our timing. Isaac's beautiful bride, Rebekah, had to learn these two difficult lessons.

The marriage of Isaac and Rebekah began in the right way—covered by prayer. It was truly a marriage made in heaven. But there was one flaw. Twenty years passed and there was no baby to love. To continue the family line. To stand as a flesh-and-blood testimony of God's faithfulness to His promises (Genesis 12:2).

Consider how such heartache is often handled today. Doctors are consulted. Parents are informed. Best friends are updated daily. Husbands or wives can become the target of much anger, blaming, belittling, and criticism. Emotions swing from shock to sorrow, from fear to panic. Arguments and complaints, mixed with tears of discouragement and depression, often ring through homes where the happy blessing of children has been withheld.

What advice would Rebekah and Isaac have for us today when our dreams are thwarted? In a word, "Pray!" "Isaac pleaded with the Lord for his wife, because she was barren; and the Lord granted his plea, and Rebekah his wife conceived" (Genesis 25:21). Prayer was the means by which Rebekah entered into God's plan and His timing. Indeed, God's ways and His will come in His own perfect time.

> Like coral strands beneath the sea,
> So strongly built and chaste,
> The plans of God, unfolding, show
> No signs of human haste.[5]

What are you waiting for? Leave the desires of your heart with God through prayer and live each day in full contentment and confidence that your life—just as it is—is part of God's perfect plan and His perfect timing. Enjoy God's peace that passes all understanding.

## 45 The Power of Prayer

*She went to inquire of the LORD.*
GENESIS 25:22

Rebekah was growing in the Lord. One of the lessons she learned was that prayer is the best way to handle difficulties. Two major blessings in her life happened when people prayed:

- Abraham's servant prayed for a bride for Isaac—and God led him to Rebekah. Prayer was the key factor in Rebekah becoming Isaac's wife.
- When Rebekah was barren after 20 years of marriage, Isaac prayed and Rebekah conceived. Prayer was the primary reason she was able to get pregnant.

But now Rebekah was having a "problem pregnancy." As the pregnancy and her worries continued, Rebekah's spiritual growth showed. She "went to inquire of the LORD." Her understanding of God's power encouraged her to depend on Him more fully. And she was not disappointed. The Lord spoke to her!

Like Rebekah, you can depend more fully on God's power and His love by praying during difficulties. Asking through prayer helps you see your problem in light of God's power. Asking in prayer reaps other fruit too:

- Prayer deepens your insight into what you really need.
- Prayer broadens your appreciation for God's answers.
- Prayer allows you to mature so you can use His gifts more wisely.[6]

What pains, trials, temptations, or sufferings are you facing today? Follow in Rebekah's footsteps of faith and take your concerns to the Lord. Prayer should be your first option!

## 46 Approaching God

*The Lord said to her...*
Genesis 25:23

Everyone struggles. We struggle in marriage, with finances, with health problems, with family members, with career, with jobs, with friends, and with temptation. For the beautiful Rebekah, however, there was literally an internal struggle. Finally pregnant after 20 years of marriage to Isaac, she knew something wasn't right in her pregnancy. An extraordinary commotion raged inside and made her uneasy. So she went to the only Person who could help her—she prayed to the Lord. The answer to her prayer—and the relief for her struggle—was in God's hands. No one else could help.

First, only God could know Rebekah was carrying twins. God forms the inward parts of each child in the womb of its mother, and its frame is not hidden from Him (see Psalm 139:13-16). Rebekah's twins were the first recorded in Scripture.

Second, only God could know the futures of Rebekah's twin sons. He answers Rebekah's question, "Why am I like this?" with a prophecy regarding her twins: "Two nations are in your womb, two peoples shall be separated from your body; one people shall be stronger than the other, and the older shall serve the younger." Her twins would reverse the traditional roles—the older would serve the younger—and the two would struggle as each became a great nation.

When perplexed, disturbed, anxious, and distressed Rebekah responded by approaching God. Is this your practice too? I hope so! Take your struggles and routinely...

go into the sanctuary of God (Psalm 73:17),
spread your case before the Lord (2 Kings 19:14), and
ask counsel at the Almighty's throne (Hebrews 4:16).

## 47 T-R-U-S-T

*She is my sister.*
GENESIS 26:7

So far Rebekah had successfully weathered a series of significant faith ventures.

- *Separation*—Rebekah left family and home to marry Isaac, heir to God's promise to make Abraham's descendants into a great nation.
- *Marriage*—Rebekah made the necessary adjustments to married life and her marriage partner.
- *Childlessness*—Two decades passed as Rebekah and Isaac waited for a child.
- *Motherhood*—Finally two babies were born. I'm sure being the mother of the world's first-recorded twins stretched Rebekah's faith.

But Rebekah's beauty endured...and presented another test of faith. There was a famine, but God instructed Isaac to stay put. Because he was afraid the Philistines would kill him for his beautiful wife, Isaac told the king, "She is my sister." (Remember—Abraham, his dad, said the same thing about Sarah!)

What would you have done? If you're frozen with fear...

**T**rust in God—not your husband (1 Peter 3:1-2).

**R**efuse to succumb to fear (1 Peter 3:6).

**U**nderstand God always watches over you (Psalm 23:4).

**S**trengthen your spirit with God's promises (2 Peter 1:4).

**T**hank God for His promised protection (Isaiah 41:10).

To better understand what it means to trust God, look up each verse listed with T-R-U-S-T. Ask God to help you rely on Him when you're tested.

## 48 God Is Always Working

*Rachel came with her father's sheep.*
GENESIS 29:9

Experts on proper etiquette tell us to include personal information when we introduce someone. At this point in our journey through the Bible, God introduces us to another amazing single woman named Rachel. Note her personal information.

- *Her family*—Rachel was the daughter of Laban, Rebekah's brother, and therefore in the line of Abraham.
- *Her occupation*—Rachel was a shepherdess. In fact, the name Rachel means "ewe."
- *Her appearance*—"Rachel was beautiful of form and appearance." Like her Aunt Rebekah, she was lovely to look at.

God also introduces us to Jacob, another person important to Him...and who will soon be important to Rachel.

- *His family*—Jacob and his twin brother, Esau, were the sons of Isaac and Rebekah, who came from Rachel's homeland. Jacob and his brother were also grandsons of Abraham.
- *His predicament*—Favoritism, jealousy, and deceit led Jacob to flee to Rachel's homeland to escape being murdered by Esau. Furthermore, Isaac advised Jacob to find a wife from among his own people (Genesis 28:2).

God brought Rachel and Jacob together by working through *people, events,* and *circumstances.* We'll soon learn exactly how He did it. For now, look back over the last few days and weeks. How did God work through people, events, and circumstances to bring about good for you? Some happenings may not seem good in this lifetime, but trust a loving God that there is and will be good!

## 49 Don't Look for Miracles

*Rachel came with her father's sheep.*
GENESIS 29:9

The day began like every other day. As Rachel mentally ran through her list of chores, she saw no hint that today life would be dramatically transformed. At the top of Rachel's to-do list was one very necessary responsibility: "Water father's sheep." As she approached the well that afternoon, Rachel noticed a stranger. He stood with other shepherds talking and presumably waiting for a larger group to gather before rolling the stone away from the well's mouth so the sheep could drink. Rachel was surprised when the handsome stranger ran to the well, lifted off the rock, and began watering her sheep. Then he kissed her, wept, and explained they were relatives.

That was the beginning of the courtship of Rachel and Jacob! Rachel's ordinary day became extraordinary.

How does a single woman meet the man of her dreams? Here are two keys from Rachel's experience:

> *Rachel was busy.* She was where she was supposed to be (at the town well) and doing what she was supposed to be doing (watering her father's sheep).
>
> *Rachel was faithful.* Tending and watering her father's sheep were Rachel's responsibilities. As she faithfully discharged her duty, God was leading her to her destiny.

If you're single and looking for a marriage partner, don't look for miracles. Don't look for the extraordinary. Continue in your usual manner. God often reveals His divine plans in small, ordinary events.

"Don't look for miracles" also applies to married women. Pray for your husband, but don't wait for him to change. Please God by being the best wife you can be.

# 50 A Woman After God's Own Heart

*Leah's eyes were delicate.*
GENESIS 29:17

"Your beauty should not come from outward adornment, such as braided hair and the wearing of gold jewelry and fine clothes. Instead, it should be that of your inner self, the unfading beauty of a gentle and quiet spirit, which is of great worth in God's sight" (1 Peter 3:3-4 NIV). These few verses give us God's standards for beauty. Take to heart His beauty tips!

*Nurture the beauty of your heart.* God values Christian character, which shines in positive, outward conduct. Fashion your heart after Jesus'!

*Cultivate the beauty of a gentle and quiet spirit.* God treasures the soft graces of a calm, quiet spirit—not costly clothes and jewels. Focus on what's inside.

*Concern yourself with inner beauty,* which is precious in the sight of God. Your supreme goal in life is to be pleasing in His sight. Fix your eyes on Him.

Leah was destined to live her life in the shadow of Rachel's exquisite beauty. Not only was Leah—whose name means "wearied" or "faint from sickness"—less than beautiful, but her eyes were delicate, weak, and dull—a serious blemish at the time. But even great beauty fades.

Aren't you glad God is more concerned about inner beauty? Aren't you thankful "the LORD does not see as man sees; for man looks at the outward appearance, but the LORD looks at the heart" (1 Samuel 16:7)?

Tend to your inner beauty by spending time each day in the presence of the Lord, discovering more about Him and how you can better please Him. Let Him transform you into a woman of true beauty...a woman after His heart.

# 51 Turning Ashes to Beauty

*He took Leah…and brought her to Jacob.*
GENESIS 29:33

Leah's father, Laban, was a master of deception. Thanks to her own father, Leah was used, mistreated, and rejected!

- Jacob, a distant cousin to Leah and Rachel, came to their home to seek a bride.
- Rachel, Leah's beautiful sister, met Jacob at the city well, and the two instantly fell in love.
- Laban, Rachel's father, contracted with Jacob for seven years of indentured service in exchange for Rachel's hand in marriage. On the wedding night, however, Laban secretly substituted Leah for Rachel.
- The result? Leah was used by her father, unloved by her husband, and envied by her sister (Genesis 30:1).

Disappointment is a fact of life. Have you been unfairly used? Deceived? Rejected? Let God comfort you! Leah wasn't beautiful—and neither were her circumstances. But God exchanged her sorrow for blessings. What emerged from Leah's disappointment?

- She had a husband. With her imperfect eyes, she may have never married.
- She had six boys and one girl. She may never have had children.
- She was the mother of 6 of the men who led the 12 tribes of Israel.
- She was the mother of Judah, through whom Jesus Christ would come.
- She was the first or "recognized" wife of Jacob.

# 52 God Acts on Your Behalf

*The LORD saw that Leah was unloved.*
GENESIS 29:31

The lowly...the downtrodden...the suffering. People who know affliction also know the protection of God's promises. Indeed, we are assured that "the LORD is near to those who have a broken heart, and saves such as have a contrite spirit. Many are the afflictions of the righteous, but the LORD delivers him out of them all" (Psalm 34:18-19).

Leah knew affliction. She was deceived, used, and rejected. Her heart was broken and crushed. As the less-than-beautiful sister of the stunning Rachel and the daughter of the deceptive Laban, Leah ended up in a loveless marriage. To make matters worse, her husband later married her sister, Rachel, and "he also loved Rachel more than Leah."

But God knows all there is to know about His beloved children and sees all that touches their lives. He knows all that harms or hurts them, all that causes them pain. God took note of the lowly condition of Leah and then acted. He opened her womb so she could have many children, while Rachel remained barren.

When you're suffering, remember nothing happens to you that is unnoticed by God. He sees and understands everything that goes on in your life.

> For the eyes of the LORD run to and fro throughout the whole earth, to show Himself strong on behalf of those whose heart is loyal to Him (2 Chronicles 16:9).
>
> Behold, the eye of the LORD is on those who fear Him, on those who hope in His mercy (Psalm 33:18).

In His time, God will act on your behalf! So look to Him for comfort, purpose, and fulfillment.

## 53 *Proof of God's Love*

*The LORD has surely looked on my affliction.*
GENESIS 29:32

What's in a name? Plenty! In Bible times, names given to newborns were very significant. A name expressed the parents' feelings and many times alluded to circumstances in the family's history. Often the relationship the parents enjoyed with God was evident in their baby's name. Through the names they bestowed, mothers and fathers passed on their expectations, their faith, and a bit of their hard-earned wisdom. Such is the case of Leah. As you follow Leah on her journey, you'll see that the names of her children mark her spiritual growth. Here's what happened.

Leah had the misfortune of sharing her husband, Jacob, with her stunning sister, Rachel. The Bible tells us Jacob loved Rachel more than Leah and that Leah was unloved. Both Leah and Rachel were barren for awhile, but the Lord eventually opened Leah's womb, and she conceived and bore a son.

When she held her new baby, Leah christened him "Reuben"—"See, a son!" or "Behold a son!" Leah exclaimed, "The LORD has surely looked on my affliction. Now therefore, my husband will love me." The name "Reuben" reveals Leah's longing for love. She hoped Jacob would turn his heart toward her as he held his first child.

But buried deeper in the naming of her tiny boy was her joyful surprise at God's compassion. "Reuben" also acknowledges God's kindness and providence. He'd noticed her trouble and looked favorably upon Leah. She treasured that thought so deeply she passed it on to her son. To Leah, Reuben would always be proof of God's loving care.

*Lord, thank You for the proof of Your love for me that came with Jesus' death on the cross. Help me remember that any momentary affliction is a small price to pay for the hope of the life to come I have in Jesus. Amen.*

## 54 A Budding Prayer Life

*The LORD has heard that I am unloved.*
GENESIS 29:33

Sharing her husband with her sister, Rachel, was becoming increasingly difficult for Leah. Neither Leah nor Rachel had been able to have children...until the Lord opened Leah's womb. How she hoped her firstborn son would help her win her husband's love. But nothing changed.

Then Leah conceived again. Perhaps a second child—a second son—would make a difference in Jacob's heart? Maybe Jacob would love her then. But nothing changed. In fact, things were worse. The King James Version says "Leah was hated" (Genesis 29:31).

Swaddling her second son, Leah called him "Simeon," meaning "hearing." She said, "Because the LORD has heard that I am unloved, He has therefore given me this son also." Hidden in this name is evidence of Leah's budding prayer life. With her first child, she hoped to gain her husband's love. When those hopes died, Leah turned to prayer. A second baby had come because God heard Leah.

Is there any difficulty, any trial, any lack in your life? Are there sorrows you bear from sunup to sundown? Do terrible burdens weigh you down? Pray! Pour out your troubled heart to God, knowing He loves and cares for you. As one person shared,

> Trouble and perplexity drive me to prayer, and
> prayer drives away perplexity and trouble.[7]

# 55 *Two Steps Forward*

*I have borne him three sons.*
GENESIS 29:34

Each year Leah's problem intensified. Her husband loved her less and Rachel more. But year by year Leah's family grew. First Reuben was born, then Simeon, and now she held yet another newborn. And Leah's faith grew. While waiting for her first two children, she'd come to know God better and trust Him more. He'd removed her barrenness and opened her womb. Her first baby's name, Reuben, reflected her deep gratitude to God. The name sounds like "the LORD has surely looked on my affliction" and means "Behold a son." She knew Reuben was a gift from God. Then the second baby arrived, another answer to her prayers. With "Simeon" Leah again gave credit to God, saying, "The LORD has heard that I am unloved."

Even after bearing two of his babies failed to win Jacob's heart, Leah still hoped. She became pregnant a third time. "Now this time my husband will become attached to me, because I have borne him three sons," she wished. Brimming with hope and confident in her ability to bear children, Leah looked at her new babe and named him "Levi," meaning "joined, attached." This reflects an emphasis on pleasing Jacob rather than thanking God.

After taking two steps forward in her growing faith, has Leah taken a step back? It's hard to tell. For now though, let's focus on her two giant steps forward and two life principles we can use:

- Always acknowledge God in each event of life.
- Always ask God for direction and wisdom about each event.

Making these two steps part of your approach to life will help you center your heart and mind on God. How can you apply them in your present situation?

## 56 A Vibrant Rainbow

*Now I will praise the* Lord.

Genesis 29:35

Everyone experiences disappointment and lack, loss and sorrow. Everyone has thwarted dreams and hopes. Everyone contends with problems and conflicts. Whatever clouds and storms you've encountered, your victory over them stands as a brilliant rainbow of God's grace.

Leah, the wife of Jacob, lived a life ravaged by hardship. Aren't you glad she enjoyed such a brilliant victory in her problem-filled life? Locked in a loveless marriage, Leah also shared her husband with her younger, more beautiful sister. Yet Leah was the wife God blessed with bearing most of Jacob's children.

Child #1 was named Reuben.

Child #2 was christened Simeon.

Child #3 was called Levi.

And now came the fourth child— "Judah," meaning "praise." The arc of the rainbow was clear and complete as praise rang through Leah's tent. "Now I will praise the Lord!" she exclaimed.

What made the rainbow complete was Leah's apparent submission to the Lord and victory over her circumstances. Leah finally ceased fretting about the absence of Jacob's love and instead rested in God's love. She found in Him joy and reasons to praise. And through Judah the Messiah would come! Every generation would know who Leah's fourth son was.

Will you follow Leah's path to victory? Will you praise your all-wise, ever-loving, forever-faithful Father...even through tears and in dark times? Rest in God's love and offer Him praise that fills in the vivid, joyful colors of the rich rainbow of His grace to you.

## 57 *Nurturing Strong Roots*

*Now I will praise the LORD.*
GENESIS 29:35

What does it take to become strong in the Lord? What can you glean from the following story?

> In bygone days there was a process used for growing the trees that became the main masts for military and merchant ships. The great shipbuilders first selected a tree located on the top of a high hill as a potential mast. Then they cut away all of the surrounding trees that would shield the chosen one from the force of the wind. As the years went by and the winds blew fiercely against the tree, the tree only grew stronger until finally it was strong enough to be the foremast of a ship.[8]

Fierce winds blew in Leah's life. Her father's mistreatment, her husband's hatred, and her sister's envy hurled against her. But Leah deepened her faith and received from God what she needed. She shouted, "Now I will praise the LORD!"

> Stand up in the place where the dear Lord has put you, and there do your best. God gives us trial tests...Out of the buffeting of a serious conflict we are expected to grow strong. The tree that grows where tempests toss its boughs and bend its trunk often almost to breaking, is often more firmly rooted than the tree which grows in the sequestered valley where no storm ever brings stress or strain. The same is true of life.[9]

Buffeting, conflicts, tempests, storms, stresses, strains—all are God's prods to help you attain greater faith and strength.

# 58 Might from Meekness

*And [Rachel] gave him Bilhah her maid.*
GENESIS 30:4

Jesus taught, "Blessed are the meek, for they shall inherit the earth." Paul wrote, "When I am weak, then I am strong." Hannah prayed, "The LORD...brings low and lifts up." Do you see the common theme? In God's world, "might" comes from "meekness." If you find yourself in a lowly position, or if you are struggling under oppression, or if you're living in a God-ordained season in the shade, take heart!

Sentenced to a life of slavery, Bilhah had little to look forward to. Her life wasn't her own. In fact, she was passed from person to person and was given to Rachel by her master when Rachel married Jacob. Yet Bilhah discovered God's blessings in the midst of her lowly existence.

Bilhah couldn't help but notice the domestic tensions in her new home. Jacob's two wives, Leah and Rachel, were constantly at odds. Jacob loved Rachel more than he did Leah. And Leah gave birth to son after son, while the barren Rachel burned with envy.

During a heated argument with her husband, Rachel announced, "Here is my maid Bilhah; go in to her, and she will bear a child on my knees, that I also may have children by her." Bilhah had been given away again! But this time from meekness would arise might...through Bilhah's offspring.

Dan was Bilhah's firstborn by Jacob. From Dan sprang the mighty Samson, the renowned judge and deliverer of Israel, whose exceptional physical strength was greatly used by God. Naphtali was Bilhah's second son by Jacob. He too grew strong and became the founder of a large tribe of people.

This lowly servant was blessed with two sons who inherited a portion of Jacob's vast wealth and became powerful leaders of 2 of the 12 tribes of Israel!

## 59 Strength and Dignity

*[Leah] took Zilpah her maid and gave her to Jacob.*
GENESIS 30:9

In Proverbs 31:25 King Solomon describes the ideal clothing for women: "Strength and dignity are her clothing, and she smiles at the future" (NASB). Now meet a woman most unlikely to be clothed with such splendor. Zilpah, whose Arabic name means "dignity," was a slave owned by Leah's father, Laban. He gave Zilpah to Leah when she married Jacob. Little did Zilpah know that being Leah's servant would require her to bear children! "When Leah saw she'd stopped bearing children, she gave Zilpah to her husband Jacob as a wife." And God blessed Zilpah with two sons who became great men of strength and the fathers of two tribes of Israel.

Leah named Zilpah's first son "Gad," meaning "fortune." He was the forefather of a strong, warlike race that bravely defended their country and aided their relatives in the conquest of Canaan.

Zilpah's second son was called "Asher," meaning "happiness." I'm sure Zilpah smiled with happiness too. And that smile extended through history as Asher's line brought forth Anna, another woman of strength and dignity who devoted her life to prayer. She was the prophetess who recognized the infant Jesus as the Messiah (Luke 2:36-38).

And how about you? Are you clothed in the strength and dignity available to you as one of God's children? Devote yourself to developing character and conduct that pleases the Lord. Pour your life into your family. Contribute wholeheartedly to God's plan. Pass your faith on to your children. Assist your brothers and sisters in Christ in their tasks for the Lord. Bring happiness, encouragement, and comfort to those around you. And apply yourself to prayer...for others and for God's church.

## 60 *Radiant Glory*

*God listened to Leah, and she conceived.*
GENESIS 30:17

Leah had weak eyes and her name meant "faint." But centuries later her life still shines like a brilliant star with a sparkling trail stretched across a black velvet sky. Leah wasn't beautiful, she wasn't loved, and she wasn't wanted by her husband. Yet her legacy through her six sons leaves a luminous path through Scripture.

The background against which Leah's star shines was indeed dark. On the night her sister Rachel was to marry Jacob, Leah's scheming father sent Leah instead. Trickery, lies, and scheming were the starting points of her loveless marriage to Jacob. But out of her difficult circumstances, Leah began to shine as—through prayer—she pressed herself closer to the awesome, dazzling glory of God. She bore four sons—Reuben, Simeon, Levi, and Judah as she looked to God for His understanding, His mercy, and His help.

Leah's season of luster slowed as "she stopped bearing" children (Genesis 29:35). Once again she applied what she'd learned about handling heartaches. She prayed passionately for the blessing she most desired—to be part of God's promise of land and numerous descendants to Abraham and now to Jacob. She prayed Jacob's seed would be as the stars of heaven and perhaps one might be the Messiah.

God heard Leah, and she conceived and bore Jacob a fifth son named Issachar, a sixth son named Zebulun, and a daughter named Dinah.

Is your trust in God blazing a trail of faith that causes others to marvel and consider Him?

> *Lord, I want to reflect Your glory to those around me. May Your brilliant presence in my life draw people to Your Son Jesus. Help me keep my life pure, free from unrepentant sin, so Your light loses none of its intensity.*

## 61 *Waiting's Classroom*

*God remembered Rachel, and God listened to her.*
Genesis 30:22

"Second only to suffering, waiting may be the greatest teacher and trainer in godliness, maturity, and genuine spirituality most of us ever encounter."[10] Rachel definitely put in her time waiting! Her expectation that she would one day be a mother grew out of God's promise to Abraham that his seed would become a great nation equaling in number the stars in the sky and the grains of sand on the seashores (Genesis 12:2-3; 22:17). Yet Rachel and Jacob waited...and waited...and waited.

How long did Rachel wait? It probably seemed like forever. She waited while 10 children were born to Jacob by her sister, Leah, and two servants named Bilhah and Zilpah. It's possible that a quarter of a century passed while Rachel remained childless.

What spiritual lessons did she learn? And can what she learned help you in your faith journey?

*The lesson of prayer.* Rachel discovered the power of prayer. Genesis 30:22 says, "And God listened to her and opened her womb." Prayer will still your fretting heart as you look to God for what is lacking in your life. Prayer also sculpts your heart into the beautiful posture of humility.

*The lesson of faith.* In naming her long-desired son, Rachel exhibits extraordinary faith. "She called his name Joseph [meaning "God will add"] and said, 'The Lord shall add to me another son.'" Rachel's faith—enshrined in the name of her son—reaches out and presses on for more than God has yet given.

How patient are you? Are you waiting for healing? Are you waiting for reconciliation, renewal, or revival? What are you learning as you wait? And what blessings are you reaching for by faith? Pray faithfully as you wait on the Lord.

## 62 Stepping into the Unknown

*Whatever God has said to you, do it.*
GENESIS 31:16

From the beginning of time God gave a divine principle for marriage: "Therefore a man shall leave his father and mother and be joined to his wife, and they shall become one flesh" (Genesis 2:24).

After running away from Esau, Jacob spent many years with relatives. Now he wanted to return home. Detailing God's leading and pointing to His hand of blessing, Jacob asked Rachel and Leah to go with him. He wanted to take a willing family on his pilgrimage home...a family filled with faith. Would Rachel and Leah stay in their father's familiar house or go with their husband to a foreign land?

Leaving and cleaving is always a test of faith.

- It tests our obedience to God's Word and His way.
- It tests our faith in God's leading through a husband.
- It tests our trust in our husbands' wisdom.
- It tests our commitment to our husbands.

How did Rachel and Leah answer? "Whatever God has said to you, do it." What amazing faith and support! They joined other women of faith as they stepped out and followed God.

Are you a wife? Is your husband Number One in your life (after God)? Is there stress and conflict surrounding your marriage and your parents? Consider signing an agreement that spells out your status as a wife. The wording might be: "I am no longer accountable to my parents. I am free from that authority and now bound joyfully and securely to my mate."[11]

Are you a mother of married children? If so, consider signing such a statement that releases them to follow after God with their mates.

# 63 Devoted Service

***Deborah, Rebekah's nurse, died.***
GENESIS 35:8

As Rebekah's faithful nursemaid, Deborah made the arduous 500-mile trip from Haran to Hebron when Rebekah went to marry Abraham's son Isaac. Deborah also weathered Rebekah's ups and downs during her 20 years of waiting for a child. When Rebekah's twin boys finally arrived, Deborah lovingly and tenderly cared for Jacob and Esau, who eventually grew up and left home to start their own families. Jacob married in Haran, and his family quickly grew into a large one. Because Deborah was with Jacob's family on their travel back to Canaan (Genesis 35:8), it's probable she was sent to him when he married to help nurse yet a third generation—a duty that required a tedious trek back to Haran. She cared for Rebekah, for Rebekah's children, and now for Rebekah's grandchildren.

Age brought an end to Deborah's active role of caregiver, and then Jacob's family cared for her. She loved them, and they loved her. After approximately 100 years of life, Deborah was buried under "the oak of weeping" and was lamented with sadness and tears usually reserved for family.

Deborah is a beautiful portrait of devoted service. Are you following in her steps? As a representative of God, you're called to love all with God's love. The ultimate expression of love is service given freely and abundantly. Take to heart these truths...

> Love bears all things,
> Love believes all things,
> Love hopes all things,
> Love endures all things,
> Love never fails.[12]

Servanthood is a hallmark of the Christian faith. What can you do today to demonstrate your heart of love and service?

## 64 *Ministering God's Love*

*You will have this son also.*
GENESIS 35:17

Rachel, wife of Jacob, died in childbirth. She was buried near Bethlehem, and her grave is marked by a pillar raised in her memory by her devoted husband. She is survived by Jacob, her sister Leah, her firstborn son Joseph, and her new baby Benjamin.

Rachel's hypothetical obituary offers us two fascinating firsts.

- Rachel's death is the first instance of death during childbirth recorded in the Bible. Journeying from Bethel to Ephrath, Rachel "labored in childbirth, and she had hard labor." In an effort to encourage and comfort the distraught Rachel, her midwife said, "Do not fear; you will have this son also." Her words came true, but the beginning of Rachel's second son's life marked the end of her own.
- The pillar the grieving Jacob set up on Rachel's grave is the first grave marker on record in the Bible.

Rachel's life was marked by great love and marred by many struggles. Two phrases could have been engraved on the pillar erected in her honor:

- *A loved wife.* Rachel was Jacob's true love from the moment they met.
- *A loving mother.* At one time Rachel demanded of Jacob, "Give me children, or else I die" (Genesis 30:1). Eventually God blessed Rachel, and she poured love into her son Joseph, who grew up and became the godliest and greatest of the 12 sons of Jacob.

Rachel's chief contribution to God's kingdom happened in her home and in the hearts of those nearest and dearest to her. Like Rachel, are you ministering God's love at home and to those around you?

## 65 *Forging Ahead*

*There I buried Leah.*
Genesis 49:31

We don't know how Leah's life ended. The only mention of her death is when Jacob said, "I buried Leah."

Leah's life was filled with pain and sorrow, discouragement and disappointment, setbacks and letdowns. Yet even as she lived her life in the shadow of Jacob and Rachel's bright love, she enjoyed three tremendous blessings as she forged ahead.

- Leah was blessed by God with six sons and one daughter. One of her sons was Judah, through whose line the Savior Jesus Christ would come.
- Leah was buried with her husband. Leah, not Rachel, lay next to Jacob in the family tomb.
- Leah is mentioned in God's Who's Who (Genesis 49:31). Leah (meaning "weak" and "faint") is among those forever remembered, along with Abraham, Isaac, and Jacob, and their wives, Sarah and Rebekah.

Every life—including yours—has its shadowlands. How can you move on through heartache? Follow what Leah learned—

*Lesson #1:* Take a long-range view. God's purposes are achieved through the whole of your life, not in fragments of a moment, a day, or a year. What counts most is the sum of your contributions. Being a devoted wife, a loving mother, and a benefit to those around you are contributions to God's kingdom that can never be fully measured.

*Lesson #2:* Give your love generously to as many as you can. It's not what you get, but what you give that is God's true measure of a life.

## 66 Rewards Come

*There I buried Leah.*
GENESIS 49:31

Far better than reading a volume of *Who's Who in Church History* is reading the Who's Who lists of men and women who shaped the nation of Israel. One such list appears in Genesis 49. Leah is included in this roll call of very important people, which shows us something very important about who matters in the kingdom of God.

As Jacob, the son of Isaac and grandson of Abraham, lay dying in Egypt, he first blessed his 12 sons. Then, having pronounced his blessings, Jacob charged his sons to bury him in the field of Machpelah in the land of Canaan and explained why:

> There they buried Abraham and Sarah his wife,
> there they buried Isaac and Rebekah his wife,
> and there I buried Leah.

At long last Leah is honored by her husband. During Leah's life Jacob never pretended to love her and never hid his love for her sister, Rachel. But in the end he requested to be buried alongside Leah. And Leah—not Rachel—is listed in the Who's Who of patriarchal couples through whom God extended the promise of a Savior. Leah is mentioned right beside Abraham, Isaac, Jacob, Sarah, and Rebekah. Faithful Leah finally received the honor she never knew during her days on earth.

Your calling—like Leah's—is to remain faithful…to the end. Honor is not always bestowed along life's way. Flowers may be thrown across your path, but the winner's wreath is not awarded until the end of the contest. Regardless of obstacles en route to glory, regardless of sorrow or mistreatment on your journey to paradise, look only to the Lord. He is standing at the end to receive you…at the end to reward you. Wait for God's "well done." It will come!

## 67 *Early Women of Faith*

***Israel took his journey with all that he had.***
GENESIS 46:1

In a country ruled by a monarch, a crown is usually passed down from generation to generation. The crown—generally magnificent, ornate, and bejeweled—is an emblem of the ruler's exalted position. But no position or title is more exalted or prestigious than "woman of faith." Through the ages many women who loved God have worn that crown of eternal righteousness. Let's look back at some of those women.

- Eve fell in sin but went on to walk with God.
- Noah's wife accepted God's invitation to salvation.
- Sarah followed where God led her husband.
- Hagar cried out to God twice and He preserved her.
- Rebekah prayed to God for a child.
- Servants Bilhah and Zilpah entered into God's blessings.
- Rachel died giving Israel a godly leader.
- Leah shone brilliantly in the shadows of suffering.

The Lord blessed each of these women and made her beautiful. They endured hardship, adversity, shame, and failure. They were called upon by God to make hard choices and demonstrated their faith. Many showed their faith in God by a forward gaze, by a decision to not look back at loss, at things forsaken, at failure, at mistreatment. Most chose to greet every sunrise with fresh hope. Each endured and pressed on as she drew great strength from the Lord.

Are you a woman of faith? Are you actively looking to the Lord for His help, His wisdom, His enabling, and His grace? As one writer remarked, "Our part is to trust Him fully, to obey Him implicitly, and to follow His instructions faithfully."[13] In doing so, you live in a way that points to the majestic beauty of faith, grace, and excellence.

## 68 Choose God's Way

*You shall kill him.*
EXODUS 1:16

Every problem requires a solution, and the Pharaoh of Egypt had a big one—Joseph, the son of Rachel and Jacob. During a devastating famine the only food available was in Egypt, so Jacob and his family moved there. They were reunited with Joseph and enjoyed many wonderful years together.

"Now there arose a new king over Egypt, who did not know Joseph. And he said to his people, 'Look, the people of the children of Israel are more and mightier than we'" (Exodus 1:8-9).

- *The problem*—The rapid increase in the number of Israelites.
- *The solution*—Murder every male baby.
- *The means*—The Hebrew midwives Shiphrah and Puah.

Shiphrah and Puah were professionals who assisted Hebrew women with childbirth and the initial care of their newborns. When these two women were commanded to kill the babies they were helping bring into the world, they faced a huge dilemma.

- *The problem*—Ordered to kill every male baby born to the Hebrews.
- *The solution*—Because they feared God, the women quietly disobeyed the order.

Every problem tests the mettle of your allegiance to God. Every problem says, "Whom will you obey?" Take courage from Shiphrah and Puah, who risked their lives by disregarding Pharaoh's command to kill. Be bold every time a problem comes up and choose God's way.

## 69 The Fear of the Lord

*The midwives feared God.*
Exodus 1:17

What does it mean to "fear" God? The meaning is twofold. One aspect is reverence, and the other is terror. As a woman of God—a woman who fears the Lord—your life will be characterized by both aspects. You'll...

- dread God's displeasure
- desire His favor
- revere His holiness
- cheerfully follow His will
- be grateful for His benefits
- sincerely worship Him
- carefully obey His commandments[14]

Shiphrah and Puah show these qualities. Midwives by profession, these women were commanded by the Pharaoh of Egypt to kill every Hebrew male child born. What would you do in such a situation? The midwives chose to disobey Pharaoh's command, revealing their great courage and tremendous love for God. They counted the cost (and the cost was their lives!), but their love and respect for the Lord helped them make the right decision. They obeyed God rather than man. They lived out their fear of the Lord in practical faith.

Do you fear the Lord? Be sure your love for God shows in the practical details of daily life. Spend some time in prayer and commit yourself to the Lord. Determine to more fervently revere His holiness, follow Him, and obey His Word. Pour out your gratitude for His many blessings. "The mercy of the Lord is from everlasting to everlasting on those who fear Him" (Psalm 103:17).

# 70 Practical Daily Faith

*[God] provided households for them.*
EXODUS 1:21

The number of Israelites in Egypt was greatly increasing, so the Pharaoh of Egypt ordered the midwives to kill every male baby. But Shiphrah and Puah, two women who were probably Egyptian and oversaw other midwives, refused. They feared God and risked their lives to save many Jewish infants.

The kindness these two midwives showed to God's people didn't go unnoticed. God saw their practical daily faith and blessed them for obeying His ways—

*Blessing #1:* God protected them from Pharaoh. Because they chose to disobey Pharaoh's edict, "God dealt well with the midwives." He preserved their lives. Those who fear the Lord receive His protection.

*Blessing #2:* God provided them with families. "Because the midwives feared God...He provided households for them." Shiphrah and Puah were probably older, unmarried women. In return for their goodness, God blessed them with what they most wanted—families of their own. He gave them husbands, built them up into families, blessed their children, and prospered them in all they did.

What does God require of you so He may abundantly bless you? In a word, *obedience.* What can you do to cultivate this? Ask...

- What does God command in His Word?
- What is the right thing to do?
- What would Jesus do?

# 71 Faith for Every Day

*She hid [her baby] three months.*
Exodus 2:2

Have you wondered what true faith looks like in everyday life? Meet Jochebed, a true picture of faith in action. Note a few key facts about this great woman of faith.

*Her heritage.* A daughter of Levi, Jochebed married Amram, a man of the house of Levi (Exodus 2:1; 6:20). Through Levi, Jochebed and Amram inherited the faith of Abraham, Isaac, and Jacob.

*Her situation.* As the mother of a newborn boy, Jochebed faced a frightening dilemma. She knew the Egyptian Pharaoh had ordered every son born of the Jews to be cast into the Nile River (Exodus 1:22).

*Her faith.* Motivated by her trust in God and her love for her child, Jochebed took a bold step of faith and hid little Moses. This singular act of faith qualified her as one whose life testifies of faith in God. Only three women—Sarah, Rahab, and Jochebed—are noted among God's heroes of faith (Hebrews 11). Of Jochebed Scripture says, "By faith Moses, when he was born, was hidden three months by his parents, because…they were not afraid of the king's command" (verse 23).

*Her decision.* Jochebed's faith fueled her courage. Deciding to neither obey Pharaoh's command nor fear him or any consequences, she trusted God and kept her baby alive.

Every day how does your faith show? What acts or choices might people notice that reveal your love for Him? As a child of God, hold up your frightening, seemingly impossible situations to your Father in heaven. Realize that worry ends when faith begins…and that faith ends when worry begins. Declare with David, "Whenever I am afraid, I will trust in You" (Psalm 56:3).

## 72 Take the Risk!

*She took an ark...and laid it...*
*by the river's bank.*
EXODUS 2:3

The wise writer of Ecclesiastes tells women who love God to "cast your bread upon the waters, for you will find it after many days" (11:1). This principle for living a life of faith alludes to the agricultural practice of throwing seed upon water or soggy ground and then waiting for it to produce a harvest. Like a farmer, at times you must take a risk to enjoy the rewards of faith. You must step out *before* you can receive God's blessing.

When the Egyptian Pharaoh ordered every male baby born to the Jews to be drowned in the Nile, Jochebed was forced to take a chance with her "seed"...with her tiny baby, Moses. She hid her little babe for three months. Then, realizing she could no longer conceal a vigorous infant and trusting God, Jochebed "took an ark of bulrushes...put the child in it, and laid it in the reeds by the river's bank." She was casting her bread—her beloved son—upon the waters.

In His great providence, God brought Pharaoh's daughter to the riverbank. She found the ark and had compassion for the infant. Needing a nursemaid for the baby, the princess found Jochebed—further evidence of God's providence. Jochebed was allowed to keep and nurse the precious babe she'd placed into the hands of God by putting him into the river. Jochebed's seed of faith sprouted!

What challenge in your life requires a risk of faith? Are you sending your child off to school or college, off to a new married life, off to a job in another city or state, off to serve God on the mission field? Do you feel you're losing him or her? Have the faith of Jochebed. Take the risk and let go. Trust God that you will eventually reap blessings.

# 73 An Amazing Rescue

*The daughter of Pharaoh...had compassion on him.*
EXODUS 2:5-6

Are you ready to explore a stunning instance of God's providential use of people, events, and circumstances in the lives of His children? The times were dark—deathly dark!—for the Jewish people in Egypt. The Pharaoh sentenced every Hebrew baby boy to death by drowning (Exodus 1:22). But one woman of faith, Jochebed, defied Pharaoh's order. She hid her baby boy for three months and then placed him in a handmade basket and put it at the river's edge.

By God's sovereign providence, into this grim scene waded the Pharaoh's daughter. Walking along the riverbank, she spotted the basket and had it fetched out of the water. She knew of her father's detestable edict, but his evil hadn't hardened her heart. With compassion she responded to the baby's cries and later adopted the infant as her own. Imagine, the daughter of the Pharaoh saving the life of a baby her father ordered killed! Only God could design such an amazing rescue!

As God's child, you're the apple of His eye (Deuteronomy 32:10). That means you're guarded, protected, and kept by Him just as Jochebed and her baby were. Despite the appalling edict of one person (the Pharaoh), God used another person (Pharaoh's daughter) to honor Jochebed's faith and save her son Moses. In the midst of Israel's difficult circumstances, God was at work preparing for their future deliverance.

And now for you...Are you facing unfair treatment, perhaps even from someone cruel and evil? Are you oppressed? Hang on to your faith and wait for God's gracious providence and overruling power. Trust that He is going before you, as He went before Moses and Jochebed. With His great power, God will keep you, care for you, and guide you...and afterward receive you to glory.

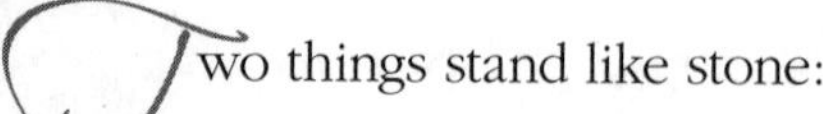

# 74 A Heart of Compassion

*The daughter of Pharaoh...had compassion on him.*
Exodus 2:5-6

Two things stand like stone:

Kindness in another's troubles;
Courage in one's own.[15]

Little is known about the mysterious daughter of Pharaoh, but her kindness and courage have endured through the ages. The Scriptures tell of that sunny day when this princess approached the Nile River for her bath. While wading along the river's edge, she caught sight of a floating basket, which she discovered held a small baby boy. This woman knew the baby was one of the Hebrews' children her father had ordered killed, but she had compassion for him. The Pharaoh's daughter had a very big heart!

- *She was compassionate.* Hearing the baby's cries, the daughter of the powerful Pharaoh drew the infant out of the water and named him Moses.
- *She was kind.* At the risk of jeopardizing her relationship with her father, this princess thought it too cruel to murder the little infant she held. She offered kindness to someone in trouble.
- *She was courageous.* Compassion and kindness kindled courage in the princess and overshadowed any fear she had of disobeying her father.

Although Pharaoh's daughter was a pagan, God used this woman's kindness and courage to benefit His people. This tender woman of the past—whose name we don't even know—challenges us today. Will you pray to be more kind to others in distress? To be courageous and compassionate when the need arises?

## 75 Cultivating Family Values

*His sister stood afar off.*
EXODUS 2:4

Miriam was probably between 7 and 12 years old when her baby brother Moses was born. For three months she helped her mother, Jochebed, hide the babe and care for him as their family defied the Pharaoh's edict to kill every newborn Hebrew boy (Exodus 1:22). When the baby became too vigorous to hide, Miriam's mom placed Moses into a floating basket that she set among the reeds of the Nile River.

Miriam watched Moses. When the opportunity arose—when Pharaoh's daughter discovered the baby and responded positively—Miriam ran up and offered to find a nurse for the infant. Because of her quick actions, Moses would be cared for at home by his mother.

As a mom, a devoted grandmother, a loving aunt, you can help instill such loyalty and love in your family by...

- *openly expressing kindness and concern for others.* Children repeat what they hear and mimic what they see. Be a living model of Jesus Christ.
- *expressing love openly.* Be affectionate and verbal. Say "I love you" every time you say goodbye or talk on the phone to your children.
- *teaching siblings to love one another.* Encourage brothers and sisters to pray for one another and to do secret acts of kindness for one another.
- *cultivating strong family ties.* Promote a "one for all and all for one" attitude in your family.
- *praying for God's love to be revealed by and through your children.*

# 76 *Clever and Gutsy Miriam*

*So [Miriam] went and called the child's mother.*
Exodus 2:8

Traditionally Jewish girls remained under the guidance of their mothers until marriage. So by the time Moses was born, Miriam had been taught the valuable qualities of diligence, faithfulness, responsibility, and wisdom by Jochebed. The young Miriam clearly exhibited each of these virtues.

Since Pharaoh had commanded that every Hebrew boy be drowned, when Moses' parents gave birth to a little boy, they hid him until he could no longer be kept quiet. The distressful day came when they placed Moses in a basket on the river. Even though they knew God would watch over him, it was still heartbreaking.

Perhaps Moses' mother couldn't bear to watch what might happen to her dear baby. Or perhaps her presence at the riverbank would've been too obvious. Did she ask Miriam to stand nearby and watch over the basket? Or did the spunky, devoted sister stay on her own to look out for her baby brother? However it happened, she was there when Pharaoh's daughter came to bathe and ended up rescuing the infant. Thinking fast, the clever and gutsy Miriam stepped forward and asked, "Shall I go and call a nurse for you from the Hebrew women, that she may nurse the child for you?" Given permission by the princess, Miriam brought Jochebed to feed him! Because of Miriam's quick thinking, a double blessing was reaped by her family.

- Jochebed received her baby back.
- Jochebed received wages for nursing Moses.

Teaching your little ones love, mercy, caring, and compassion, along with diligence, faithfulness, responsibility, and wisdom—the kinds of traits we see in Miriam—begins with you! They will grow up to mirror your merits. What are they seeing in you and learning from your actions?

## 77 Nurturing Children

*Take this child away and nurse him for me.*
EXODUS 2:9

If you're a mother, grandmother, or aunt, God calls you to devote yourself to children. You have the important role of teaching your growing family members about Him, of nurturing them up for Him, of giving Him a man or woman to use for His great purposes. Today's look at Jochebed focuses on her faithful mothering.

*Her name.* Jochebed is the first person in Scripture to have a name compounded with "Jah," or "Jehovah." Jochebed means "glory of Jehovah," "Jehovah is her glory," or "Jehovah is our glory." This is the woman the pagan daughter of Pharaoh asked to "take this child away and nurse him for me."

*Her son.* Pharaoh's daughter didn't know the infant she'd taken out of the basket floating in the Nile River was Jochebed's. To save her child from a death decree, Jochebed placed him into that homemade basket and, by faith, positioned it and its precious cargo in the water at the river's edge.

*Her assignment.* The opportunity to nurse Moses gave Jochebed two-and-a-half-years to teach her son about Jehovah. She had these few years to help her child become a man God could use. When Moses was weaned, Jochebed would have to deliver him to Pharaoh's daughter.

Just a few years! Did you know 50 percent of a child's character and personality development takes place by age three and 75 percent by age five? Jochebed used those critical years to train her son in the ways of the Lord. I urge you to take seriously your role in the lives of your children. Even a few years devoted to God's little ones can make a world of difference!

## 78 Making Each Day Count

*[Jochebed] took the child and nursed him.*
Exodus 2:9

God gives Christian parents the assignment of training up children for Him. Proverbs 22:6 says, "Train up a child in the way he should go." Jochebed raised Moses, her youngest child, for his first three years and then had to turn him over to his adoptive mom. Can you imagine how much her heart hurt when she had to give Moses to Pharaoh's daughter to raise? But Jochebed's faithful training bore fruit in her son's life. The second half of Proverbs 22:6 came true, "When he is old he will not depart from it." At age 40 Moses chose to identify with God's people rather than remain in Pharaoh's palace (Hebrews 11:24-26). That was his first giant step toward the important role God had for him.

Deuteronomy 6:5-7 gives us two guidelines for training children:

> *Love God.* "You shall love the Lord your God with all your heart, with all your soul, and with all your strength." Devote yourself to your heavenly Father. Love Him more than anyone or anything else.
>
> *Teach God's Word.* "You shall teach [My words] diligently to your children and shall talk of them when you sit in your house, when you walk by the way, when you lie down, and when you rise up." Faithfully communicate the truths of Scripture.

An axiom of teaching warns, "You can't impart what you don't possess." Is God the focus of your life? Is pleasing Him the overarching concern of your life? With a foundation of deep love for God and His Word hidden in your heart, you definitely have something crucial to share with your children. Consciously and constantly make each day count—talk to your children about God!

# 79 Four Cs of Wisdom

*She brought [Moses] to Pharaoh's daughter.*
EXODUS 2:10

All around you is evidence that evil is in this fallen world. Terrible news comes in from all over the world. But take heart! You can make a difference. Take Jochebed, for instance. She lived in an evil world that was growing darker every day. When her third baby was born, the Egyptian Pharaoh put forth his evil hand of oppression. He ordered that every boy born to the Jews be murdered (Exodus 1:16, 22)! What could Jochebed—a godly woman and devoted mother—do against such evil? She could take action in faith!

- *Courage*—Jochebed decided to keep her baby rather than kill him, thereby preserving him to bless the world.
- *Creativity*—Jochebed made a basket from bulrushes, covered it with tar and mud for waterproofing, and then put her baby in it so he would float in the Nile River close to where Pharaoh's daughter came regularly.
- *Care*—During the brief time she had Moses, Jochebed lovingly nursed and diligently trained him in the ways of the Lord.
- *Confidence*—After giving her son loving care and spiritual instruction, Jochebed returned her son to Pharaoh's household, trusting God would care for her boy.

God used Jochebed's courage, creativity, care, and confidence to position her son inside the house of Pharaoh. There he would be educated and become familiar with Egyptian ways. God would later use Moses to deliver His people from oppression.

If you're a mom, don't fret because of evildoers. Devote yourself to raising children who love God. And take heart! The prince of darkness is helpless against the power of the truth you plant in your children's hearts and minds.

# 80 Light the Fire of Faith!

*She brought [Moses] to Pharaoh's daughter.*
EXODUS 2:10

The Proverbs 31 woman excelled in her God-given role of mother. Her children even "rose up" and blessed her. This "blessing" means her grown children lived in a way that brought honor, joy, and credit to their mother. Although the Bible doesn't say much about Jochebed, it does reveal much about her three children that reflects on their mom. Who were her celebrated children?

- *Aaron* became Israel's first high priest, marking the beginning of the Aaronic priesthood (Exodus 30:30).
- Her daughter *Miriam* was a gifted poetess and musician who led the Israelite women in a victory song after God delivered them from Pharaoh's army. Along with her brothers, she was involved in God's deliverance of Israel from Egyptian oppression.
- *Moses,* the baby Jochebed gave to Pharaoh's daughter in order to save his life, led God's people out of Egypt. He also communicated God's law to them.

Where did these three get their flame of faith? Answer: From their mom! Jochebed took seriously her relationship with God and her role as a mother. She lived her life for the Lord, and her sons and daughter lit their torches of faith at her flame.

You too are called to light the fires of faith in your home. Does your soul burn energetically with love for the Lord, with the bright joy of salvation, with a shining commitment to your family? Yes, having such a fire of faith is costly, requiring energy and commitment. But when you use your life to fuel the faith in those you love, as you burn brilliantly and intensely, your children have many opportunities to light their own flame of love for God.

# 81 Moms Partnering with God

*She brought [Moses] to Pharaoh's daughter.*
EXODUS 2:10

Look into the heart of Jochebed. She was a fierce, protective, caring mom. How can you grow these qualities?

*Begin early.* "Let every Christian parent understand when the child is three years old that they have done more than half they ever will for his character."[16]

*Embrace motherhood.* "The most important occupation on the earth for a woman is to be a real mother to her children. It does not have much glory in it; there is a lot of grit and grime. But there is no greater place of ministry, position, or power than that of a mother."[17]

*Live with integrity.* "Only as genuine Christian holiness and Christlike love are expressed in the life of a parent, can the child have the opportunity to inherit the flame and not the ashes."[18]

*Partner with God.* "Parenthood is a partnership with God. You are not molding iron nor chiseling marble; you are working with the Creator of the universe in shaping human character and determining destiny."[19]

God's calling to teach little ones is noble. So partner with God. Cultivate a fierce passion for God's Word and keep His wisdom in your heart. Consider these checkpoints:

- Do you spend time daily feasting on God's Word and sharing life-giving truth with your children?
- Are you giving the Bible a reigning position in your home and family life?
- Is there a regular family time for teaching, memorizing, and reciting Bible passages?

## 82 The Gift of Generosity

*[Moses] became [Pharaoh's daughter's] son.*
EXODUS 2:10

Remember when we looked at the admirable qualities in Pharaoh's daughter? She was compassionate, kind, and courageous as she defied her father's death sentence for Jewish baby boys and saved little Moses. To this fearless daughter's credit, we now add the gift of generosity. Not only did she save Moses' life, but she also took him into Pharaoh's palace as her son and raised him as royalty. What blessings and benefits did Moses enjoy as the adopted son of Pharaoh's daughter?

- Her care helped build a solid foundation so Moses would be an effective leader of God's people. Being raised in Pharaoh's home, he saw government up close.
- Her kind act was God's means of delivering the child who would one day lead His people out of Egypt.
- Her adoption of Moses afforded him the privileges of a royal son.
- Her parentage meant an education and knowledge of the Egyptian language for the man who would one day negotiate with Pharaoh, lead the Israelites out of Egypt, and write the first five books of the Bible.

Through the actions of one noble woman, God moved His servant Moses from the reeds along the Nile River into a royal household. He was transplanted from the simple home of persecuted Israelite parents to a luxurious palace. From a future of shepherding and brick-making, he was prepared to become the leader of the Hebrew nation.

Have you thought about the many advantages and blessings you've received from others? Thank God for His gifts to you through people who have helped you. Then express your gratitude to your parents, relatives, friends, teachers, benefactors, and mentors.

## 83 *Finding Your Dream Man?*

*He gave Zipporah his daughter to Moses.*
EXODUS 2:21

Meet Zipporah, the woman married to Moses. God doesn't tell us much, but we can gather some information.

*Facts about Moses.* Moses was taken into the Egyptian Pharaoh's palace to be raised and educated. However, his special status was revoked when he murdered an Egyptian who was beating a Hebrew. When Pharaoh sought to kill Moses, he fled to the land of Midian.

*Facts about Reuel's daughters.* Moses' first encounter with his distant relatives in Midian was at a well where the daughters of Reuel, the priest of Midian, watered their father's flock. After Moses helped these seven women, they invited him to their home.

*Facts about Zipporah.* Piecing together the facts about Zipporah (whose name means "little bird") reveals she was:

- *A distant relative to Moses*—Kin to Moses through Abraham, Zipporah was the daughter of a priest who was probably a God-fearing man (Exodus 18:12-13).
- *A faithful worker*—When we first see Zipporah, she's at work, drawing water for her father's flock.
- *An obedient daughter*—Zipporah served her father in her daily duties. She was also content to marry Moses, the man to whom her father gave her.
- *A hospitable woman*—After Moses helped Zipporah and her sisters, they invited him to their house.

Are you wondering how...when...if...you will meet the man of your dreams? Develop the admirable character qualities exhibited in Zipporah's life.

## 84 *God Supplies What You Need*

*Let...every [woman] ask [silver and gold] from her neighbor.*
EXODUS 11:2

Hudson Taylor, founder of China Inland Mission, once boldly and rightly declared, "God's work done in God's way will never lack God's supplies." Again and again this missionary witnessed God providing for His work and His people.

Moses was leading God's people and meeting with the Egyptian Pharaoh, demanding that he let the Israelites return home. Moses and his brother, Aaron, met with Pharaoh nine times to secure permission to leave. Then, in a final stroke against the Egyptians, God told Moses, "I will bring one more plague on Pharaoh and on Egypt. Afterward he will let you go from here." That last plague was death to the firstborn human and beast in every Egyptian household.

Before the death plague occurred, God instructed Moses, "You shall not go empty-handed. But every woman shall ask of her neighbor...articles of silver, articles of gold, and clothing" (Exodus 3:21-22). In other words, the women were to ask openly and intentionally for the Egyptians' gold and silver jewelry, drinking vessels, and clothing. What was the outcome of the women's follow through? The Egyptian people showered them with gifts!

What God requires of you, He will equip you for and see that your needs are abundantly supplied. Believe it! As God's child you will never lack the supplies you need to do His work. Indeed, your heavenly Father has promised to "supply all your need according to His riches in glory by Christ Jesus" (Philippians 4:19).

| | |
|---|---|
| Are you faithfully asking God for His supply? | Perhaps "you do not have because you do not ask" (James 4:2). |
| Are your motives pure? Are you most concerned about God's purposes and His glory? | See that you do not "ask amiss, that you may spend it on your pleasures" (James 4:3). |

## 85 Time for Ministry

*Miriam...the sister of [Moses and] Aaron...*
EXODUS 15:20

"Miriam, what advice do you have for single women?" Imagine an interviewer today asking this question of Miriam, one of God's super-singles of yesterday.

Perhaps Miriam would simply say, "Devote yourself to ministry." Based on the Bible, Miriam appears to have viewed her singleness as an opportunity to give herself fully to ministry. As a result she blossomed into one of the Bible's strongest female leaders (Micah 6:4). Throughout the deliverance of God's people from Egyptian bondage and their journey into the Promised Land, Miriam accompanied and assisted her brothers, Aaron and Moses, in their leadership of the Israelites.

If you're unmarried, join Miriam in her view of ministry. Yes, you may have your career (that is also an important opportunity for ministry), but the rest of your time is available.

Now, whether you're single or married, take time to pray about these two questions:

- How effectively am I using my "free" time—my evenings, my weekends, my children's naptimes—for God's kingdom?
- What doors of ministry are open to me now?

Just think of the myriad of ministries you could have during your free time! You could mentor another woman. You could write or e-mail a lonely missionary. You could take a special meal to a person suffering physically. You could visit a shut-in. You could help your church prepare for worship services. Take a bold step into the realm of selfless ministry. Make time for it.

## 86 *Encouraging Family Interaction*

*Miriam...the sister of [Moses and] Aaron...*
EXODUS 15:20

Miriam was the quick-thinking girl who hid along Egypt's Nile River and quietly watched the tiny floating basket that held her baby brother, Moses. She was waiting to see what would happen (Exodus 2:4). Miriam's devotion to Moses didn't end on that riverbank. In response to God's call to live her life as a single woman, Miriam devoted herself to serving her two brothers, Aaron and Moses, as they served God and His people (Micah 6:4).

In the previous reading we began an interview with Miriam by asking, "What advice do you have for single women?" Based on how Miriam lived her life, we imagined her first piece of advice would be to devote yourself to ministry. Now let's look at a second pearl of wisdom—"Devote yourself to family."

Miriam gave her heart, her love, and her energy to helping her brothers in the massive undertaking of leading the Jewish nation—over two million people!—away from the oppression of Pharaoh and into freedom. As Aaron and Moses led the entire company, Miriam was looked upon—and acted as—the leader of the women.

Are you single? If so, in what creative ways can you serve and support your family members in their various endeavors, especially those laboring for God's kingdom? Family deserves your loyalty and understanding.

Are you a mom? Are you encouraging family unity among your children? Engage your family in joint service to God. Consider "adopting" a missionary family, serving a meal at a local soup kitchen, laboring during a church workday, teaching Sunday school, or getting school supplies and backpacks for needy kids. As you promote mutual service to God and ministry to one another, your children will be well on their way to uniting in service to God just as Moses, Aaron, and Miriam did.

# 87 *Praising and Prophesying*

*Miriam, the prophetess...*
Exodus 15:20

A prophetess receives messages from God and shares it with others. She openly praises the Lord with words and songs that come from or are inspired by Him. Only a handful of women in Scripture are given this role and title. They include Miriam, Deborah, Huldah, Anna, and Philip's four daughters.[20] Miriam is the first woman noted in Scripture with this rare honor (Numbers 12:2). One occasion when Miriam spoke for God was a great day in the history of the Jewish people.

The years before Miriam's prophesying included her people's bondage under the oppressive hand of the Egyptians. When the sons of Israel cried out to God for help, God sent Moses and Aaron, Miriam's brothers, to negotiate the Israelites' freedom. Times were tense because Pharaoh increased the Jews' workload and repeatedly changed his mind about their release. After ten encounters with Moses and numerous plagues choreographed by God, including the death of all the firstborn Egyptian children and livestock, Pharaoh finally allowed the Israelites to leave. But even then he was so angry he soon sent an army in pursuit (Exodus 14:7).

This dramatic situation was the backdrop for one more mighty and supernatural act. As soon as the Jewish people walked through the miraculously parted Red Sea waters, God just as miraculously closed the waters, drowning the entire Egyptian army. What wonder! What relief for the Jews! What deliverance! Moses erupted into a song of praise, and Miriam also offered her own God-inspired song of praise. With tambourine in hand and followed by all the women dancing and playing their own tambourines, Miriam exulted, "Sing to the Lord, for He has triumphed gloriously! The horse and its rider He has thrown into the sea!" Amen!

## 88 *Inspired to Serve*

*All the women went out after her.*
Exodus 15:20

Do you have aspirations for leadership? Consider a few principles of spiritual leadership. Then ask God to help develop them in you.

- *A leader is a follower.* To be a good leader you must first be a follower. Leadership is a discipline, and in the process of being a faithful follower you gain discipline.
- *A leader is a pray-er.* Prayer brings to leadership the power and energy of the Holy Spirit. Missionary and leader Hudson Taylor was convinced that it is possible to move others, through God, by prayer alone.
- *A leader is an initiator.* Authentic leaders take risks and move out courageously to make their vision happen.[21]

If you want a great model for leading—look to Miriam!

- *Miriam was a follower.* She faithfully served and assisted her brothers, Aaron and Moses, as they led God's people (Micah 6:4).
- *Miriam was a pray-er.* As a prophetess and woman of prayer, Miriam was filled with the Holy Spirit, who inspired her words.
- *Miriam was an initiator.* Moved by God's miraculous defeat of the Egyptian army in the midst of the Red Sea, Miriam "took the timbrel in her hand" and led the women in a song and dance of joy.

May God's Spirit and Miriam's example inspire you!

## 89 *Celebrate!*

***All the women went out…
with timbrels and with dances.***
EXODUS 15:20

Have you ever felt like a rubber band? Stretched…and stretched…and stretched…until you were ready to snap? That's what the Israelites felt. For more than 350 years God's people suffered oppression as slaves in Egypt. And when God sent Moses to deliver them, tension increased as the Pharaoh refused again and again to let God's people go and even made their work harder (Exodus 10:27).

The Jews labored and waited…for a long time. They worried about much. They wondered about Moses' leadership and God's faithfulness. Then they witnessed many powerful miracles, including the Pharaoh's release of them and the drowning of his army.

Now, safe on the other side of the Red Sea, they worshiped. Their release from bondage and the long-awaited relief from tension resulted in a spontaneous outburst of praise. Moses and the people of Israel sang to the Lord, and all the women went out after Miriam playing their timbrels and dancing.

God tells us in Ecclesiastes 3:4 and 7:

> There is a "time to weep, and a time to laugh;"
> There is a "time to mourn, and a time to dance…."
> There is a "time to keep silence, and a time to speak."

And it was time for the Israelites to laugh, dance, speak, sing, shout, and celebrate! So with their lips they exalted Jehovah, spoke of His wonders, and sang His praises.

Why not add your own voice to the Israelites' mighty chorus of praise? Celebrate…

- your release from a trial
- your deliverance from bondage
- your escape from eternal darkness

Magnify the Lord! Exalt His name! Celebrate!

## 90 Sing with Joyful Abandon!

*Miriam…answered [the men's song].*
EXODUS 15:21

"Music is God's gift to man. It is the only art of heaven given to earth, and the only art of earth we take to heaven."[22] Throughout time God's people have expressed their praise and worship and joy to God through music. In fact, the Bible charges everything that has breath to "Praise the Lord!" with voice and with trumpet, lute, harp, timbrels, stringed instruments, flutes, and cymbals (Psalm 150: 1-6). It's natural to sing and shout when you experience a blessing. Music allows you to express pure praise to God and participate in an activity of heaven.

Miriam sang! As the leader of the women in the two-million-plus assembly of God's people who escaped slavery to the Egyptians, she praised God. After they crossed the miraculously parted waters of the Red Sea and the sea just as miraculously closed on Pharaoh's pursuing army (Exodus 12–14), Miriam couldn't contain her joy. She sang and praised God's power and faithfulness: "Sing to the LORD, for He has triumphed gloriously! The horse and its rider He has thrown into the sea!" And the women joined in!

How can you follow Miriam's heartfelt and joyous example of praising God in unashamed exaltation?

- *Praise God spontaneously.* Miriam grabbed a tambourine and answered the male singers with a chorus of joyful praise.
- *Praise God for who He is.* Miriam celebrated God's power and His unchallenged supremacy and justice, truth and mercy.
- *Praise God heartily.* Miriam and the women sang and danced as they praised God. As Colossians 3:23 says, "Whatever you do, do it heartily, as to the Lord."

## 91 A Lifetime of Serving

*Sing to the LORD.*
EXODUS 15:21

One of the most encouraging characteristics of the women in the Bible who loved God is that they walked with Him and served His people until they died. As we say farewell to Miriam, one of God's terrific senior saints, please notice the many wonderful ways the 92-year-old-plus woman expended her energies. Her pattern makes wonderful lifetime goals for you and me.

- *Miriam loved the Lord.* As the Israelites emerged from the parted waters of the Red Sea and witnessed God's destruction of their enemies, Miriam's heart burst into praise and song as she worshiped the Lord.
- *Miriam led the women.* Ever the leader, when Miriam's hands reached for a timbrel and her soul sang in tribute to God, the other women joined her. Miriam was the leader of the women on the journey to the Promised Land.
- *Miriam served her brothers.* The young Miriam cared about her baby brother, Moses, as his basket floated in the Nile. The spunky older Miriam assisted her brothers Moses and Aaron as they led God's two million people out of slavery, into Egypt, and through the desert on the way to the Promised Land.
- *Miriam praised God.* She was never too old or too tired to praise Jehovah for His goodness and wonderful works for His children. Her worship was public, expressive, exuberant, and heartfelt.

Whatever your age, continue to be a woman who loves God and serves His people!

## 92 *Giving Generously*

*[Women] came...as many as had a willing heart.*
Exodus 35:22

The Dead Sea is a vast body of salt water located in the desert land of Israel. In ancient times the Dead Sea basin was regularly flooded by the Red Sea, which is where the salt comes from. Geological events such as earthquakes eventually closed off the Dead Sea. Forty-nine miles long, 10 miles wide, and 1300 feet deep, the Dead Sea is fed by the Jordan River at the rate of six million gallons of fresh water a day. Despite that influx of clean water, the Dead Sea is...dead! One of the reasons is because it has no outlet.

There is a lovely sorority referred to by many as "the willing-hearted women." Before the great Israelite exodus from Egyptian slavery, the women were told to ask for—and they received—gifts of gold and silver jewelry from the Egyptians (Exodus 11:2). Later, when the Israelites were encamped, Moses issued a call from God for an offering to finance and furnish a place of worship (Exodus 25:8). How did the willing-hearted Israelite women respond? They contributed by bringing earrings, nose rings, rings, necklaces, and other gold jewelry as offerings to the Lord.

How lovely to have a generous heart! Like flowing water, money and possessions are less useful when they're hoarded. Don't be like the Dead Sea—useless—because your assets have no outlet! Prayerfully consider these questions:

- What is my attitude toward my belongings?
- Do I have a plan for regular giving?
- What can I contribute to the Lord's work today?

Notice how this section of Exodus ends. The people gave so generously Moses finally told them to stop giving!

# 93 *Giving What You've Received*

*[Women] came...as many as had a willing heart.*
EXODUS 35:22

More than 3000 years ago a group of grateful Jewish women modeled a wonderful way to express heartfelt appreciation to their Deliverer. God had miraculously spared their firstborn children and orchestrated the deliverance of the Jews after long years of slavery in the land of Egypt. So when Moses said, "Whoever is of a willing heart, let him bring...an offering to the LORD" (Exodus 35:5), these women responded generously. Their striking example offers several precepts for giving to God from our hearts.

*Precept #1: Give your treasure.* When the call came for an offering, the Israelite women brought jewelry, fine linen, goats' hair, animal skins, and acacia wood. Even though they'd spent hundreds of years as slaves, now that they had treasure they chose to give.

What about your treasures? Where did they come from?

- "And what do you have that you did not receive?" (1 Corinthians 4:7). The answer to this question is a loud and clear, "Absolutely nothing!" After all, it is the Lord who gives power to get wealth (Deuteronomy 8:18).
- In the New Testament James reminds us that "every good gift and every perfect gift is from above, and comes down from the Father of lights" (James 1:17).
- The apostle Paul reminds us that "we brought nothing into this world, and it is certain we can carry nothing out" (1 Timothy 6:7).

Jesus said "Freely you have received, freely give" (Matthew 10:8). Amen!

## 94 Treasure Is More than Gold

*All the women who were gifted artisans spun...with their hands.*
Exodus 35:25

"Where your treasure is, there your heart will be also" (Matthew 6:21). When Moses called for a freewill offering to fund the tabernacle, many Israelite women gave out of hearts overflowing with gratitude to God. Along with giving "traditional" treasure, some followed a second giving principle.

*Precept #2: Give your talent.* Supplied with raw materials given by some of the women, others used their God-given talents to spin and weave. They produced fine linens and fabrics as offerings to God.

How do you view the skills God has given you? Do you use them to bring glory to Him? Imagine the beauty the Israelite women contributed to the house of the Lord! They worked the hair of goats and the skins of animals into gorgeous hangings to adorn their place of worship.

Evaluate your own aptitudes, skills, abilities, and expertise. Since they all come from God, how can you use them for His purposes? Share your talents to benefit people and enhance the worship of God! If you have a flair for arranging flowers, why not supply pulpit flowers each week? If you know how to clean, consider tidying up the ladies' room between services. If you're an artist, why not offer to embellish the church bulletin? If you crochet, think about creating an afghan made with love for one of your church's shut-ins. Give back to God the talents He's given to you.

## 95 The Gift of Time

*All the women whose hearts stirred with wisdom spun yarn of goats' hair.*
EXODUS 35:26

Nineteenth-century essayist and poet Ralph Waldo Emerson likened the minutes of our lives to uncut diamonds. Just as uncut diamonds gain value by being cut and used in jewelry-making, our minutes are raw commodities that increase in value as they're shaped and used for the Lord.

Imagine how brilliantly the diamond-like minutes—and hours—the Israelite women gave for God's tabernacle shine in heaven! When God told Moses to involve the people in outfitting a place for worship, God's faithful women answered generously. Their response gives us another important guide for our giving.

*Precept #3: Give your time.* The women of Israel worked diligently to furnish the tabernacle. With grateful hearts and busy hands, they turned raw materials into masterpieces of beauty fit for God. They spent hours weaving 10 curtains of "fine twined linen" (highlighted with blue, purple, and scarlet yarn and decorated with cherubim) and making 11 curtains of goats' hair, goats' skins, and rams' skins needed for a top covering. Each curtain measured 42 feet long and 6 feet wide—large enough to cover the 30-foot-high, 75-foot-wide wooden framework of the tabernacle![23]

Time is a precious gift from God you can give back for His purposes—time at a church workday to make your place of worship more beautiful, time at a prayer meeting to make the lives of those you pray for more beautiful, and time in God's Word to make your soul even more beautiful in His eyes.

Watch your minutes and spend them wisely. As a little poem declares, "Just a tiny little minute, but eternity is in it!" Use your minutes, hours, and days for timeless endeavors.

## 96 God's Blessings for You!

*[All the] women whose hearts were willing...*
EXODUS 35:29

Before we count more of the blessings the women of Israel enjoyed from God, pause, bow your head before Him who is mighty, and note some of the great things He's done for you. Take all the time you need to give praise, worship, and thanksgiving to your awesome God!

Now, note a few of God's rich and miraculous blessings He gave His own:

- *Safety*—God protected the Israelites through the 10 plagues He sent to the land of Egypt.
- *Family*—God spared the Hebrews' firstborns during the death plague.
- *Life*—God saved His people's lives by parting the Red Sea so they could walk to safety.
- *Deliverance*—In miraculous ways God ended the bondage and affliction His people had long experienced at the hands of the Egyptians.[24]

The Almighty has done wonders for you too! Why not echo the response of the Israelite women to God's overwhelming blessings? Give to the Lord...

*Volume*—they gave generously,
*Value*—they gave their best,
*Variety*—they gave treasure, talent, and time,
*Vigorously*—they gave enthusiastically.

## 97 *Beautiful Devotion*

*The bronze mirrors of the serving women...*
Exodus 38:8

When God speaks, His people need to listen...and obey. In the days of the great patriarch Moses, God spoke about using the gifts of the people to build a tabernacle for worship (Exodus 35:5). The hearts of the Israelites were so moved they brought more than enough and had to be instructed to stop giving!

Once the materials were gathered, preparations began. The coverings and structure were assembled. Next, the inner and outer veils were made. Then came the articles for the Holy Place—the ark of the covenant, the mercy seat, the table of show-bread, and the golden lampstand. Finally, the altar of incense and the altar of burnt offering were crafted (Exodus 36–38).

One last utensil remained to be created. That was the giant bowl where the priests could wash their blood-stained hands and soiled feet after offering the required animal sacrifices and before going into the Holy Place to worship the Lord. For this most important basin, Moses "made the laver of bronze and its base of bronze, from the bronze mirrors of the serving women."

God records forever this selfless act of the Israelite women who gave up their highly prized possessions for the priests' washbasin. They freely surrendered their beautiful brass mirrors—undoubtedly fine examples of Egyptian handiwork. From these melted-down objects of personal vanity, Moses formed an item that helped the priests be pure and holy before God. These women loved God more than their possessions—and more than their outward beauty.[25]

Have you dedicated to God all you own? Is all you are and have His? If the answer is yes, you possess the highest beauty of all—devotion and dedication to God.

## 98 Set Apart for God

*The vow of a Nazirite...*
NUMBERS 6:2

As a believer in Jesus Christ, you're set apart to God. You've been delivered from the power of darkness and translated into the kingdom of God's Son (Colossians 1:13). Jesus accomplished these wonders for you!

In the time of Moses, a group of women chose to go beyond giving material possessions and time. God allowed for a special heart offering—a vow—for those laypeople who wanted to dedicate even more to Him. The law stated that when either a man or woman takes the vow of a Nazirite to separate himself to the Lord, he shall separate himself from certain items and practices.

What did a woman who took a voluntary Nazirite vow avoid? God's unusual list included wine, grape products, haircuts, and touching dead bodies. By submitting to these restrictions in their daily lives, the people visibly and publicly set themselves apart from the world and declared their dedication to God.

How about you?

- Are you set apart to God in your heart and in your practices?
- Can others tell by your behavior, words, and attitudes that you are set apart from the world?
- Do people sense an otherworldliness about you, an aura of holiness?
- Have you set your affections on things above? Is your heart seeking those things that are of value to Christ (Colossians 3:1-2)?
- What will you do today to dedicate yourself afresh to God?

## 99 *Still Amazing Despite Flaws*

*Miriam died there and was buried there.*
NUMBERS 20:1

Why is it so easy for us to let the memory of one negative action in a person's lifetime overshadow all the good he or she accomplished? We've noted many aspects of Miriam's life of service to God. Four books of the Bible—Exodus, Leviticus, Numbers, Micah—tell us about this amazing woman who loved God. Just look at her list of outstanding accomplishments for God:

- She cared for her baby brother, Moses (Exodus 2:4).
- She served God shoulder to shoulder with her two brothers, Moses and Aaron, as they led God's people to freedom (Micah 6:4).
- She prophesied for God, speaking and acting under His inspiration (Exodus 15:20).
- She led the Israelite women in joyous worship after their deliverance from the Egyptian army (Exodus 15:20-21).
- She served God into her nineties, earning the tribute of "senior saint."

Yet there was one incident that casts a shadow on Miriam. In jealousy, Miriam (and Aaron) verbally attacked Moses. Miriam was severely punished by God and stricken with leprosy (Numbers 12). But, like God, let's not condemn Miriam for her lapse.

Beginning today, make an effort to graciously note and remember all that is good in other people. Don't let flaws or momentary sins color your overall view. As the Bible reminds us, "Whatever things are...noble...lovely...of good report...[and] praiseworthy—meditate on these things" (Philippians 4:8).

# 100 Women Can Inherit

*Then came the daughters of Zelophehad.*
NUMBERS 27:1-11

Question: What happens to a man's property when he dies without sons? The five daughters of Zelophehad asked this question. When their father died before the Israelites took possession of the Promised Land, these young women went to Moses for a ruling.

Answer: Moses consulted the Lord, and God gave Moses a new statute. The daughters of Zelophehad would receive their father's inheritance.

The record of their request stands forever in praise of these women. Mark well their positive qualities:

*Bold*—As women without relatives to speak for them, they took their case directly to Moses and, thus, before God. God values each of His children and is interested in what's happening.

*Balanced*—Their request was not a matter of greed. They only asked for the land that would have been assigned to their father when Canaan was settled. They wanted their father's name attached to the land, which would provide for them and be handed down through the generations.

*Believing*—These brave, wise daughters of Zelophehad never doubted that every man among the Lord's people would receive his portion in the land of promise (Joshua 21:43).

*Blessed*—These sisters received the reward of faith...the inheritance of their father.

Follow their example. Go boldly before God with your praise and requests. Believe He answers prayer. And receive with gratitude the blessings that come with depending on Him.

# 101 Vows Reveal Dedication

*If a woman makes a vow to the Lord…*
NUMBERS 30:3-16

We've seen the devotion of the Israelite women who voluntarily took a Nazirite vow. Now let's look at vows we make to God. Be sure to scan Numbers 30 (it's an exciting, thought-provoking chapter) and then consider…

- *The definition of a vow*—In the Old Testament, *vow* means a bond or a binding obligation. In the New Testament it means a prayer to God.
- *The significance of a vow*—A vow is a pledge or oath that's religious in nature. It's a transaction between a person and God. The person dedicates himself, his service, or something valuable to God.
- *The kinds of vows*—Besides being promises made to God, vows can also be voluntarily imposed self-discipline for building character and reaching certain goals.[26]

At the core of making a vow to God is a tremendous dedication to Him and a longing to grow in holiness. Do you want to make a vow? Take these two critical guidelines to heart:

- *Keep your word*—Whether vows, oaths, or promises, Jesus charges, "Let your 'Yes' be 'Yes,' and your 'No,' 'No'" (Matthew 5:37).
- *Take vows seriously*—God does! Proverbs 20:25 says, "It is a snare for a man…to reconsider his vows." In other words, "It's better not to make a vow or a promise than to make one and break it."

## 102 Before and After

*[They] came to the house of a harlot named Rahab.*
Joshua 2:1

"Rahab-the-harlot." Throughout the Bible, these three words refer to a remarkable woman who appears in faith's Hall of Fame (Hebrews 11). And she's got a before-and-after story to tell.

*Before*—Rahab was an idolatrous Amorite. Ra was the name of an Egyptian god, and Rahab's full name meant "insolent and fierce." The Bible also reports that Rahab was a harlot, a prostitute.

*God intervenes*—God touched Rahab's heart and transformed her into a new creature. For Rahab, old things passed away, and all things became new (2 Corinthians 5:17).

*After*—After her many heroic acts of faith, God abundantly blessed her life. What were some of the tangible blessings Rahab received?

- Rahab married Salmon, a prince in the house of Judah.
- Rahab bore Salmon a son named Boaz...whose son was Obed...whose son was Jesse...whose son was David...through whose line Jesus was born (Ruth 4:20-22; Matthew 1:1 and 5).

Thank God for your own story. To the praise of the glory of His grace, God accepts you, redeems you, and forgives your sins (Ephesians 1:6-7).

# 103 A Beautiful Cameo

*The woman took the two men and hid them.*
JOSHUA 2:4

Have you ever admired a carefully crafted cameo? Do you know how they're created? The process begins with a multilayered stone or shell. An engraver etches a design (usually the profile of a woman) on the piece and then carves a relief of it in the top layer. Lower layers serve as the background for the portrait. Cutting through the tiers of colors in the stone or shell creates a striking effect, and cameos are the most breathtaking when a light color is set against a dark background.

The life of Rahab offers us one of the Bible's most dramatic cameos of courage. Her beauty is brilliant because of the dark background against which it shines. Consider her situation.

The future was bleak for Rahab and her hometown of Jericho. Joshua had sent his warrior spies into the Promised Land to scout the area. Why? Because the Israelite army was planning to cross the Jordan River and take possession of their new kingdom, beginning with the godless city of Jericho.

God, the Master Artist, shows us in Rahab a stunning relief against the grim backdrop of evil. In her we see layer upon layer—and act upon act—of faith displayed. How was Rahab's faith evidenced?

When Joshua's spies entered Jericho, Rahab hid them, cared for them, and helped them escape. She also elicited a promise of future protection from them. Within the rough stone walls of a dark and doomed city, the faith of one woman—a moral leper in her day—glows and reflects the hands of the ultimate Craftsman—God.

What difficult events, circumstances, and trials serve as the backdrop for your daily life? How will your faith shine against such darkness to create an exquisite cameo?

## 104 An Astonishing Faith

*For the* Lord *your God, He is God.*
Joshua 2:11

Are you able to state clearly what you believe? Rahab did—and her statement of faith saved her life! Here's what happened.

The time came for God's people to enter the land God had promised them. Joshua, God's appointed leader, sent two of his warriors to check out the walled city of Jericho. While there, they lodged at Rahab's house. When the king of Jericho demanded Rahab hand over the men, Rahab quickly hid them and told the authorities they'd already left.

Why did this harlot and resident of a godless town take such a risk? Hear Rahab's words to the spies…and her heart of faith!

- I know that the Lord has given you the land.
- We have heard how the Lord dried up the water of the Red Sea for you when you came out of Egypt.
- The Lord your God, He is God in heaven above and on earth beneath.

Rahab's statement of faith clearly reveals her astonishing faith and knowledge of God. She obviously knew who God was and what He'd done for His people. She knew of His plan to give the land to His chosen race. And she knew He was the God of all heaven and earth. Rahab definitely had her facts about God straight!

How would your statement of faith read? How much do you know about God and His dealings with His people? How many of His attributes are you familiar with? Take time to think…and pray…and articulate your beliefs. Search the Scriptures too. Know what you believe…and then, as Rahab did, declare your faith to others.

# 105 *Choices*

*She let them down by a rope.*
JOSHUA 2:15

Did you know only three women are included in God's honor roll of Old Testament saints found in Hebrews 11? Standing tall in this lineup with Sarah (the mother of faith) and Jochebed (Moses' faithful mom) is Rahab. What is the glaring, even shocking, difference between Sarah, Jochebed, and Rahab?

- Sarah was married to Abraham, the friend of God (James 2:23).
- Jochebed was married to Amram, of the house of Levi, in the line of Abraham, Isaac, and Jacob (Exodus 2:1).
- Rahab was a pagan prostitute.

Rahab had no godly heritage, no devout husband, no pious parents. But her choices qualified her to join the ranks of Sarah and Jochebed! Ponder this truth:

To every man there openeth a way
And the high soul climbs the high way
And the low soul climbs the low...
To every man there openeth
A high way and a low;
And every man decideth
Which way his soul shall go.[27]

Rahab's choices exhibited her faith and altered her earthly and eternal destinies. On that notable day in Jericho when God sent His agents to Rahab's house, two ways opened up for her. Would she choose the way of faith—the high way? Or would she continue on the way of the world—the low path? Rahab's brave choices reveal a remarkable faith that reaped a fulfilling future.

What choices are you making that affect your destiny? How high are your sights—and your faith—set?

## 106 Risking All for God

*She let them down by a rope.*
Joshua 2:15

Time moves along in a predictable rhythm. We get up at a predicted time. We work our way through the day doing predictable tasks. We go to bed, finishing a day filled with familiar people, situations, and activities. Rahab's life also followed its predictable path...until one dramatic day. She'd heard about God and the miracles He performed for His people—the parting of the Red Sea and the destruction of two kings. Then she came face-to-face with two Israelites...and suddenly had a serious decision to make. Would she turn them over to the king's men, or would she help them escape?

*Choice #1—Rahab helped the spies.* Rahab risked her life to protect her nation's enemies. Her treasonous decision was punishable by death. But Rahab feared God more than man. Her choice revealed:

- *Kindness*—Jericho's king found out about the spies and asked Rahab to turn them over. She refused.
- *Courage*—To stand against her king and betray her city took courage. Yet she acted boldly, choosing to save the two men who represented God's people.
- *Faith*—Rahab believed her country was destined for destruction. She also believed God and His people would prevail.
- *Creativity*—Thinking quickly, Rahab hid the spies, sent their pursuers in another direction, and secretly let the two men out of the city.

Does your interaction with God's people and others show kindness, courage, faith, and creativity?

# 107 *Your Chain of Faith*

*According to your words, so be it.*
Joshua 2:21

"Faith by itself, if it does not have works, is dead" and "by works faith [is] made perfect" (James 2:17 and 22). Our works are guided by our choices. Have you ever thought about faith being like a chain—a series of choices linked together? Rahab continued to make choices that evidenced her faith in God. We saw the first faith-link in her chain when she made choice #1 and helped the Israelite spies escape. Then Rahab made another faith choice.

*Choice #2—Rahab believed the spies.* When Joshua's scouts said the Israelite army would cross the Jordan River and take the land, Rahab believed them. She said, "I know that the Lord has given you the land." She'd heard of God's miraculous care for His people, was convinced of the supremacy of Jehovah, and so believed.

How long—and how strong—is your chain of faith? Is your faith growing and evident in the choices you make? For starters, do you believe God's Word? It's important because what you believe determines how you behave, how you work out your faith. For instance,

- Abraham, the father of our faith, believed God when He promised, "I will make you a great nation" (Genesis 12:2; 15:6).
- The apostle Paul exhibited faith during a severe storm when he sailed to Rome. He declared, "I believe God that it will be just as it was told me" (Acts 27:25).

You walk with Rahab, Abraham, and Paul when you believe God's Word. The next time you have the choice of faith or doubt, choose to believe...and add another link to your chain of faith.

## 108 *Claiming God's Promises*

*According to your words, so be it.*
Joshua 2:21

Sit back a moment and admire Rahab's amazing faith. Everything about her situation worked against her ever becoming a woman after God's own heart. She was a pagan. And a prostitute. And yet in Hebrews 11 (called "God's roll call of faith") Rahab stands among the great men and women. She earned that place because of her choices to follow God and work with His people including...

*Choice #3—Rahab secured a promise.* Rahab asked for—and received—a promise from the spies that they would save her life and all her family when they returned to invade the city.

Thousands of promises in the Bible apply to you! And they will come true because they're based on the very nature and character of God! For instance,

- Jesus promised, "I will never leave you nor forsake you" (Hebrews 13:5).
- Paul promised, "My God shall supply all your need according to His riches in glory by Christ Jesus" (Philippians 4:19).
- Jesus promised, "My grace is sufficient for you" (2 Corinthians 12:9).
- Paul promised, "If you confess with your mouth the Lord Jesus and believe in your heart that God has raised Him from the dead, you will be saved" (Romans 10:9).

Follow in the faith of Rahab. Accept God's promises. Look for them in the Bible. Then, in faith, make the choice to trust Him.

## 109 Rahab's Remarkable Transformation

*Joshua spared Rahab...and all that she had.*
JOSHUA 6:25

Before we leave Rahab's heroic life, notice how God worked in her heart and life.

*Rahab's life before faith*

- Occupation: Prostitute

*Rahab's acts of faith*

- *She helped the spies.* Rahab hid Joshua's spies, diverted the soldiers, and helped the men escape.
- *She believed the spies were God's people.*
- *She secured the promise* that she and her family would be spared when the soldiers attacked.
- *She acted on the promise.* After the spies left, Rahab followed their instructions and tied a scarlet cord in the window—a signal to Israelite soldiers to save everyone in that house.

*Rahab's blessings for faith*

Rahab and her family were spared during Jericho's destruction. She moved to Israel and married Salmon (Matthew 1:5). She was the mother of Boaz...who married Ruth...who bore Obed...whose son was Jesse, the father of David...through whose line came our Savior and Lord, Jesus!

*Rahab's life of faith*

- Occupation: Godly wife and mother

Your faith life and blessings will differ from Rahab's. But you're definitely a recipient of "every spiritual blessing in the heavenly places in Christ" (Ephesians 1:3). Rejoice!

# 110 *God's Word to Women*

*[Joshua read] before all the assembly of Israel...*
*with the women...among them.*
JOSHUA 8:35

At last God's people entered the Promised Land. That red-letter day was so slow in arriving! Consider their history.

- the hundreds of years of bondage in Egypt
- the 10 plagues God sent against the Egyptians
- the pursuit by Pharaoh's forces as Israel fled
- the miraculous crossing of the Red Sea
- the destruction of Pharaoh's army
- the 40 years of wilderness wanderings[28]

Even when the Jewish people finally entered Canaan, they faced wars, death, and destruction. So Joshua built an altar for worship and read God's law to the Israelites, including the women and children. What specific guidance did the Word of the Lord give for women?

*Guidance for family*—God's Word includes specifics for training children in the way of the Lord (Deuteronomy 6:6-7).

*Guidance for the heart*—The Bible contains instructions for growing a heart that pleases God (Psalm 139:23-24).

*Guidance for eternal life*—There's only one way to heaven, and that's by faith in God. Every page of Scripture points to the reality of God.

*Guidance for life on earth*—Job mourned, "Man is born to trouble" (Job 5:7). Trouble is a fact of life, but God's Word contains direction, hope, and comfort.

Before you go into the world today, be sure to stop, worship, and read God's Word for guidance.

## 111 *Boldly Asking and Acting*

*Give me also springs of water.*
Joshua 15:19

Achsah was a woman of courage and wisdom. The daughter of Caleb, Achsah learned from him to ask for what she wanted.

When Achsah married, the dowry Caleb gave included a portion of his land. Because water was critical in that arid climate, Achsah boldly said to her father, "Give me also springs of water." Like father, like daughter!

Achsah could be easily overlooked, but her life holds important messages.

*Message #1: Watch.* The wise woman "watches over the ways of her household" (Proverbs 31:27). Achsah realized water on her property would improve the welfare of her family.

*Checkup:* Are you watching over your home? Are you aware of improvements that would enhance the welfare of your family?

*Message #2: Improve.* The wise woman enhances her property. Achsah noticed what her property needed to make it better.

*Checkup:* Are you improving your residence (your house, room, or dorm room)? Do you have a plan of action (even for a good cleaning)? When are you going to start?

*Message #3: Ask.* Achsah knew what she wanted and needed to make her home improvements happen. She also knew the best person to ask—her father, Caleb, who owned the upper springs.

*Checkup:* Do you ask God for wisdom, direction, and provision? Do you consult your husband? Do you check with others who might help you?

# 112 A Remarkable Woman

*Deborah, a prophetess...was judging Israel.*
JUDGES 4:4

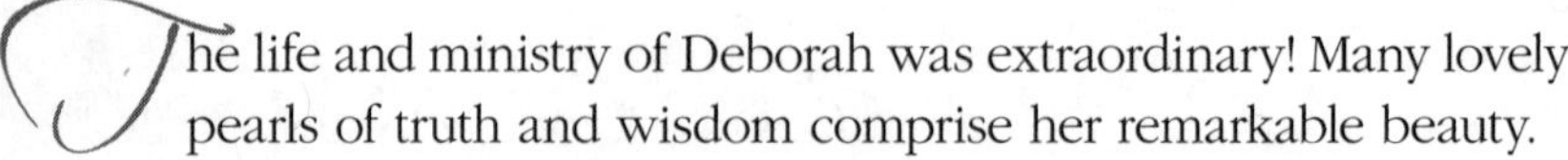

The life and ministry of Deborah was extraordinary! Many lovely pearls of truth and wisdom comprise her remarkable beauty.

- *A remarkable woman*—Deborah was a prophetess, a wife, and a judge. She also went to war with the Israelite army, sang a song to the Lord, and was called "a mother in Israel." No other biblical woman is described this way.
- *A remarkable calling*—Deborah is referred to as "a prophetess." Only a handful of women in the Bible were called to this lofty position.
- *A remarkable wife*—Along with the unique roles God called Deborah to fulfill, she was also "the wife of Lapidoth."
- *A remarkable leader*—Deborah served in her home and as one of God's judges over His people. Her leadership extended beyond her place of judgment—"the palm tree of Deborah"—to the plain of the battlefield where she was shoulder to shoulder with Barak, the army commander.
- *A remarkable faith*—Although others wavered, including Barak, Deborah's faith in God's sure victory never faltered, even when the odds were against Israel.
- *A remarkable poet*—Inspired by God and from a heart of gratitude, Deborah sang. She offered a tribute to God.

"Remarkable!" Does this rich word describe your life? While the specifics will differ, your commitment to God and your heart attitude can match Deborah's. How? Be diligent. Be devoted. Be dedicated. Be available. Be prepared. The rest is up to God!

## 113 *What Wives Do*

*Deborah...the wife of Lapidoth...*
JUDGES 4:4

How do people introduce you to someone? If you're married, consider yourself successful if you're introduced as the wife of your husband. These words of tribute mean you've become known as a faithful, dedicated, supportive mate.

When God introduces us to Deborah, He calls her "the wife of Lapidoth." Yes, Deborah was a prophetess and a judge, but she was also a wife. Nothing is known about Deborah's husband, but we can safely assume Deborah extended every form of respect and honor that was due to her husband.

God used Deborah mightily on behalf of His people because she followed God and obeyed His Word, including His guidelines for her as a wife.

Here's a quick overview for wives.

- *A wife helps her husband.* "The LORD God said, 'It is not good that man should be alone; I will make him a helper comparable to him'" (Genesis 2:18).
- *A wife follows her husband.* "Wives, submit [adapt yourselves] to your own husbands, as to the Lord" (Ephesians 5:22).
- *A wife respects her husband.* "Let the wife see that she respects [praises and honors] her husband" (Ephesians 5:33).
- *A wife loves her husband.* "Admonish the young women to love [to be affectionate to] their husbands" (Titus 2:4).

Yes, Deborah was entrusted with leadership and service opportunities. But she was also a faithful wife. God is honored when you help, follow, respect, and love your husband.

## 114 *Answers for Troubled Times*

*The children of Israel came up to [Deborah] for judgment.*
JUDGES 4:5

Look at a painting. Did you notice that the background sets off the subject and helps give the painting impact? As we look at Deborah we can't help but notice the background against which her dazzling life is lived out.

*The period*—"In those days there was no king in Israel; everyone did what was right in his own eyes" (Judges 21:25). The Israelites were characterized by disobedience, idolatry, and defeat. They were in the Promised Land but the many pagan strongholds influenced them spiritually and they faced the constant threat of war.

*The problem*—During this turbulent, disobedient time God let the Israelites fall into the hands of Jabin, the king of Canaan, who harshly oppressed them for 20 years.

*The prophetess*—God's solution to Israel's problem was Deborah. She became His witness, His prophetess, discerning and declaring God's mind. She ministered as a mediator between God and His people and poured out His wisdom, knowledge, and instruction when the people came to her for help.

*The purpose*—God's purposes in using Deborah as a judge were to lead His people into successful battle against the Canaanites and ignite spiritual revival. Hearing God's Word awakened God's people to their sagging spiritual condition and stirred up their hearts.

Like Deborah, you live in a spiritually dark time. People today need God. And Christians need encouragement and exhortation. Every time you speak and share truth from Scripture, you're proclaiming God's Word and wisdom. Follow in the footsteps of Deborah. Open God's Word to encourage your heart and learn His wisdom. Then help others develop and strengthen their faith.

# 115 Remarkable Leadership

*She said, "I will surely go with you."*
JUDGES 4:9

"Wisdom is oftentimes nearer when we stoop than when we soar." These words of William Wordsworth perfectly describe a key to Deborah's success. Her wisdom was exhibited through humility.

- *Deborah didn't seek to be a judge.* The judges of God's people were raised up by God (Judges 2:16).
- *Deborah called upon Barak to lead.* When Israel suffered at the hands of Jabin, the king of Canaan, Deborah sent for Barak, told him to deploy troops, and shared God's promise, "I will deliver him into your hand."
- *Deborah warned Barak about the consequences of her going into war.* Barak refused to go into battle without Deborah. Deborah explained that if she were present there would be no glory for him. "The LORD will sell Sisera [Jabin's army commander] into the hand of a woman."
- *Deborah went with Barak.* Ever the patriot, Deborah declared, "I will surely go with you." Only after calling on Barak and advising him of the consequences of her presence on the battlefield did Deborah go to the front.

The way to greatness in God's kingdom is humble service. Never seeking, never aggressive, never too assertive, Deborah waited on God, encouraged others to take the lead, and assisted when needed. How can you apply these truths to your life today?

## 116 Mentally and Physically Strong

*Then Deborah arose and went with Barak [to war].*
JUDGES 4:9

"Who can find a virtuous woman?" (Proverbs 31:10 KJV). Well, in Deborah God found one! A virtuous woman possesses power of mind (moral principles and attitudes) and power of body (ability and effectiveness). Deborah, a prophetess and judge in Israel, had both. She administered God's laws and managed and counseled His people. Strong physically, she accompanied Barak to the battlefield. While some may struggle with the mental image of a woman with a sword in her hand, God has nothing but praise for this remarkable woman and warrior (Judges 4–5).

The Hebrew word for virtuous is used more than 200 times in the Bible to describe an army. It also aptly describes Deborah. This Old Testament term refers to "a force" and means "able, capable, mighty, strong, valiant, powerful, efficient, wealthy, and worthy." The word is also used in reference to a man or men of war and men prepared for war. Simply change the masculine to the feminine, and you'll begin to understand the power at the core of a virtuous woman, the power at the core of Deborah![29] To lead God's people into battle against their oppressors, Deborah called upon her mental toughness and physical energy, which are primary traits of a successful army.

Do you desire to be a virtuous woman? The day-in, day-out duties you encounter call for significant power of mind and body. Mental toughness and physical energy will keep you from giving up, giving in, dropping out, or quitting short of God's goal for you as you serve Him.

Take a moment to ask God for strength—*His* strength. Tell Him your desire to become a woman who moves through the challenges and duties of life with valor, courage, bravery, stamina, endurance, and power—*His* power.

# 117 A Song of Praise and Adoration

*Then Deborah...sang.*
JUDGES 5:1

How to chronicle the important event was the predicament Deborah was in. The occasion was God's victory over Israel's enemies (Judges 4:23). The day and age was a time when the law of Moses was still being written on stones (Joshua 8:32). Yet when God "fought from the heavens" and "the stars from their courses fought against" Israel's adversaries (5:20), Deborah wanted to share the victory and keep the memory alive. So what did she do? She sang.

Just as Moses, Miriam, and King David sang after God's mighty conquests, so did Deborah. Judges 5 contains Deborah's poem of praise—words of a joyful heart overflowing with gratitude. Deborah gave testimony to and praised God for...

- marching against the opposing armies
- His righteous acts
- acting on Deborah's behalf

"A good man out of the good treasure of his heart brings forth good" (Luke 6:45). Deborah's song spilled from a heart filled with treasure. Her song reveals her worship and reverence, honor and love, joy and exultation, praise and adoration.

What's in your heart? What lyrics would you write for the song in your heart? Consider these guidelines from Scripture:

> Let the words of my mouth and the meditation of my heart be acceptable in Your sight (Psalm 19:14).
>
> With...psalms and hymns and spiritual songs, be singing and making melody in your heart to the Lord (Ephesians 5:19).

## 118 "A Mother in Israel"

*Deborah arose...a mother in Israel.*
JUDGES 5:7

Do you think Golda Meir, former prime minister of Israel, knew about Deborah, a judge and leader of Israel? Probably. Golda Meir (1898–1978) once said, "I have no ambition to be somebody," and yet Mrs. Meir became great in her lifetime as she dreamed of a Jewish state and then witnessed its birth![30] In her day Prime Minister Golda Meir was something of a mother to Israel.

The title "a mother in Israel" was originally attributed to the prophetess Deborah by God. Because of her roles among God's people as leader, judge, warrior, motivator, deliverer, and protector, Deborah became a spiritual mother to those in Israel. Her remarkable faith gave strength and courage to God's people. Her dedication to God enabled her to arouse the Israelites from spiritual lethargy. Her commitment to God and His people energized her to serve. Under Deborah's judgeship Israel enjoyed 40 years of rest.

Do you desire the remarkable, wholehearted devotion to God Deborah had? Ponder these factors that contribute to a fervent, wholehearted commitment to God and foster great faith.

- *A life spent in God's Word*—All Scripture is profitable for instruction in righteousness. God's Word equips you for good works (2 Timothy 3:16-17).
- *A life spent in prayer*—Do you want to do great things for God? Then ask great things of God. The Bible says, "You do not have because you do not ask" (James 4:2). So *ask* for greater strength and perseverance, greater faith and devotion.
- *A life spent in obedience*—As you dedicate your life to being "a doer of the word," God promises you will be blessed (James 1:22, 25).

# 119 Jael's Shocking Act

*Most blessed among women is Jael.*
JUDGES 5:24

Jael's story can, at first glance, cause confusion. The Bible praises her for assassinating someone! Let's unravel a few facts before we consider God's description of this woman who showed her love for God in a most unusual way.

- Israel was at war against the king of Canaan (Judges 4:10).
- Jael and her husband, Heber the Kenite, were dwelling in a tent about 15 miles from the battle.
- As Israel routed the Canaanite army, God's people pursued Sisera, the captain of the enemy forces.
- A tired and famished Sisera arrived at Jael's tent.
- While Sisera slept, Jael took a tent peg and drove it into his temple with a hammer.

Although Jael's actions are startling and anything but lovely, God has nothing negative to say about her. Indeed, God considered Jael a heroine, a woman who was "the friend of Israel." In their God-inspired song of tribute, Deborah, the reigning judge of Israel, and Barak, the captain of Israel's army, offer praise for Jael, the woman who was God's instrument for victory over Israel's enemy. They praise the faith of Jael, a foreigner, who acted out her faith in her family's tent in the only way she, a Bedouin tent-woman, knew. Using the tools and skills of her daily life, Jael battled for God in time of war.

God gave praise where praise was due. File this distinctive "friend of Israel" story in your heart and pray for opportunities to help God's people and His purposes. I'm certainly not advocating violence or mayhem, but God may have some unusual plans for you.

## 120 *Your Children's Faith*

*His daughter [came] out to meet him.*
JUDGES 11:34

What do parents who follow God dream for their children? That they will love God with all their hearts, souls, and might! If you have children, be diligent to...

- live in a way that reveals your love for God
- nurture them in the training and admonition of the Lord
- speak continuously of the Lord—when you're at home, in the car, before bed, when you wake up

Jephthah, the ninth judge of Israel, was called on to lead the Israelites into battle. He exhibited a heart of faith, "spoke all his words before the LORD," and was visited by "the Spirit of the LORD." Jephthah vowed that if God gave him victory, "whatever comes out of the doors of my house to meet me...shall surely be the LORD's, and I will offer it up as a burnt offering."

Unfortunately, when Jephthah returned home victorious, his daughter—his only child—was the first to come out to meet him. How did this godly father react? He tore his clothes and explained, "I have given my word to the LORD, and I cannot go back on it."

What did his daughter do? She affirmed his vow. "If you have given your word to the LORD, do to me according to what has gone out of your mouth."

Jephthah successfully brought his daughter up to love God, and it cost him and his daughter dearly as they honored God by keeping the vow he'd made.

When people—adults and children—live for God, there are always costs involved, along with the many benefits. Pray that your children's devotion to God will always grow despite any difficulties and hardships.

And a special word of caution: Be careful what you vow!

## 121 *A Light in the Darkness*

*Do to me according to what has gone out of your mouth.*
JUDGES 11:36

It was a time of rampant sin, defilement, confusion, anarchy—and painful judgment from God as "everyone did what was right in his own eyes" (Judges 21:25). Yet Jephthah and his daughter proved to be a vein of gold, shining bright for God amid the dirt and darkness of the era of the judges. As part of God's punishment of His people's sin and rebellion, Israel was at war with their heathen neighbors. Jephthah was summoned to lead the Israelites into battle. What happened next?

- Jephthah invoked God as a witness to his agreement to serve his country as judge and warrior.
- Jephthah was graciously empowered by the Spirit of the Lord to benefit His people.
- Jephthah vowed to God to sacrifice whatever came out of the doors of his house if he experienced victory in battle.
- The Israelites were victorious.
- Jephthah's daughter—his only child—was the first creature to exit his house when he arrived home.
- He tore his clothes and explained his vow.
- His daughter nobly accepted her role as a sacrifice and encouraged her father to follow through on his vow. This woman of golden character viewed her destiny as a worthwhile price to pay for God's victory over Israel's enemies.

You are also called to shine. A woman who loves God is a light in darkness, a witness of the Light, a city set on a hill. "Let your light so shine before men, that they may see your good works and glorify your Father in heaven" (Matthew 5:16).

## 122 *The Flower of Humility*

*His wife was barren and had no children.*
JUDGES 13:2

Do you love flowers? Can the sight of a beautifully arranged floral bouquet take your breath away and stir your soul? As we stroll through the life of another woman of God, you'll notice a few of the blooms God, the Master Gardener, selected to make her life a lovely tribute to Him.

The first flower for this lovely woman's bouquet is the most fragrant—the flower of humility. Just as the fragrance for perfumes comes from crushed flowers, so the beauty and godliness of the wife of Manoah came from her humbling life circumstances. "Now there was a certain man...whose name was Manoah; and his wife was barren and had no children." These words sear their way into a woman's heart, causing her head to hang and her soul to sigh. And this was especially true in the days of Manoah, when many people looked with reproach at those without children. Some even thought childlessness was punishment from God.

So what does a woman without children do? Identified only as "Manoah's wife," this woman probably spent time praying. We know her husband did. When Manoah's wife told him an angel appeared to her, Manoah prayed that the angel would return. Like other childless women of the Bible (Sarah, Rebekah, Hannah, and Elizabeth), this woman's inner pain presumably pressed her more closely to God.

What's your life situation? Is there something you deeply desire that has so far been denied? Is there something you yearn for? A life of faithful prayer has the lovely fragrance that comes from godly humility, from kneeling before Almighty God. Bow your head. Submit your soul. Allow God to do His exquisite work in your life.

# 123 *The Flower of Faith*

*And the Angel of the Lord appeared to the woman.*
Judges 13:3

The vase God selected for the flowers He's gracing the life of Manoah's wife with is fit for an abundant bouquet. Yet right now it contains only a single stem—a bending-but-fragrant flower of humility (see the previous devotion). But the Master's not finished arranging the lovely existence of Manoah's wife. A second rare blossom is added—the flower of faith. Note its beauty—

- "The Angel of the Lord appeared to the woman." Whenever "the Angel of the Lord" appeared the occasion was significant—and Manoah's wife paid attention!
- The angel announced, "You shall conceive and bear a son." Certainly this barren woman's heart leaped!
- Next the angel gave Manoah's wife specific, personal instructions: "Please be careful not to drink wine or similar drink, and not to eat anything unclean." These restrictions made up a Nazirite vow and set a person apart for God's purposes.
- The angel offered further instructions regarding the baby-to-be: "No razor shall come upon [your son's] head, for the child shall be a Nazirite to God from the womb."

Such an overwhelming moment! How did Manoah's wife cope? By faith! She asked no questions, requested no signs, and showed no hint of doubt. She responded with the rare and precious silence of belief. What a gracious flower of faith!

Do you yearn for this delightful flower in your life and character? Love God with all your heart and study His Word. Trust in God's promises. Develop a faith marked by an accepting silence (no questions asked), a gentle spirit (no details needed), and a sweet submissiveness (no struggling against the unknown) to God and His will.

# 124 The Flower of Vision

*[He] shall be a Nazirite to God.*
JUDGES 13:5

In the most striking of floral designs, several stalks of flowers shoot out far beyond the others. These big, bold flowers contribute height and interest to the arrangement, magnifying the bouquet's impact. For the wife of Manoah, one far-reaching, radiant blossom was God's flower of vision for her son.

God has been busy transforming Mrs. Manoah into the beautiful masterpiece He created her to be. Into the empty life of oppression (the Lord had delivered the Israelites into the hands of the Philistines for 40 years) and sadness (this woman had no children), God granted grace and positioned two glorious blossoms—the fragrant flower of humility and the precious blossom of faith—in the vase of this woman's life. They stand in place, waiting on His selection of still more beauty.

Through the angel sent to Manoah's wife, God added the dramatic flower of a vision of the future to her life. When the angel of the Lord appeared to this childless woman, he announced she would bear a son and he would be "a Nazirite to God from the womb; and he shall begin to deliver Israel out of the hand of the Philistines." What a wonderful blessing to the long-aching heart of this mother-to-be!

- *Blessing #1. Her son had a special calling.* He would be a Nazirite from the womb to the day of his death.
- *Blessing #2. Her son had a special career.* He would deliver God's people from the reign of the Philistines.

God's vision for her son gave Manoah's wife immense hope for the future. If you have children, pray now and every day for God to reveal His vision for your offspring to them and to you.

## 125 The Flower of Obedience

*[He] shall be a Nazirite to God.*
JUDGES 13:5

What kind of flower do you imagine when you think of obedience? How about a blossom that's sturdy, solid, and long-lasting? After all, obedience is evidenced by a strong will and a commitment to the long haul. The obedient spirit of Manoah's wife warrants another flower in her bouquet of great traits. What did God ask of this strong woman?

- *To follow the law of the Nazirite.* She was to "be careful not to drink wine and not to eat anything unclean" (Judges 13:4). Following these commands placed this nameless wife and mother alongside Hannah and Elizabeth in terms of their calling (1 Samuel 1:11; Luke 1:15).
- *To make sure her son followed the law of the Nazirite.* "No razor shall come upon his head, for the child shall be a Nazirite to God from the womb." This godly mom's obedience ensured her son partnership in the purposes of God.

Consider for a moment where Mrs. Manoah's obedience led. What was in the heart of God...was passed on to the mother. What was in the heart of the mother...was passed on to the child. What was in the heart of the child...was passed on to God's people.

How does your heart check out? Do you listen to God and do what His Word says? Do you faithfully pass on what's in your heart to your children? Do you pray that your children will pass what is in their hearts from the Lord to others? Ask God to help you nurture the flower of obedience in your heart and in those of your family so you will all serve Him with full, rich, compliant hearts.

## 126 *The Flower of Worship*

*So Manoah...offered [an offering] to the LORD.*
JUDGES 13:19

Oh, let us worship the Lord and bow down! Let us worship the Lord in the beauty of holiness! Let us worship at His footstool![31] Worshiping God reveals a true heart of adoration and love. As Manoah and his wife offered God heartfelt worship, God added a radiant flower of worship to the glorious spray representing the life of this unnamed woman.

A quick review leads us to join Manoah and his lovely wife in faith and worship—

- The couple was childless.
- The angel of the Lord appeared to Manoah's wife.
- They were promised a son who would serve God.
- The angel next appeared to Manoah and his wife.
- The promise for a son was repeated.
- The angel was "wonderful" and did "wondrously" (KJV).

When Manoah and his wife saw the wondrous act of the angel ascending in the fire of their offering to the Lord, they fell facedown and worshiped! They praised God for who He is—the Giver of blessings, the Answerer of prayers, the Protector and Deliverer of His people, the Sovereign Ruler of all time, the Keeper of promises, the God of the universe.

Now add your own thoughts to this list of God's great attributes. Take to heart this definition and spend time in praise—

> Worship is an inward reverence, a bowing down of the soul in the presence of God, an awesome dependence on Him...a solemn consciousness of the Divine, a secret communion with the unseen.[32]

## 127 *The Flower of Motherhood*

*So the woman bore a son.*
JUDGES 13:24

We often honor mothers with roses on Mother's Day. Today let's honor Manoah's wife with a single beautiful stem—the flower of motherhood. This blossom has been long in coming, and we rejoice with this *formerly* barren woman.

Known throughout the Bible as "Manoah's wife," at last another phrase can be used to describe this lovely lady: She's "Samson's mother." This gentle woman lived her life in the shadow of two men—her husband, Manoah, and her famous son, Samson, a judge of God's people and the strongest man who ever lived. Being a wife and mother appears to have been enough for her happiness and fulfillment.

Aren't you glad the Bible paints such a positive picture of parenting? From it we learn these divine truths about being a mom:

- Children are a heritage from the Lord (Psalm 127:3).
- The fruit of the womb is a reward from God (Psalm 127:3).
- [God] settles the barren woman in her home as a happy mother of children (Psalm 113:9 NIV).

And aren't you glad the Bible gives parents sound advice for raising children? Here are a few bits of wisdom:

- Train up a child in the way he should go (Proverbs 22:6).
- Bring [your children] up in the training and instruction of the Lord (Ephesians 6:4 NIV).
- Love your children (Titus 2:4).

If you're a mom, your calling is a high and noble one, a momentous stewardship as God entrusts precious children—His special creations—to you. Pray daily for your kids. Teach them God's Word diligently, model Jesus, and worship together regularly.

## 128 A Future and a Hope

*[Elimelech and] his wife and two sons, went to live for a while in the country of Moab.*
RUTH 1:1 NIV

The famous opening words of Charles Dickens' *A Tale of Two Cities* declare, "It was the best of times, it was the worst of times." These words also describe 10 years in the life of a woman named Naomi.

*The best of times.* Because of a great famine Naomi and her family—her husband, Elimelech, and their two sons, Mahlon and Chilion—left their hometown of Bethlehem and settled in Moab where there was food. Yes, times there were good. They feasted and prospered. And, oh, how Naomi must have rejoiced when her two sons married. Each one met his mate in Moab. Those days were truly sweet!

*The worst of times.* But then the death knell sounded. First Naomi's beloved husband died, and then she lost her two precious sons—a triple blow to the heart of this wife and mom. How could something that had been so good turn so sour? Naomi seemed alone in the world...except for her sons' wives.

Have you felt like Naomi must have? Have you moved into what was supposed to be an ideal future, experienced temporary bliss and blessing...and then faced great loss and pain? If your answer is yes, God has two strong promises for you—

> "For I know the thoughts that I think toward you," says the LORD, "thoughts of peace and not of evil, to give you a future and a hope" (Jeremiah 29:11).
>
> And we know that all things work together for good to those who love God, to those who are the called according to His purpose (Romans 8:28).

As you cling to the One who made these promises, you'll walk the path of "a future and a hope" with Naomi.

## 129 Learning to Trust

*She went out from the place where she was.*
RUTH 1:7

When you hit a hard place in life, it's not the time to collapse, cave in, fall apart, or break down. It's time to trust God!

The day Naomi and her family left for Moab, Naomi "went out full." But tragedy struck. Her husband and then her two sons died. Naomi was devastated. When she heard the famine was over, she decided to return to her homeland. But it was a long journey.

- Naomi's daughters-in-law, Orpah and Ruth, started the journey with her.
- Naomi urged these young women to return to their respective parents' homes.
- Naomi kissed the two women goodbye.
- Orpah returned to her home.
- Ruth chose to stay with Naomi.

Certainly sorrow was not how Naomi envisioned her life, but she was learning to trust God more to work in her life through people, events, and circumstances.

- *The people*—Where once Naomi depended on her husband and sons, she would now depend on a young, widowed daughter-in-law.
- *The events*—Naomi certainly didn't choose to have her husband and sons killed. But now she needed to trust God to work through their deaths.
- *The circumstances*—Never had Naomi imagined she'd be returning home without her husband or sons. Yes, she would have to trust God.

## 130 *In Times of Distress...*

*The two of them went until they came to Bethlehem.*
RUTH 1:19

People love reunions. Relatives from far away gather for fun, sharing, and love. Best friends meet often to catch up on each other's lives. Military men and women arrange get-togethers to renew wartime friendships. High schools and colleges host class reunions and homecoming events so graduates can stay in touch.

A different kind of reunion took place thousands of years ago. It wasn't by choice, and it wasn't for pleasure. There was no joyful anticipation. Naomi, who'd left Bethlehem and moved to Moab with her family, was now returning without her husband and sons. Their deaths turned Naomi's dreams into disaster. She was returning as a widow and accompanied by Ruth, a Moabite daughter-in-law.

Naomi, whose name means "pleasant," walked 70 dusty miles from their place in Moab to Bethlehem. As her former friends greeted her with, "Is this Naomi?" she replied, "Do not call me Naomi; call me Mara [Mara means "bitter"]...I went out full, and the LORD has brought me home again empty."

God works in our lives through people, events, and circumstances, but never to make us bitter—only to make us better! Remember these two promises: God's thoughts toward you are of peace and not of evil, to give you a future and hope, and He will work everything out for your good (Jeremiah 29:11; Romans 8:28). What can you do to be fruitful while enduring difficulties?

*Give thanks always.* It's impossible to be bitter and thankful at the same time (Ephesians 5:20).

*Pray without ceasing.* Even through tears, prayer is your heart's song to God (1 Thessalonians 5:17).

*Reach out.* Comfort others with the comfort God gives you (2 Corinthians 1:4).

## 131 *A Coincidence?*

*She happened to come to…*
*the field belonging to Boaz.*
RUTH 2:3

Bethlehem was the place.
Food was the pressing need.
A field of grain was the setting.
Ruth was the woman.

There's no such thing in the life of God's children as happenstance or coincidence. There is only the great sovereignty of God Almighty who watches over His children and guides their steps, sometimes obviously and other times not.

In her new homeland Ruth ventured out to glean in the grain fields. She went without a guide, without a companion…alone except for God, who directed her steps to one particular field, owned by one particular relative, who would later became her husband! As you look at Ruth's life, consider this quote—

> God wisely orders small events; and those that seem altogether…[conditional] serve his own glory and the good of his people. Many a great affair is brought about by a little turn, which seemed…[lucky or accidental] to us, but was directed by Providence with design.[33]

Are you looking for God's hand in all the events, the coincidences, the chance happenings, the luck, and the flukes of your life? If you believe in a sovereign God, if you believe in His loving providence, you know that everything that touches your life is Him at work! So…

- look for the hand of God.
- believe God works in your life in all you encounter and experience.
- trust God to work all things, even "happenstance," together for your good (Romans 8:28).

## 132 Sheltered by God's Wings

*Under whose wings you have come for refuge.*
RUTH 2:12

The book of Ruth includes a pair of heartfelt "hymns."

*Ruth's hymn.* Although raised in the pagan nation of Moab, Ruth placed her trust in the God of Israel. In her faith-filled declaration to Naomi, Ruth's words of devotion read like a song:

> Wherever you go, I will go;
> And wherever you lodge, I will lodge;
> Your people shall be my people,
> And your God, my God.
> Where you die, I will die,
> And there will I be buried.

*Boaz's hymn.* Boaz was a devout follower of God, a landowner, and a distant relative of Ruth. Upon meeting Ruth, he blessed her and encouraged her with a delightful melody of words:

> The Lord repay your work,
> and a full reward be given you
> by the LORD God of Israel,
> under whose wings you have
> come for refuge.

Perhaps Boaz saw the struggling Ruth—a woman who'd wandered into his barley field and labored diligently to gather food for herself and her widowed mother-in-law—as a fragile baby chick. In Psalm 36:7 God is portrayed as a mother bird who shelters her young chicks with her wings. What a great metaphor Boaz used to bless Ruth for her remarkable trust in God.

Do you trust in God...and God alone? Do you depend totally on the One who provides for His own? Your heavenly Father is responsible for protecting you. Your responsibility is to trust Him.

# 133 Beautiful Melodies

*Under whose wings you have come for refuge.*
RUTH 2:12

In the previous devotion we were blessed by the delightful outpourings of two hearts filled with love for God. Couched in the words of Boaz was the comforting thought of finding refuge under the strong and mighty wings of God.

We can't leave this rich image of resting under God's wings without appreciating a hymn written in 1896. William Cushing's personal expression of trust comes after being told devastating news for any preacher—that his voice was going out permanently. He went on to write more than 300 hymns.[34] Whatever difficulties and pain you face, find refuge "under His wings."

*Under His Wings*

Under His wings I am safely abiding,
Tho the night deepens and tempests are wild;
Still I can trust Him—I know He will keep me,
He has redeemed me and I am His child.

Under His wings, what a refuge in sorrow!
How the heart yearningly turns to His rest!
Often when earth has no balm for my healing,
There I find comfort and there I am blest.

Under His wings, O what precious enjoyment!
There will I hide till life's trials are o'er;
Sheltered, protected, no evil can harm me,
Resting in Jesus I'm safe evermore.

REFRAIN
Under His wings, under His wings,
Who from His love can sever?
Under His wings my soul shall abide,
Safely abide forever.

## 134 *A Glimmer of Understanding*

*The Lord...has not forsaken His kindness.*
Ruth 2:20

What would you do if...

- you were a widow
- your sons died
- your daughter-in-law was your only companion
- you needed food?

This was Naomi's predicament. Too old to labor herself, Naomi depended on Ruth for the basics of life.

The law of Moses stipulated that grain dropped by reapers as they brought in the crops could be gleaned by the poor. This law was tailor-made for women in Naomi and Ruth's position. So Ruth went out daily to glean barley. One day she "happened"—by God's sovereign design!—into the field of a distant relative named Boaz. Boaz noticed Ruth and inquired about her. Then he introduced himself and blessed Ruth for finding refuge under the wings of the Lord. Boaz gave Ruth extended privileges when reaping in his fields. He also gave her extra food, extra grain, and protection.

When Ruth told Naomi of the goodness of Boaz, hope and joy pushed their way through the bitter, hard crust that encased Naomi's once-happy heart. "Blessed be he of the Lord, who has not forsaken His kindness to the living and the dead!" In Naomi's cold heart appeared a glimmer of understanding of God's steadfast lovingkindness and His mercy.

God's gracious dealings offer at least two messages:

- Look for the kindness of the Lord extended to you through the good deeds of others.
- Extend the kindness of the Lord to others through your good deeds.

## 135 Looking Out for Others

*All that you say to me I will do.*
Ruth 3:5

We know very little about the customs in the small town in Israel where Ruth and Naomi lived. What we do know is found in Ruth 3. As you know, Naomi was Ruth's mother-in-law, and both women lost their husbands. Returning to Bethlehem, they found themselves looking straight into the face of a dim future...until one of Naomi's relatives came on the scene. Boaz generously blessed the lives of these two widows with food from his fields.

Now let's consider the actions of these two women toward each other. They obviously loved and looked out for each other.

*Naomi wanted the best for Ruth.* Naomi noticed the budding respect Ruth and Boaz had for each other. Naomi saw a hopeful future for Ruth. So Naomi, an older, wiser woman, coached the younger in the customs of her land—customs for securing a marriage partner. Naomi told Ruth...

- how to look ("wash yourself and anoint yourself, put on your best garment") and
- how to act ("when he lies down...uncover his feet...and he will tell you what you should do").

*Ruth wanted the best for Naomi.* By now Ruth knew Boaz could—and wanted to—provide for the aged and needy Naomi. Ruth too wanted that security for her mother-in-law. So Ruth followed Naomi's instructions and basically proposed to Boaz!

Naomi and Ruth are beautiful portraits of selflessness. Each clearly wanted what was best for the other. What picture are you painting with your life? Are you loving others? Do you desire what's best for them? Ask God for a more generous, selfless attitude toward others.

## 136 Upright, Loving, and Honest

*You are a virtuous woman.*
Ruth 3:11

Ruth was from the pagan country of Moab and a widow. Yet she left her homeland, her family, and her religion to follow Naomi to Bethlehem. Everyone there saw Ruth's love and concern for her widowed mother-in-law. As the landowner Boaz declared to Ruth, "All the people of my town know that you are a virtuous woman."

Read Proverbs 31:10-31, God's portrait of a "virtuous woman." Then hear what one scholar shares:

> The "virtuous" wife of Proverbs 31:10 is personified by "virtuous" Ruth of whom the same Hebrew word is used (3:11). With amazing parallel, they share at least eight character traits...Each woman was:
>
> 1. Devoted to her family
> (Ruth 1:15-18; Proverbs 31:10-12, 23)
> 2. Delighting in her work
> (Ruth 2:2; Proverbs 31:13)
> 3. Diligent in her labor
> (Ruth 2:7, 17, 23; Proverbs 31:14-18, 19-21, 24, 27)
> 4. Dedicated to godly speech
> (Ruth 2:10, 13; Proverbs 31:26)
> 5. Dependent on God
> (Ruth 2:12; Proverbs 31:25, 30)
> 6. Dressed with care
> (Ruth 3:3; Proverbs 31:22, 25)
> 7. Discreet with men
> (Ruth 3:6-13; Proverbs 31:11-12, 23)
> 8. Delivering blessings
> (Ruth 4:14-15; Proverbs 31:28, 29, 31)[35]

Ask God to work these eight godly qualities into your heart!

## 137 A Virtuous Man

*Boaz went up to the gate.*
RUTH 4:1

In Ruth 3 and Proverbs 31 we meet virtuous women, but did you know Ruth 4 details the qualities of a virtuous man? God's list of virtues exhibited by Boaz's sterling life includes:

- *Diligent*—Boaz is described as "a man of great wealth" (Ruth 2:1), and we see him carefully and thoughtfully overseeing his property.
- *Friendly*—Boaz greeted his workers with warmth and even welcomed a stranger named Ruth (2:4, 8).
- *Merciful*—Noticing Ruth at work, Boaz asked about her situation and acted on her behalf (2:7).
- *Godly*—Boaz asked Jehovah to bless Ruth in return for her care for Naomi (2:12).
- *Encouraging*—Boaz pointed out Ruth's strong qualities and spoke of them to cheer her on (2:12; 3:11).
- *Generous*—Boaz gave Ruth extra food even though Ruth was willing to work for it (2:15).
- *Kind*—Naomi thanked God for His kindness shown to both of them through Boaz (2:20).
- *Discreet*—Boaz sent Ruth home before daylight to protect her reputation (3:14).
- *Faithful*—Following through on his promise to Ruth, Boaz "went to court" to clear the way to marry her.

*Are you single?* Look for these qualities in the man you seek. Don't settle for less than the best. Check this list often! *Are you married?* Prize, praise, and pray for these qualities in your husband. *Are you a mom?* Instill these qualities in your daughters and sons.

## 138 *Clothes of Love*

*Ruth...became his wife; and...bore a son.*
RUTH 4:13

Here's a thought to prop up by your kitchen sink, attach to your computer, and tape to your bathroom mirror:

*True service is love in working clothes.*

Perhaps Ruth's most outstanding distinction was her servant heart. She consistently ministered to Naomi. Ruth rose before dawn, put on work clothes of love, gleaned in the barley fields, and returned home at night with food and grain for them (Ruth 2:17-18). When God gifted the widowed Ruth with a new, wonderful husband and a precious baby, her joy was complete. She now had an entire family to serve and love again!

What clothes of love can you put on?

*Service to others*—Nurturing a servant's heart begins with the decision to serve others. Jesus models this heart attitude for us. He "did not come to be served, but to serve" (Matthew 20:28).

*Service to your husband*—God's Word is clear: "Whatever you do [including serving your husband], do it heartily, as to the Lord and not to men" (Colossians 3:23).

*Service to your children*—Every meal prepared, every piece of clothing washed, every room tidied, every floor swept, every ride given is love in action.

*Service to your church*—Married or single, you can exercise your servant heart at church. There are meals to take to those in need, pew racks to stock, chairs to set up, and Sunday school classes to teach.

The Bible points out many beautiful services rendered by women, including giving people food and places to stay, washing the feet of fellow believers, offering relief to the afflicted, and diligently performing good works (1 Timothy 5:10). Why not join their inspiring ranks?

## 139 *Being a Grandma*

*Naomi took the child and…*
*became a nurse to him.*
Ruth 4:16

During her life Naomi traveled from a mountaintop existence of bliss into a deep, dark valley of sorrow—marrying and living near family and friends, moving to Moab, losing her husband, losing her two sons, moving back to Bethlehem with one daughter-in-law. But God didn't leave Naomi in her valley of despair. He didn't leave her hopeless and empty. God blessed her with a grandchild, and she knew happiness again. How she must have welcomed the warmth of a delightful grandbaby!

Tiny Obed was Naomi's first grandchild. Decades had passed since she'd held a little one in her arms. What did this babe signify to her?

- a continuation of the heritage of her husband
- a "son" to love since losing her own sons
- a child to care for and an opportunity to serve as nursemaid
- an offspring who would help care for her in her old age
- a "restorer of life" and a hope for the future

Being a grandmother is a great privilege! It also provides new opportunities, plenty of challenges, and myriad responsibilities. Here's a delightful acrostic to help you live out the "grand" in "grandmother."

**G**ive a godly example
**R**emember important occasions
**A**lways love your grandchildren's parents—no matter what
**N**ever show favoritism
**D**evelop a personal relationship with each grandchild

And if you're not a grandmother yet, pray for your grandma!

## 140 Precious Treasure

*Now this is the genealogy of...Boaz.*
Ruth 4:18, 21

Proverbs 12:4 proclaims, "A virtuous woman is a crown to her husband" (KJV). And Ruth was such a woman. After her first husband's death she married Boaz, a man of godly character. The union of this noble couple created a lineage that extended through time and for eternity. Take a moment to admire these gems in Ruth and Boaz's descendants.

> *"Boaz begot Obed"*—As one Bible scholar noted, "Through the birth of Obed, God wove the thread of Ruth's life most intricately into the web of the history of His people. She became the chosen line through which later the Savior of the world appeared."[36]
>
> *"Obed begot Jesse"*—Just as Isaiah had prophesied, "There shall come forth a Rod from the stem of Jesse, and a Branch shall grow out of his roots" (11:1). That Rod and that Branch was the Lord Jesus Christ.
>
> *"Jesse begot David"*—The hope of a messianic king and kingdom was fulfilled in Christ through the lineage of David, his father (Jesse), and his grandfather (Obed), who was born to Boaz and Ruth.
>
> *Jesus Christ*—The family tree or "the book of the genealogy of Jesus Christ, the Son of David" includes Boaz, Obed, Jesse, and David (Matthew 1:1, 5-6).

Do you have children or grandchildren? If yes, you're blessed! They are precious treasure and stars in your crown. Pray for them fervently. Encourage them in the Lord mightily. Ensure they know about Jesus abundantly. Support their spiritual growth heartily.

## 141 *The Master Weaver*

*[Her] name...was Hannah.*
1 Samuel 1:2

Get ready to meet one of the most gracious women in the Bible! Her name is Hannah, which means "gracious, graciousness, grace, and favor." Hannah is one of the few women in the Scriptures about whom nothing negative is reported. How did she become such a testimony to God's great grace? Short, simple answers include bitter words—difficulty, pain, suffering, and sacrifice. For Hannah—and for all women who love God (including you and me)—God used some dark threads to weave the rich tapestry of her life.

Before we look at Hannah's life, here's a beautiful poem. I don't know who wrote it, but take its message to heart.

*The Divine Weaver*

My life is but a weaving
Between my Lord and me;
I cannot choose the colors
He worketh steadily.

Oft times He weaveth sorrow
And I, in foolish pride,
Forget that He seeth the upper,
And I the under side.

Not till the loom is silent
And the shuttles cease to fly,
Shall God unroll the canvas
And explain the reason why.

The dark threads are as needful
In the Weaver's skillful hand,
As the threads of gold and silver
In the pattern He has planned.

## 142 Dark Threads

*He had two wives: the name of one was Hannah.*
1 SAMUEL 1:2

Girls often dream of someday getting married. They may even spend years imagining and planning the perfect wedding day, honeymoon, and married life. In fact, most bridal magazines and books are purchased by young women who aren't even engaged or dating! These girls are simply fantasizing about their futures.

If, as a young girl, Hannah dreamed of the perfect marriage, her dreams were eventually met by harsh reality. She did marry, and her husband's name was Elkanah, a Levite from one of the most honorable families of priests. Hannah's husband may have been a terrific man, but there were some not-so-wonderful facts about Hannah's marriage to him. These dark threads of pain were woven throughout Hannah's life.

- *Hannah shared her husband.* Hannah's husband had two wives at the same time. (Yes, it was legal then!) Hannah's name is listed first, probably indicating she was Elkanah's first wife.
- *Hannah had no children.* The Bible simply states, "The LORD had closed her womb." Hannah didn't receive the blessing of children. Instead of ringing with laughter and the noises of active children, Hannah's house may have echoed with muffled sobs.
- *Hannah was harassed by the other wife.* Insult was added to injury for the lovely Hannah. Peninnah, Elkanah's second wife and Hannah's rival, "provoked her severely, to make her miserable."

Gather together the dark threads of pain in your life and place them into the wise and wonderful hands of God. He'll use them to make your life a beautiful masterpiece and testimony to His glory!

## 143 Golden Threads of Worship

*She went up to the house of the LORD.*
1 SAMUEL 1:7

Woven into the texture of Hannah's soul alongside the dark threads of suffering were glorious gold threads of reverence for God. Hannah's life had problems, but it was also filled with fervent worship. At the appointed time each year, Hannah journeyed with her husband to the house of the Lord to worship and make the requisite sacrifices to Him. Such devotion is clear evidence of a woman after God's own heart! What is worship? What are the benefits?

- *Worship is fellowship with God.* We don't know whether Hannah talked to her husband about the persecution she suffered from his other wife. We do know Hannah worshiped God and told Him her troubles.
- *Worship is the first step toward wisdom.* How do you handle a hard situation? Hannah went to God for wisdom about dealing with the daily difficulties of her life. As she worshiped, God led her in the path of His wisdom.
- *Worship is inward reverence.* It's relatively easy to do things for God—give money, serve in church, attend Christian events. But true worship is a matter of the heart rather than external activity.
- "*Worship quickens the conscience* by the holiness of God, feeds the mind with the beauty of God, opens the heart to the love of God, and devotes the will to the purpose of God."[37] Is any other activity more important?

When you suffer—worship. When you're confused—worship. When you're lonely—worship. When you're anxious—worship. When you're criticized—worship. Give God your reverential worship every day. Allow Him to weave an abundance of this dazzling gold into your life.

## 144 The Rope of Prayer

*She...prayed to the Lord.*
1 Samuel 1:10

Hannah's afflictions were heavy. She shared her husband with his second wife. She had no children. She was relentlessly provoked by the other wife. Bitterness of soul and anguish of heart clouded her spirit. But instead of giving up or blowing up, Hannah clung to the rope of prayer that connected her to God. Her soul may have been dark, but her faith was radiant as she poured out her distress to God.

The Hebrew language has many words for the act of prayer. The term used to describe Hannah's heartfelt prayer in 1 Samuel 1:10 means "to entreat, to make supplication."[38] She pleaded with the Lord in her trouble and made her requests known.

Take an inventory of your life. Hannah had marital problems. Do you? She was denied motherhood—something she desired. What do you long for but haven't been given? Provocation, cruelty, and ridicule were part of Hannah's everyday life. Do you regularly suffer mistreatment?

Suffering from what she didn't have, Hannah grabbed on to what she did have—the rope of prayer—and drew herself and her situation up to God's heavenly throne. Though weak from sadness, Hannah's hands were strong enough to seize her link to God.

When you experience difficulties, do what Hannah did...and enjoy the benefits!

- Holding on to the rope of prayer helps show you God's will.
- Handling the rope of prayer develops spiritual muscle.
- Hanging on to the rope of prayer in turbulent times gives you an anchor, however rough or long-lasting the storm.
- Hitching yourself to God by the rope of prayer moves you along His path for you.

## 145 *Threads of Devotion*

*She made a vow.*
1 Samuel 1:11

The threads were gathered. The shuttle was flying. God was weaving His divine design for Hannah's life. He included dark threads—the black and charcoal-gray hues of trial—as well as the glittering golden threads of worship. We've also noted the sturdy, powerful rope of prayer that securely attached Hannah to God. Now sterling silver makes its appearance!

Terrible tension mounted at home. Hannah's relationship with her husband's second wife was unbearable. Hannah was miserable... heartbreakingly miserable. And her situation seemed hopeless. True, her longing for a baby was a very personal desire. A baby would bring joy to her heart, brighten her life, and silence her critics. But as time—the preordained and perfect timing of God's plan—went on, Hannah's desire slowly grew beyond her personal yearnings and focused instead on God. The time Hannah spent wanting and waiting gave Him time to work in her a desire for something more worthy than a child merely for herself. She came to desire a man *for* God.

Hannah vowed: "O Lord of hosts, if You will...give Your maidservant a male child, then I will give him to the Lord all the days of his life." If God would give her a son, she would give that son back to God.

What about you? Do you want what you want for your own pleasure or fulfillment? Or do your desires focus on God and His purposes? Take time today to evaluate...and, if necessary, adjust... your desires and the motives behind your prayers.

# 146 Shimmering Threads of Grace

*I am a woman of sorrowful spirit.*
1 SAMUEL 1:15

In her pain—the pain of childlessness and the pain from cruel, relentless goading—Hannah turned to God. At the house of the Lord, weeping in anguish and bitterness of soul, Hannah prayed, crying out in her heart to the Lord rather than lashing out with her mouth. Never had she felt such agony. Never had she prayed so passionately. Never had she made such a serious vow to God.

As Hannah poured out her heart, the priest Eli saw her silently mouthing her cries to God. He concluded she was drunk and reprimanded her, "How long will you be drunk? Put your wine away from you!"

And what was Hannah's response? Did she say "But you don't understand!" or "Wait a minute—that's not true"? Even though misunderstood *and* falsely accused, she responded gently. The soft hues of graciousness were woven into her life and were shimmering despite her difficult circumstances.

She didn't argue or get defensive. She quietly explained, "I am a woman of sorrowful spirit." She knew and lived the truth of Proverbs 31:26—"She opens her mouth with wisdom, and on her tongue is the law of kindness." She followed God's wisdom for communication...

- Speak with wisdom and kindness (Proverbs 31:26).
- Think before you speak (15:28).
- Learn to speak softly (15:1).
- Add sweetness to your speech (16:21).
- Be instructive when you speak (16:23).
- Err on the side of less (10:19).

And how did Eli respond to Hannah's gracious speech? He gave her his priestly blessing!

# 147 Incredible Faith

*Her face was no longer sad.*
1 Samuel 1:18

At last Hannah's ordeal was over. Her trials had been many...and intense. Sharing her husband with another wife. Dealing with the heartbreak of being barren. Enduring harassment by the other wife. Being misunderstood by the temple priest.

But when Hannah explained to Eli about her prayer, she suddenly found her misery pushed aside by joy. What prompted this radical change? First Samuel 1:17 says Eli responded to her gentle reply by giving Hannah a blessing with a promise: "Go in peace, and the God of Israel grant your petition which you have asked of Him."

A new color is being woven into Hannah's life story. Perhaps the color blue to highlight her faith that spanned the sky and connected her to her heavenly Father. She placed her trust in God and the God-inspired blessing from Eli.

Nothing had really changed in her circumstances. She was still in a two-wife household, she still wasn't pregnant, and no doubt Peninnah would still harass her. But Hannah believed in God, and so she found joy in the promise of her petition being granted. What great faith! After Eli pronounced his blessing, this woman who fasted, wept, and prayed in anguish and bitterness "went her way and ate, and her face was no longer sad." She didn't have a son—she wasn't even pregnant yet!—but she knew she'd have a son someday.

Are heavenly blue threads of faith woven throughout your daily existence? Is your faith revealed in the everyday events of life? Faith is believing what God says He will do. Trust Him even when your situation doesn't seem to be improving. God is at work!

## 148 The Brilliance of Joy

*Hannah conceived and bore a son.*
1 SAMUEL 1:20

Joy is brightest in the person whose life has been darkest. And dark, sad colors appeared throughout the life tapestry of God's servant Hannah. Yet suddenly there was a splash of brilliance! A new color—riotous threads of joy—appeared. And it's quite a sizable patch!

As you know, Hannah knew dark times. She had marital problems because her husband, Elkanah, divided his love between her and another wife. She had personal problems as, year after year, she bore no children. She had people problems as Peninnah, the other wife who'd given Elkanah several sons and daughters, relentlessly mocked and reviled her. And she had a problem in public when the temple priest scolded her for allegedly being intoxicated while praying.

But joy finally burst on the scene! Hannah received the priest's blessing and later conceived and gave birth to a baby boy. Never would she forget who'd given her this precious baby! God, the Creator of life, heard her prayers and answered with the gift of a son! Hannah named him Samuel, meaning "name of God" and "asked of God," saying, "Because I have asked for him from the LORD."

Do you share Hannah's joy? Even if the weaving of your life contains many dark threads, can others spot the brilliant threads of joy? Regardless of your circumstances, thank the Lord for His goodness and mercy. The psalmist calls us to "bless the LORD…and forget not all His benefits" (Psalm 103:2). So rejoice in the Lord always (Philippians 4:4). Rejoice in the forgiveness, redemption, and relationship with God that Christ made possible on the cross and through His death and resurrection. May the brilliant threads of joy brighten your darkness.

## 149 *Threads of Love*

*The woman...nursed her son until she had weaned him.*
1 Samuel 1:23

Rich and warm, the violets and roses are the perfect tints for the threads of love God wove into Hannah's life. After praying fervently and believing faithfully, Hannah birthed a son! And now she only had a few brief years to train her son for God. Samuel had been "asked *of* God" and given *by* God, and he also was vowed *to* God before he was conceived. How long did Hannah have to pour her love and God's truth into little Samuel? Two or three years—only until he was weaned.

Question: How does a mother train a child for God? Answer: By following these guidelines for child-raising:

- *Love the Lord with all your heart* (Deuteronomy 6:5). Training a child for God requires you love Him totally.
- *Teach your child God's Word* (Deuteronomy 6:7). The Bible will teach, convict, guide, and train your kids as they grow (2 Timothy 3:16).
- *Teach your child God's ways.* Proverbs 22:6 advises, "Train up a child in the way he should go." And the way he should go is God's way!
- *Remember the Lord always* (Deuteronomy 6:7). In the moment-by-moment unfolding of life, acknowledge God's lordship and power, His sovereignty and love, His protection and provision. Your children will notice.
- *Worship the Lord* (Deuteronomy 6:13). Your devotion to God and Jesus points your child to eternal life.

Don't let another minute slip by! Do whatever you can to train each child your life touches for the Lord.

## 150 The Color of Giving

*I...have lent him to the* L*ORD.*
1 SAMUEL 1:28

How Hannah cherished her little boy, never forgetting he'd been given to her by God. And she never forgot her promise to give her son back to God for a lifetime of service. She kept her vow as she lovingly raised Samuel in the Lord. Finally the momentous day came when Samuel was to move to the Temple to serve God.

As Hannah and her husband approached the house of the Lord with their son and the required sacrifice, Hannah knew this day would require the most personal gift of all. She was giving God her best, most precious possession—her Samuel.

As you picture this little family walking toward Shiloh, imagine the rich red threads added to the tapestry of Hannah's life. Red seems the most suitable color for sacrifice.

What can you give to God that reveals your love?

- *Your children?* God gave His only Son for you (John 3:16). Have you given your children to Him to use in any way and in any place?
- *Obedience?* "Has the LORD as great delight in burnt offerings and sacrifices, as in obeying the voice of the LORD? Behold, to obey is better than sacrifice" (1 Samuel 15:22). To what obedience is God calling you?
- *Time?* Every moment is valuable to God.
- *Money?* As he placed his silver on the altar, King David revealed his heart, "[I will not] offer...to the LORD my God...that which costs me nothing" (2 Samuel 24:24). Gifts of love cost.

Hold all things lightly and nothing tightly when it comes to God. "All" includes your best, most costly treasures.

## 151 *Where Is Your Focus?*

*And Hannah prayed.*
1 Samuel 2:1

As brave Hannah entered her hardest hour—the hour appointed for her to leave her long-awaited and much-prayed-for son at the house of the Lord to be raised by someone else—her focus was not on herself...her problems...her sacrifice. Instead it was riveted on God. Expressions of exultation and glory tumbled out of Hannah as she praised God.

Hannah loved God, so we shouldn't be surprised by her worship at this difficult moment. Her heart and words are revealed for you and me to read, enjoy, learn from, and imitate. Note the contents of Hannah's impassioned prayer:

- *God's salvation*—"I rejoice in Your salvation" (verse 1).
- *God's holiness*—"No one is holy like the Lord" (verse 2).
- *God's strength*—"There [is no] rock like our God" (verse 2).
- *God's knowledge*—"The Lord is the God of knowledge" (verse 3).
- *God's power*—Only God has the power to make the mighty weak, the full hungry, the barren fertile, the dead alive, the sick well, the poor rich, and the humble exalted (verses 4-8).
- *God's judgment*—"The adversaries of the Lord shall be broken in pieces" (verses 9-10).

Why not memorize Hannah's psalm of praise and make it your own? Meditate on the attributes and actions of God she mentions and worship your almighty God.

## 152 Long-Distance Loving

*His mother used to make him a little robe.*
1 Samuel 2:19

How does a woman who loves God and her family fill her days when her nest is empty? That's the challenge Hannah now faced. After her many years of suffering, grief, and prayer, God graced Hannah with a son (1 Samuel 1 tells the whole story). As she loved and trained Samuel, her days were happy, full, and rich. But she'd wanted a baby so badly that she vowed to "give him to the Lord all the days of his life" if she got pregnant. Because her love for God was genuine, Hannah kept her promise and took her young son to the house of the Lord.

So how does a mom fill her days when her children have moved out? Rather than give in to sadness, Hannah worked on long-distance love. Each year she made Samuel a robe and took it to him. Hannah, whose life was such an exquisite weaving, became a weaver herself—making clothing for the next generation.

Imagine the rich variety of colors she carefully selected for Samuel's warm and beautiful coats. And imagine the memories evoked by the necessary darks, the splashes of blue, the sparkling silver and gold, the brilliant yellows, and the crimson reds—memories of lessons she'd learned from the Lord through the years. And don't you think Hannah, who prayed so fervently for a son, prayed for him still as she made his robes?

What can you do today to love your children and grandchildren across the miles? As a loving, praying mom, reach out to your children today—and every day!—with your prayers and your love. Call, write letters, send emails, give gifts (large and small), and tell them you love them.

## 153 A Vibrant Tapestry

*Hannah...bore three sons and two daughters.*
1 Samuel 2:21

Hannah experienced great loss when she left him at such a young age at the house of the Lord. Seldom would she see or interact with him after that time. After fulfilling her vow to God, "the Lord visited Hannah, so she conceived and bore three sons and two daughters." Five more children filled Hannah's empty home after Samuel left. The grain of Hannah's sacrifice sprouted and bore much fruit. Hannah's faith grew, her family grew, her love grew, her joy grew, and her influence grew as she raised five additional children. (And Samuel was used mightily by God too.)

Can you see the vivid green threads of spiritual growth running through the weaving of Hannah's life? What can you take from her life to help yours become vibrant and strong?

- Hannah knew firsthand the heartache that accompanies barrenness. Are you sympathetic and sensitive to those who have no children?
- Hannah took her problems to God. Do you tell Him your problems...or only your friends?
- Hannah faithfully communicated with the Lord. Have you learned the value of earnest prayer and petition (James 5:16)?
- Hannah discovered children are gifts from the Lord. How does seeing your children as God's gifts to you impact your parenting (Psalm 127:3)?
- Hannah understood the importance of training up a child for God. Are you diligently training your children—on loan to you from God—for service in His kingdom?

## 154 Loving & Supporting Your Guy

*Michal let David down through a window.*
1 Samuel 19:12

Meet Michal, the younger daughter of Israel's first king, Saul, and the first wife of David, an Old Testament hero, warrior, and king. Life was rough for Michal and David...

- David was to marry Merab, Saul's first daughter. But Saul gave Merab to another man (1 Samuel 18:19).
- David was supposed to die. Saul's premarital requirement for David was that he kill 100 Philistines. Surely he would die in the process. But David slew 200 Philistines and lived (18:20-27)!
- David was targeted for murder. Saul sent messengers to David's house to kill him. But Michal acted quickly and helped her husband escape.

Although Michal was hardly an ideal match for David, she contributed to God's purposes. Because Michal helped her husband escape her father's men, the righteous David was spared. Far from being a snare to David, as her father hoped, Michal was instrumental in saving his life.

Do you support your husband as provider? Do you refrain from criticizing him in front of others? Do you stand with him, presenting a solid front to your parents and his? Do you follow as he leads, trusting God to guide him? Nurture a solid union with your husband by...

- *speaking well of him.* Titus 3:2 says to speak evil of no one, and that includes your husband.
- *looking for his positive qualities.* And don't forget to praise him.
- *praying for him.* Prayer changes both husband and wife.

## 155 *Parenting: A Partnership with God*

*Let my...mother come here with you.*
1 SAMUEL 22:3

Imagine having a son who was "a man after God's own heart in the making." David was such a boy, and his mother must have been a mother after God's own heart who contributed greatly to her son's growth. Here are some facts about David from 1 Samuel:

- David was one of the eight sons of Jesse.
- He was a responsible shepherd.
- He was a singer.
- He faithfully delivered food to his brothers.
- He obeyed his father.
- He trusted God as he stood against the giant Goliath.
- He was a blameless fugitive.
- He sent for and protected his mother, father, and brothers.
- He was a man after God's own heart.

How can you rear children who wholeheartedly love God? Who will do great things for His kingdom? Partner with God!

- *Pursue God* with your whole heart (Luke 10:27).
- *Plant the seed of faith* in your children's hearts (1 Corinthians 3:8).
- *Pray* for your children (Proverbs 31:2).
- *Prepare your children* for greatness in God's service by teaching God's ways (Proverbs 22:6).

## 156 A Diamond from Dust

*Abigail...was a woman of good understanding.*
1 Samuel 25:3

*Abigail.* Mark this woman's name well. Her name means "cause of joy," and you'll experience great insights as you discover glistening diamonds made from dust—jewels of godly virtue—mined out of the adversity that filled Abigail's daily existence.

There was little cause for happiness in the soil of Abigail's life. Her marriage appears to have been loveless and childless. Her husband was a fool, "harsh and evil in his doings," "a scoundrel," and a drunk.

Yet the first dazzling, diamond-like quality we gather from the dust of Abigail's life is faithfulness. We see it in her loyalty, trustworthiness, steadfastness, and reliability. It's evidenced in her faithfulness to God's Word and to the people in her life. The Bible instructs God's women to build their homes and to watch over their households (Proverbs 14:13; 1:27). Abigail did both.

When her husband foolishly refused to be kind to the powerful warrior David, Abigail acted quickly to appease the angry man and save the lives of her husband, her servants, and herself. The flashing diamond of Abigail's faithfulness glistened. Even in her problem-ridden situation, she was faithful to her husband, to her household, to her work in the home, and to God.

Does your life seem buried beneath generous layers of dust and dirt? Let your belief in God—regardless of your circumstances—shine brightly as you remain "faithful in all things" (1 Timothy 3:11). Never underestimate the brilliance and beauty of faithfulness in the eyes of God. After all, He is more concerned about you being faithful to His standards than He is about you being successful in the eyes of the world. And the people around you will notice your trust in God and be drawn to Him.

## 157 A Woman of Wisdom

*Then Abigail made haste.*
1 Samuel 25:18

"How could he do it? How could my husband say no to David?" Perhaps faithful Abigail thought this. She learned from her servants—who also couldn't believe what Nabal had done—that her household was at risk. David's band of men needed food so he sent his messengers to the wealthy Nabal. The men treated the servants with respect as they asked for food. But Nabal, whose name means "foolish," turned him away! Since David and his warriors kept Nabal's shepherds and herds safe, Nabal should have gladly sent provisions. And now David was angry, and since he'd slain tens of thousands of people, keeping on his good side was the best thing to do (1 Samuel 21:11).

"What do I do, Lord?" Abigail may have prayed. And God granted her wisdom. With the help of her servants, she quickly sent David the food he'd requested and more. Then she humbly approached David, bowing low. After offering him the food and drink, she begged for mercy and asked that David spare her foolish husband and their household.

When crises arise, be wise and take action—

- *Know the Lord.* "The knowledge of the Holy One is understanding" (Proverbs 9:10).
- *Fear the Lord.* "The fear of the Lord is the beginning of wisdom" (Proverbs 9:10).
- *Acknowledge the Lord.* "In all your ways acknowledge Him, and He shall direct your paths" (Proverbs 3:6).
- *Ask the Lord.* "If any of you lacks wisdom, let him ask of God...and it will be given to him" (James 1:5).

Ask God for guidance...*before* you take action!

## 158 *A Time to Speak*

*So she fell at his feet.*
1 SAMUEL 25:24

Consider this paradoxical principle in Proverbs 25:15—"A gentle tongue breaks a bone." A woman with beauty and brains, Abigail was caught in a face-off between two powerful men—her husband and famed warrior David. When David needed food for his warriors, Nabal foolishly refused to provide it. And David foolishly decided to slay Nabal and destroy all that was his.

If ever there were a time to speak soft words that could break strong bones (and strong wills!), it was now. Approaching David, Abigail spoke gently, respectfully, and intelligently. She appealed to his future kingship, a purpose higher than revenge.

With Nabal Abigail wisely waited to speak because he was "very drunk." He wouldn't understand what was happening or his narrow escape from death.

Abigail's discretion saved the day. She could have lost everything—including the lives of her innocent servants. She acted quickly and carefully. She exhibited good judgment in her timing, her choice of words, and her manner. Her gracious speech was effective, and the mighty will of the angry David was broken.

How can you can improve in discretion?

- *Value discretion*—Understand its importance in human relations.
- *Desire discretion*—A mark of the wise is the desire for godly traits.
- *Learn discretion*—Study wise Abigail's discretion.
- *Use discretion*—Call on the Holy Spirit to help you exercise restraint and calm your emotions.
- *Pray for discretion*—Ask God to give you this valuable quality.

## 159 God Knows Every Detail

*So Abigail...became his wife.*
1 SAMUEL 25:42

Our God is an awesome God! He knows every detail about our situations. He knows why they exist and how He'll use them to accomplish His work in our lives...just as he did in Abigail's life.

*An end.* Gentle Abigail's husband was a vile, unreasonable, disrespectful man who endangered those in his care by offending the powerful David. What happened to this fool? The Bible reports, "The LORD struck Nabal, and he died."

*A beginning.* With the end of Nabal's life came a marriage proposal to Abigail from David. In God's plan—and in His timing—Abigail went from marriage to a beast to marriage to God's best. David, a man after God's own heart, took care of Abigail for the rest of her days.

*A blessing.* Apparently Abigail and Nabal had no children, but God blessed her marriage to David with a beautiful son named Chileab, which means "God is my Judge" (2 Samuel 3:3). Surely Abigail knew the truth of this name well!

God carefully crafted the details of Abigail's life, and you can be sure He's doing the same in yours. Take comfort in His presence and care. As God commands, "Be still, and know that I am God" (Psalm 46:10). There is a time to act, but there is also a time to trust, to be still, to know that in His time and in His way God makes all things beautiful. Calmly and patiently wait to behold the Lord's work in your life.

## 160 *Breathtaking Character*

*So Abigail...became his wife.*
1 Samuel 25:42

It's hard to say farewell to Abigail. Her life was a model of feminine grace revealed by sterling character. Whenever Abigail is spoken of—whether in Bible commentaries, Sunday school lessons, in Jewish circles, or Christian ones—the words are glowing. Abigail is described as intelligent and beautiful, warm and winsome, a prudent manager, and the beautiful voice of reason and faith. She earned these accolades as she walked the tightrope challenges involved in managing the household of a foolish, alcoholic husband.

Before we move on, take one final gaze at the stunning mosaic of Abigail's character. In Abigail's life, beauty rose from the arrangement of these traits:

- *Wisdom*—Abigail acted and spoke wisely, approaching peacemaking according to God's principles.
- *Discretion*—Rising above the din of David's strong emotion, recklessness, and rage, Abigail's clear voice of reason calmed everyone. Abigail reminded David of God's justice, His ability to act on David's behalf, and His great future for David. Later God gave Abigail the right words and timing when she dealt with her contemptible husband.
- *Faithfulness*—Abigail was faithful in all things—as a wife to Nabal, as a mistress to her servants, as a messenger to David, and later as his wife.

When others look at your character, what do they notice? Do they see the qualities of humility, wisdom, faithfulness, and godliness?

## 161 *Tragedy Set Aside*

*His nurse took him up and fled.*
2 SAMUEL 4:4

Confusion and fear reigned in Israel. The Philistines were on the move! Israel's King Saul was dead on the battlefield, as were his sons, including Jonathan. When word of their deaths reached the person taking care of Jonathan's son Mephibosheth, she had a critical decision to make.

Acting quickly, this loyal and brave servant snatched up the five-year-old boy and fled for safety. In their haste, however, the prince fell and became lame for life. How did this courageous woman handle such a disastrous consequence? We can imagine she may have blamed herself and carried the guilt all her days. Yet she'd tried to do what was right and acted with a heart of love.

Has any act of your devotion failed or backfired? Take heart from the outcome of this faithful nurse's heroic deed according to God's balance sheet:

| *Negatives* | *Positives* |
|---|---|
| Mephibosheth was permanently maimed. | Mephibosheth's life was saved. |
| | The line of Saul and Jonathan continued. |
| | Mephibosheth enjoyed the favor of David's care for life. |
| | David was able to fulfill a vow he'd made to Jonathan, Mephibosheth's father. |

Consider the balance sheet of your life. What is the Lord doing despite, or even with, the negatives you list? Rest in the comforting truth that God uses all things, including the negatives, for your good (Romans 8:28-29).

## 162 A Bright Future

*She bore a son.*
2 Samuel 12:24

Forgiveness! The sound of this comforting word brings joy to the heart of each and every repentant sinner. How we rejoice that our gracious and merciful God declared, "I will forgive their iniquity, and their sin I will remember no more"!

Take a moment to consider Bathsheba. The initial facts about her life hardly glow with godliness. In fact Bathsheba is best known for being an adulteress with King David. This sin resulted in her pregnancy, her husband's murder, and her newborn baby's death.

Yet like the sun after the rain, God's cleansing forgiveness shone brilliantly and warmly once Bathsheba's new husband acknowledged their sin. Hear David's words flowing from his penitent heart:

> I acknowledge my transgressions...
> Create in me a clean heart, O God...
> Restore to me the joy of Your salvation
> (Psalm 51:3, 10, 12).

After David's restoration to a right relationship with God, Bathsheba enjoyed the goodness of the Lord. Soon He blessed her with another baby, whom she named Solomon, meaning "beloved of the Lord." God chose Solomon to be king of Israel, and he is numbered among the ancestors of Jesus Christ (Matthew 1).

Everyone's life is spotted and stained with sin. Yet you too can enjoy the promise and reality of God's forgiveness. As one commentator wrote, "When we brood over sins God has said He will remember no more against us, we actually doubt His mercy and rob ourselves of spiritual power and progress."[39] No single sin should ruin an entire life. Instead, acknowledge your transgressions before God, receive His cleansing and forgiveness, and with joy over the salvation you have through Jesus Christ, enter a bright future.

## 163 The Right Time to Speak Up

*Bathsheba went into the chamber to the king.*
1 Kings 1:15

A lovely line of Scripture prompts us to adorn our hearts with "the incorruptible ornament of a gentle and quiet spirit" (1 Peter 3:4). Does this mean we shouldn't speak up about issues? In Bathsheba we see there is "a time to keep silence, and a time to speak" (Ecclesiastes 3:7). She acts with discernment according to five principles that signal the time to speak up.

- *Find the right time.* David promised Bathsheba their son Solomon would reign as king after him. Yet David lay dying without naming a successor and unaware of an uprising in progress. It was time to speak up.
- *Choose the right issue.* If David's kingly line was to continue through Solomon, he must act now. The successor to the throne was the right issue to speak up about.
- *Act out of the right motive.* God designated Solomon as the man to build the house of the Lord instead of David (1 Chronicles 22:9-10). How could this happen if Solomon weren't on the throne? This grand issue qualified as a right motive for speaking.
- *Be sensitive to the right prompting.* Nathan, God's prophet, approached Bathsheba, advised her to speak up, and told her what to say. The counsel of this godly man was the right prompting.
- *Speak in the right manner.* Bathsheba bowed respectfully, paying homage to her husband. She waited until he asked her to state her business. Humbleness and respect was the right way.

These principles are good for you to follow too. Try this approach the next time you must take care of business.

## 164 Searching for Wisdom

*The queen of Sheba…came to test [Solomon].*
1 KINGS 10:1

In the sixth century BC news traveled slowly, ever so slowly—as slowly as people walk, camels amble, and donkeys shuffle. Slowly word of Solomon, Israel's wise king who served a powerful God, made its way to Sheba, some 1200 miles south of Jerusalem. Sitting in her palace, the queen of Sheba must have mulled over the various reports. Surely no person could be so wise and no god so remarkable! And yet…what if? She decided to see for herself.

The trip to Jerusalem was long and expensive. Scholars estimate the progress of soldiers, gifts, animals, supplies, and attendants at 20 miles a day for 75 days. But no effort is too great and no price too high for true wisdom. With curiosity about Solomon, a willing spirit, and a deep hunger for wisdom, this queen set out for Israel.

What efforts are you willing to make to gain wisdom? Do you spend five minutes a day reading a chapter of Proverbs, the Bible's book of wisdom? Do you attend classes, lectures, or seminars taught by wise and godly people? Do you reserve time in your schedule to seek counsel or mentoring from someone you know to be wise?

We live in a drive-through, instant-gratification society. We want all things without effort—and we want them now! Yet in the example of this famous queen, we see a willingness to seek and sacrifice, to give whatever it takes to find answers to life's questions. Why not follow her example? Search for a precious pearl of wisdom today…and then add another to your strand tomorrow…and then another the next day. Wisdom is an ornament of grace to the soul.

## 165 *Wisdom—Worth the Price*

*She came to test [Solomon] with hard questions.*
1 Kings 10:1

Why do we take vacations? Top on most people's list is R&R—rest and relaxation. But we may also go for adventure, sightseeing, history, and the wonders of seeing new places and things.

The queen of Sheba reflects the noblest of all purposes for taking a trip. She was a true seeker of wisdom. Jesus reports that this "queen of the South...came from the ends of the earth to hear the wisdom of Solomon" (Matthew 12:42). Her journey from southern Arabia to Jerusalem by camel caravan across some 1200-plus miles of desert serves as a model for all of us. Why? Because she journeyed to see and hear the wisdom of King Solomon—the wisdom of the Lord—and to learn more about the God Solomon relied on.

Known for her legendary beauty, wealth, and magnificence, this queen appeared to have everything. But her greatest asset was a heart that desired knowledge. She gladly spent what she had to obtain the wealth of wisdom. This queen went on a quest for the keys to growing in knowledge and spiritual truth. As a woman who loves God, you need to do the same!

Proverbs 16:16 says, "How much better to get wisdom than gold!" So why not plan your own quest for spiritual truth and wisdom? Review the resources below, add your own ideas, and get started!

- books
- Bible studies
- seminars and conferences
- people who desire to learn and have wisdom
- classes at a Christian college or church

Is seeking wisdom high on your priority list? I hope so!

## 166 Taking a Bold Step for Wisdom

*Then she gave the king...talents of gold.*
1 KINGS 10:10

It's hard to imagine the fortune belonging to the queen of Sheba. This remarkable woman gave King Solomon the equivalent of 3.5 million dollars in gold and an unheard-of abundance of spices and jewels. Why? Because this rich sovereign from southern Arabia lacked one thing—true knowledge of God. And with that knowledge comes real wisdom. No price tag can be put on the knowledge of the holy, for "the fear of the LORD is the beginning of wisdom, and the knowledge of the Holy One is understanding" (Proverbs 9:10). The material abundance this wise queen presented to Solomon was nothing compared to the wisdom and understanding of God.

And the queen was well rewarded for her costly efforts. Hearing Solomon's answers to her hard questions, watching him worship, and seeing the order of his home and government gave her the wisdom she sought.

We often think very little about spending money for everyday items. Consider these approximate daily costs:

- one drive-through trip for fast food: $10 for two people
- one bottle of makeup: $10
- one new DVD: $20
- One month of cable TV: $54

Why not gladly put such amounts of money to work obtaining God's matchless wisdom? Why not spend $10 on a good book, $20 on a study Bible, $30 on a Bible course? As Jesus pointed out, "Where your treasure is, there your heart will be also" (Matthew 6:21).

Acquiring wisdom doesn't always cost money. A seeking heart and an eternal perspective on what matters are the basic requirements. What bold step will you take today to grow in wisdom?

# 167 Wisdom's Path

*King Solomon gave the queen of Sheba all she desired, whatever she asked.*
1 Kings 10:13

The queen of Sheba is truly worthy of admiration. Jesus even praised this exceptional "queen of the South." Why? Because when she learned of Solomon and his God, this woman decided to find wisdom! As one scholar noted, the queen of Sheba walked wisdom's pathway by taking these seven steps:

*Step 1:* She heard—her ears were open (Proverbs 20:12).

*Step 2:* She came with no regard for effort or expense.

*Step 3:* She communed with the wisest man of her day.

*Step 4:* She saw—her eyes were open (Proverbs 20:12).

*Step 5:* She said, "Blessed be the Lord your God!"

*Step 6:* She gave in gratitude for priceless wisdom.

*Step 7:* She returned home filled with the knowledge of God.[40]

Since you desire wisdom follow these steps today...and for the rest of your life.

- *Ask God.* "If any of you lacks wisdom, let him ask of God...and it will be given to him" (James 1:5).
- *Grow* "in the grace and knowledge of our Lord and Savior Jesus Christ" (2 Peter 3:18).
- *Desire* "the pure milk of the word, that you may grow thereby" (1 Peter 2:2).
- *Seek* "those things which are above, where Christ is" (Colossians 3:1).
- *Set* "your mind on things above, not on things on the earth" (Colossians 3:2).

God will honor your efforts and bless you!

## 168 *Letting Go*

*I have commanded a widow there to provide for you.*
1 KINGS 17:9

Drought, famine, poverty, and despair were the issues the widow of Zarephath faced. In response to sin, God's prophet Elijah prayed for a drought, which reached Zarephath (1 Kings 16:33–17:1). A widow and her son lived there and were starving. As she gathered a bundle of sticks for one last fire to bake one last bread-cake from one last handful of flour and one last drop of oil, Elijah came and asked for sustenance.

*Is he really asking me for a piece of bread to eat?* she may have thought. But she did as he asked. She didn't know that Elijah was God's way of providing for her! The widow had to trust Elijah's God as she gave her last bit of food. What faith!

Have you faced a similar decision? Are you suffering from lack of nourishment? The bitter taste of despair? Leanness of soul? "Be strong and of good courage; be not afraid, neither be thou dismayed: for the LORD thy God is with thee" (Joshua 1:9 KJV). In light of this truth, you can...

*Stop!* Stop fretting and put your faith to work! Let God know your requests and then experience His peace (Philippians 4:6-7).

*Look!* Look to the Lord in faith and He will answer you and show you great and mighty things (Jeremiah 33:3).

*Listen!* Listen to the promises of the Lord, who will supply all your needs according to His riches in glory (Philippians 4:19).

*Go!* Go on being generous. Give...and it shall be given to you (Luke 6:38).

## 169 *Freely Give*

*So she...did according to the word of Elijah.*
1 Kings 17:15

What started as a material need for the widow of Zarephath quickly became a spiritual matter as the prophet Elijah strode toward her and boldly asked for food. Did he know she was gathering sticks for a fire to make the last meal for herself and her little boy before they died of starvation? All this poor woman had was a handful of flour and a little oil. Yet in faith, choosing to trust God, this brave woman shared her meager supplies.

Others have done the same...

- Widows in the church fed and lodged those in need (1 Timothy 5:10).
- Corrie ten Boom risked her life to help Jews in World War II, which led to her arrest and being sent to a German concentration camp.
- George Muller faithfully called upon God's sharing hand to provide food for 2000 orphans for 20 years.

God is calling you to a life of giving. How can you help?

- Faithfully providing meals for your family.
- Expand this ministry at home into a ministry of hospitality by opening your door to others.
- Stock your church's food closet for those in need.
- Volunteer at your city's downtown mission project.
- Get involved in feeding the hungry.

"Freely you have received, freely give" (Matthew 140:8).

## 170 By Faith...Trust

*So she...did according to the word of Elijah.*
1 Kings 17:15

Food and faith. We don't normally think of these together. Yet in the actions of the widow of Zarephath, faith is at the core of a food issue. In this time of drought and famine, everyone was scraping bottom. But God was watching and sent Elijah!

To live this woman must give her last handful of flour to God's messenger. The Bible defines faith as "the substance of things hoped for, the evidence of things not seen" (Hebrews 11:1), and this dear woman hoped and acted in faith by...

- believing Elijah, who said, "Do not fear...for thus says the Lord God of Israel: 'The bin of flour shall not be used up...until the day the Lord sends rain on the earth' "
- opening her hands and giving what she had

What was the result of this faith? This widow, her son, and Elijah were blessed by God. For more than 1000 days He miraculously provided what they needed. The widow discovered that God's people walk by faith and God provides what they need.

| *By sight...* | *But by faith she trusted and...* |
|---|---|
| There was no more food. | God provided daily bread. |
| Supplies were limited to one handful of meal. | God supplied three years of meals. |
| Everyone was perishing. | God sustained them. |
| Death was certain. | God preserved life. |

Are you walking by faith? Is there any step you need to take, trusting God for the results?

# 171 *A Measure of Faith*

***I know...the word of the LORD...is the truth.***
1 KINGS 17:24

Have you sat on the beach and enjoyed the rhythm of the waves as they rolled up the sand? As one breaker swells and curls over, the next whitecap is forming with very little pause in between. Keep this image in mind as you remember the widow of Zarephath and how her story relates to your life. You see, your life has a rhythm too—the rhythm of trouble and trust. As the trials of life roll in, you have the opportunity to trust the Lord afresh.

The widow of Zarephath trusted God in a trial that threatened her little family's lives. When she had just enough flour for one last meal before death by starvation occurred, this dear woman used that tiny bit of flour—and her tiny bit of faith—to first make a bread-cake for Elijah. Only then did she make one for herself and her son. In honor of her faith, God opened the windows of heaven and fed her, her son, and Elijah for three years!

But then a new trial struck. This widow's little boy—her only child—died. As this wave washed over her fragile life, this desperate woman called on her faith to trust that God would help her again. She approached Elijah, and he raised the child from the dead. The widow's heart was revealed when she declared, "Now I know...the word of the LORD in your mouth is the truth."

Troubles never cease. They roll in as surely as the surf continues unceasingly, day in and day out. That's the nature of this world we live in. What are you facing today that you can give to God? Remember, God's mercy and compassion are new every morning. When troubles come, in faith reach out to Him. He'll come through for you.

## 172 Giving to the Lord

*I know…the word of the LORD…is the truth.*
1 KINGS 17:24

"Give, and it will be given to you: good measure, pressed down, shaken together, and running over" (Luke 6:38). Although these words were spoken by Jesus, the widow of Zarephath experienced the truth of their promise more than 800 years before they were uttered. When the prophet Elijah asked her for food, she gave it willingly. This was the beginning of God's great provision for this trusting woman. Note some of the blessings He bestowed:

- *The blessing of feeding Elijah.* God let this widow provide for His servant Elijah. How wonderful to be used for God's kingdom purposes!
- *The blessing of life.* After sharing her food—an act of faith in God—Elijah, the widow, and her son were miraculously provided for.
- *The blessing of a resurrected son.* When tragedy struck and her son died, Elijah called on God and the boy was brought back to life.
- *The blessing of the wonderful knowledge of God.* The provision of food gave the widow clear knowledge of God and a firm foundation for believing His Word.
- *The blessing of Jesus' praise.* Jesus bestowed His "Well done!" with these words, "Many widows were in Israel in the days of Elijah…but to none of them was Elijah sent except to Zarephath…to a woman who was a widow" (Luke 4:25-26).

What will you give to God today?

## 173 Opening Your Heart and Home

*She constrained [Elisha] to eat some food.*
2 Kings 4:8

A well-known, older woman met God's prophet Elisha, probably as he was passing by her home, and invited him home for a meal with her and her husband. When she realized he regularly came through her town, she invited him to stop for a meal or stay overnight anytime. This Shunammite woman excelled in the art of hospitality.

Your love for God and His love for people is lived out when you love others. So...

- "put on a heart of...kindness" (Colossians 3:12 NASB)
- "walk in the Spirit...the fruit of the Spirit is...kindness" (Galatians 5:16, 22)
- "be kind to all" (2 Timothy 2:24 NASB)

What does it take to open your home? A heart for others. A little preparation. A giving spirit. A slice of time. The Shunammite woman shows us how to reach out—

*Kindness notices.* This woman's habit was to watch and listen to those around her, being on the lookout for people's needs.

*Kindness cares.* She genuinely cared about Elisha and his welfare.

*Kindness takes action.* She noticed Elisha's situation and invited him to dine with her family whenever he was in town.

Saint Augustine said, "Love has hands to help others. It has feet to hasten to the poor and needy. It has eyes to see misery and want. It has ears to hear the sighs and sorrow of men." Pray for...

- a loving heart
- compassion
- resources to share
- eyes that see
- funds for provisions
- energy to serve

## 174 Reflecting God's Goodness

*Let us make a small upper room...so ...he can turn in there.*
2 KINGS 4:10

If your heart is filled with the goodness of the Lord, you can be sure the people around you know your love for God and His place in your heart. Everyone around you will be blessed by the very real presence of His love in you.

God's presence was certainly apparent in the Shunammite woman as she cared for the prophet Elisha. Noticing his need for nourishment and rest, this godly woman went into action. Goodness of heart naturally leads to goodness in deeds! This hospitable woman first insisted that Elisha join them for dinner.

But she went a lot further than that! She asked her husband if they could add a little room in their house so this man of God would have a place to sleep, study, and pray. When the chamber was finished, Elisha had a home away from home. How he must have looked forward to stopping in Shunem! And Elisha's servant, Gehazi, may have stayed there too.

Look closely at the Shunammite woman and notice the godliness of her actions:

- She took the initiative to identify and meet specific needs.
- She set aside her own comfort and willingly worked to provide for the needs of another.
- She advanced the well-being of another person.
- She gave every good thing she could think of to help Elisha.

Goodness can be nurtured in your heart. God says to do good to all, including those who dislike you or treat you unkindly. Think of several people right now and what you can do for them. Then act!

## 175 A Heart of Contentment

*And the woman...bore a son.*
2 Kings 4:17

Did the Shunammite woman slip a bill under Elisha's door during his stays at her family's home? No! She had no reason to because the account never changed:

| | |
|---|---|
| Room | $0 |
| Board | $0 |
| Balance due | $0 |

Deeply touched by this godly woman's hospitality, Elisha decided to do something for her. He called her to him and asked, but she didn't have any requests. She left and Elisha wondered aloud to his servant, "What can be done for her?" Perhaps Gehazi had been pondering the same question since he too was blessed by her graciousness. He replied, "She has no son, and her husband is old."

Can you hear Elisha exclaim, "That's it! A son for her to love and who will care for her in the future! Call her back in"? He announced to this generous woman, "About this time next year you shall embrace a son." And it happened as promised.

Don't miss the remarkable message in this story. This precious wife was apparently content even before she had children. She comes across as happily dwelling with her people, lavishing love on her husband, and extending welcoming care to the likes of Elisha and his servant. Nevertheless, she undoubtedly felt ecstatic at the birth of her son! But she'd learned greater lessons in the days and decades preceding that wondrous event:

> Contentment is understanding that if I am not satisfied with what I have, I will never be satisfied with what I want...
>
> Contentment is realizing that God has already given me everything I need for my present happiness.[41]

## 176 Peace and Joy Will Come

*[Her son] sat on her knees till noon, and then died.*
2 Kings 4:20

After years of childless marriage, the hospitable Shunammite woman was told by Elisha that she would have a baby. Oh how the home filled with joy as she and her husband praised God for the birth of their precious son! But now sorrow filled the rooms. The boy was helping his father in the fields when he suddenly screamed, "My head, my head!" Carried home, the little boy sat on his mother's lap and died.

What do you do with a heart filled with sorrow and a soul in distress? There are no easy answers, but God is here for you!

*The provision of God's grace.* Whatever your day—or life—holds, God promises His grace is sufficient (2 Corinthians 12:9-10). Do you suffer from...

- infirmities and weaknesses? God's grace is sufficient for you.
- needs and hardships? God's grace is sufficient for you.
- persecution and oppression? God's grace is sufficient for you.

*The provision of God's compassion.* What a blessing to know Jesus! God's Son walked this earth and was tempted as you are. He sympathizes and empathizes with you (Hebrews 4:15).

*The provision of God's comfort.* The "God of all comfort...comforts us in *all* our tribulation" (2 Corinthians 1:3, 4).

*The provision of God's promises.* Depend on God's promises. They can't fail. As one hymn writer put it, "When the howling storms of doubt and fear assail, by the living Word of God I shall prevail, standing on the promises of God!"[42]

It's easy to look in every direction for help, hope, and comfort. But God is the only true source of what you need. Turn to Him!

## 177 Expect Something Good!

*So she…went to the man of God.*
2 Kings 4:25

Hope—"the expectation of good." And hope is the next golden and godly quality revealed in the life of the noble woman of Shunem. But the road to hope is often strewn with sorrow and adversity. Tragedy struck the happy heart and home of the Shunammite woman when her only child suddenly died. But the Shunammite responded with faith and hope.

- Faith placed her limp, dead son on the prophet Elisha's bed…and hoped.
- Faith answered her husband's "Is everything all right?" with an "It is well"…and hoped.
- Faith saddled a donkey and traveled 30 miles to Mount Carmel to see Elisha…and hoped.
- Faith answered Elisha's servant's inquiry with an "It is well"…and hoped.
- Faith fell on the ground and grasped Elisha's feet…and hoped.
- Faith refused to follow the prophet's servant and instead waited on the prophet…and hoped.
- Faith waited outside the bedroom door as Elisha prayed to God seven times…and hoped.
- Faith and hope were rewarded as the Shunammite woman took up her son—alive!

What do you most need hope for today? What will you do as an act of faith today that reveals your hope and trust in God?

## 178 Acting on Your Heart of Faith

*The woman...did according to the saying of the man of God.*
2 KINGS 8:2

The generous Shunammite woman knew blessings from the Lord: She had a husband to love, a home to enjoy, a friendship with God's prophet Elisha, and a son. But a heart of faith is grown in the dark, and there were dark times aplenty for this godly woman.

Childless for a long time, barrenness was a humbling experience. And after finally giving birth and loving her son, the lad suddenly died. (Elisha raised him from the dead!) Then death visited her home again, and she slipped into the sorrow of widowhood. And now Elisha was predicting a seven-year famine and telling her to take her son and move away.

"He who heeds counsel is wise," says Proverbs 12:15. The Shunammite woman displayed her wisdom by acting on Elisha's counsel. With a heart of faith she disregarded the personal cost and inconvenience, packed up house and home, and moved. With a heart of faith she stepped out of her comfort zone, out of the land she loved and had been so content to dwell in, away from her friends, property, inheritance, security...and into the unknown will of God.

But that's not the end of her story! Rewards aplenty accompanied her faith. After surviving the famine, this courageous widow returned to Israel, petitioned the king of Israel for her property, and received everything she owned plus what the land had earned during her absence. With a heart of faith this noble woman believed the Word of God for what she couldn't see and later was rewarded by seeing what she'd trusted Him for.

Behold the beauty and strength of a heart of faith! Is there any difficulty in your life? Nurture a heart of faith by believing God's Word, trusting in Him, and following His instructions.

## 179 The ABCs of Ministry

*So [they] went to Huldah the prophetess…*
*[and] spoke with her.*
2 Kings 22:14

In the Old City of Jerusalem is the Temple Mount, the site of the temple first built by King Solomon. Walking the perimeter you'll come to a beautiful, double-gated entrance called "Huldah's Gate." Huldah was the wife of Shallum and a prophetess.

During King Josiah's campaign to clean up and repair the house of the Lord, workers unearthed "the book of the law." After having the book read to him, the king sent for Huldah to discover what to do. Obviously she had an excellent reputation as God's prophet!

What traits made her useful to God's people?

***A**—Available.* Sitting in the central part of the city, Huldah counseled any who wished to inquire of Jehovah.

Are you available? Do you return phone calls and answer mail? Do you go where other women are?

***B**—Believer.* Huldah held fast to God's truth and believed His Word. She boldly prophesied the doom of the kingdom of Judah because people disobeyed God's commands. The people responded in repentance and the kingdom experienced revival.

Do you believe the Scriptures—every single word? Do you passionately believe it, love it, live it, and share it?

***C**—Counselor.* Huldah shared God's wisdom and the precepts of His Word and called for obedience.

What about you? When others share problems, do you call on God for guidance? Do you share His wisdom?

Make these ABCs of ministry your guide to greater usefulness in God's kingdom.

## 180 The Beauty of Usefulness

*So [the king] made her queen.*
ESTHER 2:17

What does it take to acquire the beauty of being useful to God? We get an idea from the life of Esther, an Old Testament heroine whose name means "a star."

*Heritage*—Esther, a Jew from the tribe of Benjamin, was taken to Babylon when her people were captives around 600 BC.

> What have you learned from what your ancestors stood for, fought for, believed in, and endured?

*Parentage*—Esther's parents died while she was young, but a faithful and loving uncle brought her up as his daughter.

> If you have "missing" parents, acknowledge those whom God provided in their place.

*Tutelage*—Esther was taught by her Uncle Mordecai and Hegai, a heathen eunuch in King Ahasuerus' palace.

> Give thanks for the variety of teachers God sent your way.

*Advantage*—Esther was gifted with physical beauty, Mordecai's wisdom, and Hegai's preferential treatment.

> What circumstances and opportunities did God use to prepare you for working for His kingdom?

*Homage*—Esther's heritage, parentage, and tutelage garnered her honor when she was presented as queen.

> Consider the honor you have and that you'll receive in heaven because you're a daughter of the King!

Thank God for His active, transforming, loving presence.

## 181 *Finding Courage*

*If I perish, I perish!*
ESTHER 4:16

Let's gaze upon the beauty of two women whose courage reflects their mature faith in the Lord. The first woman is Queen Esther. This beautiful Jewess was married to a temperamental, pagan king. When she learned of a plot to kill the Jews in the kingdom, she knew she must go to her husband to plead for their lives. The problem? No one—not even a wife!—approached the king uninvited without risking death. Yet Esther's courage, rooted in her faith in God, empowered her to boldly say, "If I perish, I perish!" The urgent need to act on behalf of God's people and her fearless faith in the God she loved inspired her heroism.

The second woman is Betty Scott Stam. In 1931 Betty's courage and faith led her to serve in China as a missionary. Caught in a Communist uprising, this young woman, whose life verse was Philippians 1:21—"To me, to live is Christ, and to die is gain"—knelt beside her husband, bowed her head, and was decapitated. Later, 700 students at Moody Bible Institute stood at Betty's memorial service and consecrated their lives to missionary work whenever and wherever God called them.[43] As the gifted English preacher C.H. Spurgeon noted, "Suffering saints are living seed."

Will you put your name alongside this remarkable pair of women who loved God and displayed the beauty of courage rooted in that love and in their faith in Him? Will you value the things of God more than the things of this world? Embrace the stance of faith that announces, "For me, to live is Christ, and to die is gain."

Do you sometimes lack courage? What is your favorite verse for fighting fear? Pull it out, brush up on its truth, hold it close in your heart, and use it!

## 182 7 Steps to Wisdom

*What is your petition, Queen Esther?*
*It shall be granted you.*
ESTHER 7:2

Queen Esther learned that Haman received permission "to annihilate all the Jews" (Esther 3:13). How could she persuade the king to protect the Jews?

What a beautiful picture of grace, wisdom, and patience! Esther reveals how to effectively approach and persuade other people.

*Step 1: Stop.* Before trying to rightly handle a wrong situation, Esther paused.

*Step 2: Wait.* Time is a precious asset. Waiting gave Esther time to gather the facts.

*Step 3: Consult.* Waiting allowed time for seeking further counsel.

*Step 4: Pray.* Waiting gave Esther time to fast and pray for wisdom about how to approach the king. She asked the Jews to do the same on her behalf.

*Step 5: Decide.* Time, counsel, and prayer moved Esther to choose a plan and move forward with the triumphant attitude "If I perish, I perish!"

*Step 6: Act.* Before she asked for what she wanted, Esther prepared a special dinner for King Ahasuerus and Haman to assess the king's frame of mind.

*Step 7: Adjust.* Discerning and sensitive to the situation, Esther wisely waited and prepared a second dinner before asking her husband to save her people.

Why not follow Esther's steps when you face your next challenge?

## 183 *Sweet, Gentle, Persuasive Speech*

*What is your petition, Queen Esther?*
*It shall be granted you.*
Esther 7:2

When we act with wisdom and patience, softness can indeed accomplish hard things. Because of a plot to kill every Jew, Queen Esther approached her husband to intercede for them. How did she go about it?

Did you notice what Esther didn't do? Nowhere in Esther's story will you find anger or agitation, violence or panic, rashness or reaction. Esther knew out-of-control emotions wouldn't help her avert disaster.

Esther used sweet speech—a gentle tongue—to turn the heart of her husband against the instigator of the murderous plan. What were some of Esther's "sweet-speech patterns"?

- *Words of respect.* Esther addressed her husband respectfully, "If it pleases the king," "If I have found favor in [your] sight," and "I will do as the king has said."
- *Words of welcome.* Esther sweetly extended an invitation to dinner, "Let the king...come today to the banquet that I have prepared for him" (5:4).
- *Words of caution.* Sensing the timing for her request wasn't right, Esther asked the king to return for another dinner the next day.
- *Words that were direct.* Esther boldly asked: "Let my life be given me at my petition, and my people at my request."
- *Words few in number.* Esther's words were respectful, nonconfrontive, and direct. She chose her words carefully and said what was necessary.

What are your speech patterns like? May God grant you the beauty of sweet speech!

## 184 For Such a Time as This

*So Esther arose and stood before the king.*
Esther 8:4

Where has God planted you? Even if you're not in ideal circumstances, know that God has a plan for you...and is acting on your behalf. Esther's usefulness to God and His people grew from seeds sown in the soil of sorrow and pain. Look at her liabilities:

*Born:* Born to captives in a strange land

*Parents:* Her mother and father died young

*Address:* Taken to the king's harem against her will

*Position:* Queen to an alcoholic, impulsive, pagan king

Although these details suggest she was an unlikely candidate, God used Esther mightily in His plan. When the Israelites were threatened with extermination, as queen, Esther could help them. She had truly "come to the kingdom for such a time as this."

You can be used by the Lord today by being faithful. Discover the beauty of being part of God's plan by doing the heroic—

*The Hero*

The hero does not set out to be one. She is probably more surprised than others by such recognition. She was there when the crisis occurred...and she responded as she always had in any situation. She was simply doing what had to be done! Faithful where she was in her duty...she was ready when the crisis arose. Being where she was supposed to be... doing what she was supposed to do...responding as was her custom...to circumstances as they developed...devoted to duty—she did the heroic![44]

## 185 *A Time of Thanks*

*The Jews established…that these days should be remembered.*
Esther 9:27-28

A good time-management principle is to write events on a 12-month calendar at the beginning of each year. This ensures that important occasions are remembered. More than 2400 years ago, Queen Esther and her Uncle Mordecai did something similar.

It was a dark time for God's people because they were captives in a strange land. And then King Ahasuerus issued an edict giving his subjects permission "to annihilate all the Jews, both young and old, little children and women…and to plunder their possessions" (Esther 3:13).

Imagine the Israelites' heartache…fear…dread…despair. They could do little to save themselves. But God had a plan! He'd arranged for Esther to be in a place of influence, a place of trust. This Jewess was taken from her Uncle Mordecai and placed in the king's harem. Eventually she married the king! Now Esther was in a position to intervene for the Jews. But even as queen it was a dangerous undertaking. King Ahasuerus was impulsive, alcoholic, and pagan.

With God's help and wisdom, Esther persuaded the king to let the Jews defend themselves against the onslaught. And the Jews overpowered their enemies.

Now imagine the joy! The jubilation! The sweet taste of victory! The relief! To celebrate Esther and Mordecai proclaimed the day following their triumph an annual holiday of feasting and gift giving. To this day Jews around the world celebrate the Feast of Purim.

And what about you? Do you regularly honor the goodness of the Lord and His work in your life? Christmas (God's coming in flesh) and Easter (God's atoning work for your sin) are perfect occasions to praise God. So are spiritual "birthdays" and the day of your baptism. As the psalmist says, "Bless the Lord, O my soul, and forget not all His benefits" (Psalm 103:2).

## 186 True Beauty Shines

*Esther the queen...wrote with all authority.*
Esther 9:29 KJV

Hasn't it been lovely getting to know Queen Esther? The Bible tells us about her exquisite physical beauty—that she "was lovely and beautiful," one of the "beautiful young virgins...sought for the king." But there's so much more to Esther's timeless beauty...

- *The beauty of acceptance.* Although Esther's parents died, we see no hint of bitterness or resentment that would mar or spoil Esther's beauty. She accepted her circumstances with grace.
- *The beauty of character.* Esther's character brings to mind words such as faithful, courageous, spiritual, wise, resolute.
- *The beauty of spirit.* Esther possessed the beauty of a gentle and quiet spirit, which is precious in the sight of God (1 Peter 3:4). She was gracious, cautious, patient, and discreet.

Only the Lord can create the true beauty that shines from the hearts of women like Esther (and you!). How can you nurture this beauty? By developing a deep trust in God and reverence for the Lord. Look to Him for sustenance when times are good and when times are bad. Believe God will enable you to persevere when your faith is challenged, relationships are tense, and even when death is imminent. God's grace is sufficient for whatever life demands (2 Corinthians 12:9-10).

Reach for this internal and eternal brand of beauty—the beauty that comes from the Lord! Study the inspired words of your Bible. Pray. Ask the Lord to fill you with His strength, faith, courage, and wisdom.

## 187 The Woman of Proverbs 31

*Who can find a virtuous woman?*
PROVERBS 31:10 KJV

Have you read Proverbs 31:10-31 lately? The special woman beautifully illustrated in this passage is a treasure whose price is far above rubies. Through her God presents an overview of godly character for us to follow through every age and stage of our lives. Why not delight in the Lord as you get to know His beautiful woman?[45]

Are you hesitant? Are you thinking, "I've heard about this outstanding woman. Isn't she the 'ideal' woman? The 'impossible to achieve' dream? She makes me feel inferior, like a failure. I could never be like her!"

She is indeed a striking figure, but you can be like her! Here are some facts to encourage you to follow this God-given role model.

- Proverbs 31 is taught by a woman. This is a woman's estimate of what a woman should and can be.
- The 21 verses of Proverbs 31:11-31 answer the question "Who can find a virtuous wife?" by defining "virtuous."
- The wise mother who is teaching her son about women of character is one herself, which is why she can describe her so well.
- Knowing that women of godly character are out there, this mother encourages her son to look for one.
- "Many daughters have done virtuously" (verse 29 KJV). *Many!* The Proverbs 31 woman is not a one-of-a-kind woman. And she's not a fluke.

A woman of strength and virtue is indeed a valuable treasure. And, according to God, you can become one. How? By following God's ABCs of character. We'll explore this alphabet in the next few devotions. Discover God's definition of true beauty and how to attain it!

## 188 A Powerful Mind and Body

*Who can find a virtuous woman?*
*For her price is far above rubies.*
PROVERBS 31:10 KJV

God's use of the word "virtuous" in His description of a beautiful woman has a double meaning. Both aspects communicate positive strengths.

*A powerful mind.* "Virtuous" refers to a mind made strong by principles and attitudes. A quick glance at Proverbs 31 reveals her intelligence and how she uses it:

- She keeps herself pure (verse 10).
- Her husband trusts her, as do the people around her (11).
- She's a woman of industry (13, 15, 18).
- Ever thrifty, she provides for her loved ones (14).
- She faces life (and death!) with courage (25).
- Compassion, kindness, and wisdom characterize her life (20, 26).
- Holiness crowns her efforts as she honors the Lord in all she does (30).

*A powerful body.* "Virtuous" also describes this woman's ability to put into action what her powerful mind desires:

- She works willingly with her hands (13).
- She plants a vineyard (16).
- She operates a spindle and distaff (19).
- She works until late at night (15, 18).
- She nurses the needy (20).
- She weaves the family's clothing (21-24).
- Never idle, she watches over and builds her home (27).

Ask God today to help you strengthen your mind and body.

## 189 *Woman as Mighty Warrior?*

*The heart of her husband safely trusts her;*
*so he will have no lack of gain.*
PROVERBS 31:11

The best marriage is attained by establishing it on the rock of Jesus Christ and, in His strength, offering your husband the bedrock loyalty of a faithful wife. A trustworthy and reliable wife is definitely "a gain" for a husband. But another explanation is veiled in the word "gain" in Proverbs 31:11. In the days of Proverbs 31 "gain" was obtained in four ways:

- by working at a respectable job
- by warring and stripping valuables off the bodies of the defeated
- by working as an indentured servant
- by wrongdoing, such as lying, cheating, stealing

A husband married to a Proverbs 31 woman knows a different kind of gain. He enjoys the personal contributions his wife makes to the family's well-being. Both the Hebrew and Greek languages for this section of Scripture vividly portray this woman, this unfailing prize, as a mighty warrior who uses her abilities for the benefit of her husband's domain. Verse 11 pictures the wife going to battle for her family. She battles daily on the home front so he doesn't have to engage in war or experience a "lack of gain"![46] Not only does this wife not squander or spend her husband's earnings foolishly, but she also protects, manages, and increases them.

God considers your contribution to the finances of your home beautiful, whether you're married or single. You see, God's own beauty—all His virtues, character traits, and holiness—is to be lived out in your day-to-day life. Ask God's Spirit to open your eyes to the many opportunities you have to put the godly principles of thrift and wise money management to work—and then go to war!

## 190 A Perpetual Spring of Goodness

*She does him good and not evil*
*all the days of her life.*
PROVERBS 31:12

Can you imagine a dry and dusty land—parched and cracked from lack of water, relentless sun, and searing heat? Now imagine the joy, the value, the refreshment, and the life that a year-round spring would introduce into such a bleak existence. That's what a good woman brings into the life of her husband, the atmosphere of her home, and the lives of others. She's a spring of goodness, a welcome relief to those around her.

The woman who is intent on having her refreshing ministry overflow into the lives of those she loves does good and not evil. Are you following God's plan and fulfilling His pattern for goodness? Aren't you glad He empowers you when you plan to do the good He calls you to do and then put your plans into action?

*Step 1: Plan to do good.* Proverbs 14:22 says, "Do they not go astray who devise evil? But mercy and truth belong to those who devise good." Sharing his insights into this verse, one preacher pointed to Hitler, who masterminded the murder of millions. He noted that Hitler "devised evil" and planned evil as meticulously as a bride plans her wedding. Just as meticulously we are to "devise good."

*Step 2: Practice your plan.* Don't be content with merely planning to do good. Follow through on your good intentions. Put your plan to work.

Right now whisper a prayer to the God you love and set sail today—and every day—on a course of doing good for your husband, for your family, for your friends, for others you encounter. God wants you to be a perpetual spring of goodness.

## 191 *A Fountain of Joy*

*She seeks wool and flax, and willingly works with her hands.*
PROVERBS 31:13

In biblical times a house was generally built around an open space that was used for a garden. It often included a fountain that energetically produced the happy music of bubbles, gurgles, and splashes. You can be a fountain of joy when you willingly and happily do your work! Put the following joy-producing principles into practice.

- *Pray daily*—Talking to God *and* listening gives you His perspective that lifts your duties in the home from the physical realm and gives them spiritual significance as service to the Lord.
- *Recite Scripture*—Allow God's Word to encourage you as you work. Hide favorite scriptures in your heart so you can call on them when needed. (Read Colossians 3:23; Philippians 4:13; Proverbs 14:1.)
- *Do your work to the Lord*—Colossians 3:23 reminds us, "Whatever you do, do it heartily, as to the Lord and not to men." The What, the Who, and the Why of all your work is God!
- *Look for the benefits*—Develop a vision for your work, for the home you are building, and for the ministry you offer there.
- *Pause and rest*—There's nothing wrong with well-earned rest. Pause when you need to and refresh yourself in the Lord.
- *Value each day*—Your rewards (receiving some "well dones" and enjoying a sense of order in your home and your life) come more frequently when you willingly do your work one task at a time and take life one day at a time.

## 192 The Joys and Benefits of Shopping

*She is like the merchant ships,*
*she brings her food from afar.*
PROVERBS 31:14

With a sense of mission, God's beautiful Proverbs 31 woman sets out like the majestic merchant ships of her day, to find high-quality goods for those under her roof. Scouring shops stocked by ships that sailed the Mediterranean, this woman spared no effort in obtaining items that would contribute to the well-being and delight of those she cherished. She found genuine satisfaction in providing what was best for her family. And there were other blessings she enjoyed too...

- Health resided under her roof because she set nutritious food before her family.
- Savings resulted as she searched, bargained, and bartered to provide the necessary and beautiful for her clan.
- Culture entered her doors with goods that came from exotic places and the tales and information gained when those items were purchased.
- Variety spiced up life in her home as foods and furnishings from afar treated those within.
- Quality goods were enjoyed because of her keen eye and the uncompromising standards she maintained.
- Beauty satisfied, invigorated, and ministered to the souls of her family.

You too provide the basics and the beauty that set your household apart from others. Ask God to give you even greater resolve and renewed energy so you sail smoothly toward the endearing—and enduring—quality of an enterprising spirit.

## 193 Time-Management Tips from God

*She also rises while it is yet night, and provides food for her household, and a portion for her maidservants.*
PROVERBS 31:15

Effective time management is a challenge. There are seminars you can attend, time-management systems and notebooks you can buy, magazine articles that herald ultimate keys to success, and books proffered that promise busy women like you tools to handle the myriad responsibilities that fall to you.

But the best time-management help comes from God. He gave us His three pointers for perfect time management. You'll find them in Proverbs 31 as you watch a woman successfully walk through her busy day.

> *Step 1: An early start.* Getting up a little early each morning gave the Proverbs 31 woman a jump on the day and its to-do list. One of her first activities was tending the fire for the day's meals and warmth. The early, quiet part of the day also allowed her to tend her heart's fire by spending time with God.
>
> *Step 2: Food for the family.* Providing her family's daily bread was another important reason for rising early. Like your family, the Proverbs 31 woman's family depended on her for meals.
>
> *Step 3: A plan for the day.* When the Bible says this woman gave a "portion" to her maidens, it means she gave them their work assignments for the day. She diligently organized herself and her helpers so the housekeeping chores were accomplished efficiently.

What a privilege God has given you to set the pattern and tone for your household each new dawn. May He richly bless you as you seek Him early, see to your family's needs, and set in action a plan for the day.

## 194 Dreaming, Planning, Taking Action

*She considers a field and buys it;*
*from her profits she plants a vineyard.*
Proverbs 31:16

Our all-wise Lord shows us more helpful pointers for being successful. The Proverbs 31 woman's world extended beyond her home's doorstep. She was also a visionary and a businesswoman.

*Step 1: Consideration.* Hearing that a certain field was for sale, this wise woman most likely prayed, asked questions of others, and sought advice from her husband about purchasing the field.

*Step 2: Acquisition.* Blessed with peace of mind and spirit, practical answers to her questions, and her husband's approval, she took action. This prudent woman purchased her field with money she earned and saved through hard work and thriftiness.

*Step 3: Renovation.* With her hard-earned, well-managed, faithfully saved money, this capable woman improved her property by planting a vineyard with the best plantings her funds could buy.

Proverbs 31 calls us not only to labor, but to dream. This noble, accomplished woman dreamed—and then took action to realize them. She wanted a better life for her family, better and more food on their table, produce she could give and sell to other people, income she could invest to better her family, and the satisfaction of creatively bringing her dreams to fruition. She blessed others by using the abilities God blessed her with.

Turn off the TV, the computer, and whatever keeps you from thinking creatively, from dreaming and wondering and planning. Take time before the Lord to jot down your dreams. Then consider (ask, seek, and knock), acquire (move forward), and renovate (improve your acquisition and grow your skills).

# 195 12 Steps to Getting Everything Done

*She girds herself with strength,*
*and strengthens her arms.*
PROVERBS 31:17

The Proverbs 31 homemaker worked hard to create a "home sweet home." What can you do to maintain a "can do," energetic spirit as you do the same?

1. *Embrace God's will for your life.* The Proverbs 31 woman reflects His will for you.
2. *Stay in God's Word.* There is power in the Word, so read it every day.
3. *Develop a vision.* Create a "big picture" of what you want your home to be—a safe haven for family, a place to raise children who love God.
4. *Tap into the "why."* Knowing why you do what you do helps keep you motivated to do the tasks wholeheartedly.
5. *Pray for an eager attitude.* Ask God to help you accept with eagerness the tasks He has for you.
6. *Create a schedule.* Plan *and* accomplish your work!
7. *Develop a routine.* Routines help you fly through tasks and become more efficient.
8. *Read time-management books.* Learn the best ways to do your job.
9. *Tackle the worst first.* It makes the rest of your day easy.
10. *Play music.* Upbeat music keeps you from sagging.
11. *See how quickly you can work.* Make doing your chores a game. Beat the clock.
12. *Consider the blessings.* Praise God for what your work means to you and those who it impacts.

You don't need to apply all these at once. Pick one, say a prayer, and dig in.

## 196 The Sweet Taste of Success

*She perceives that her merchandise is good, and her lamp does not go out by night.*
PROVERBS 31:18

"Industrious" is often used to describe the Proverbs 31 woman. Women always wonder, "How does she do it? What keeps her going? How can she get up early, shop, work, garden, and then sew late into the night?"

The root of her wonderful and productive busyness is a keen motivation that pushes her along. She keeps in mind her goal and the reason for doing all she does. Her consuming love for her family compels her to excel in providing for them. Desiring the best for the family she cherishes, this wonderful woman sets out to efficiently and joyfully procure what they need and want.

Love motivates her to get up early, to shop wisely, to weave clothing and household items for her home, and to purchase and work a field for its sumptuous supply of food and helpful additional income.

This noble woman's efforts yielded a twofold harvest as she tasted the success of her endeavors. Her family was cared for and her resources grew, pushing her to work just a little longer each day: "Her lamp does not go out by night."

Do you desire the sweet taste of success? Would you like to accomplish just a little more before you turn off the light? Motivation is key, so take time before the Lord to review the whys of what you do. What fuels your efforts? Does serving your family come first, even before meeting your own needs? Motivated by love—a love based in God—you'll always try to do your best. And God will use you to bless your family and others in many ways. There's no better taste of success!

Douglas Malloch described this beautifully: "A woman's love is like a light, shining the brightest in the night."[47]

## 197 Using Your Energy Wisely

*She stretches out her hands to the distaff, and her hand holds the spindle.*
Proverbs 31:19

Jesus said if the tree is good, the fruit will be too (Matthew 7:15-20). The tree—in this case the heart of God's beautiful Proverbs 31 woman—was good, making all she did positive. And who received the firstfruits of her heart? Her family! For this woman family came first, and no task was too great for her precious ones.

Some of the work this woman did was done at night by the warm glows of a fire and lamps. What do you think this beautiful-in-God's-eyes woman did by the fireside after the sun bowed its brilliant head and God's moon and stars spangled His sky? As evening arrived and her body slowed down, she sat and did her spinning, preparing wool and flax for future weavings. She knew she had to complete the monotonous work before she could be more creative.

Do you have dreams? Are there works of art you want to create? Skills you desire to gain? Talents you want to develop? A great hidden treasure of time is accessible to you at night—a quiet time for growth, to perfect skills, to learn new arts, to read, to study. How can you begin? By planning your evenings.

Save your daylight hours—your prime energy time—for work that demands the most from you physically and mentally. When dusk darkens the day and your strength fades, instead of zoning out, kicking back, and plopping down, follow the example of God's beautiful, diligent, and wise Proverbs 31 woman. Change activities. During daylight hours, clean, cook, and cultivate your garden. After dark pay bills, fold clothes, study cookbooks, and plan menus. Proverbs 10:4 tells us, "The hand of the diligent makes rich." So plan for diligence, pray for resolve, and proceed. Why not start tonight?

## 198 Mercy Adds a Lovely Fragrance

*She extends her hand to the poor, yes, she reaches out her hands to the needy.*
PROVERBS 31:20

Keeping watch over the home is one of God's key assignments for women. The Proverbs 31 woman excels at this. Her trustworthiness, diligence, industry, thrift, creativity, organization, and management are quite impressive, aren't they? But aren't you encouraged that mercy is one of her outstanding qualities? In all she does she's intent on benefiting others, including people beyond her family. Proverbs 31:20 tells us "she extends her hand to the poor."

Note the details in this verse: Her hand (singular) suggests a generous nature as she lends aid; her hands (plural) signifies these acts of mercy require two hands. Her actions clearly reflect a heart filled with love and compassion…a heart after God.

How did this gracious woman become a model in giving? And what can you do to grow in this grace?

- *Begin at home.* Each sunrise brings fresh opportunities for you to show mercy to others, especially within your family.
- *Regularly give to your home church.* Your financial gifts to your church reach the needy throughout your community, the nation, and even the world.
- *Err on the side of generosity.* Evangelist Billy Graham smiled proudly as he said of his wife: "She manages the fiscal affairs of the household—with…more generosity than precision!"[48]

Part of excelling in your home, family, and private life is found in the beauty of mercy. Mercy reflects the presence of the Lord in your heart. It pleases Him when you extend His presence by what you say and do. Mercy adds the lovely fragrance of the Lord to who you are. Be a generous, helpful, loving, merciful woman who delights in extending a helping hand.

# 199 Twice Blessed

*She is not afraid of snow for her household, for all her household is clothed with scarlet.*
PROVERBS 31:21

Looking to the future and anticipating needs can seem unimportant or overwhelming if you're inundated by the demands of the present. But I'm sure you want to provide for your family just as God provides for you. That's why Proverbs 31:21 sets forth the sparkling virtue of preparation. The foresight of this woman and her proactive efforts to prepare for the future reveal yet another facet of her heart of love.

With wisdom and willingness, the Proverbs 31 woman plans ahead and sets her management skills into motion, providing the blessings of food, nursing care, help, and clothing to those who need it. And in winter her family is handsomely and warmly clothed with scarlet cloaks of wool.

Preparation is important to God, whose very name is "Jehovah-jireh, God will provide." As God's woman, you mirror this aspect of His character when you provide for your loved ones. And your acts of provision happen more easily (if not more bountifully) when you plan and prepare. Knowing you're ready for upcoming family needs and placing your trust in your caring, loving, gracious, all-sufficient God eliminates last-minute stress and increases your confidence in meeting future demands. Preparation and provision—the rewards, contentment, and security are significant!

How do you begin a chain of blessings for you and your family? Think of ways you can improve your family dynamics and how your home is managed. Detail the preparations you need to make and write down two or three steps you can take to get going on each task. Set a date for starting and then follow through.

## 200 Clothing—Beautiful, Practical, Heart Revealing

*She makes tapestry for herself; her clothing is fine linen and purple.*
PROVERBS 31:22

Weaving was important in Palestinian culture. A creative artist with an end product in mind, the Proverbs 31 woman spent many late-night hours spinning and weaving her wool and flax into fantastic fabrics and then using them to sew clothes for her family—in the quality and colors fit for royalty.

Clothing is significant. It's right out there for all to see and reflects the hearts of the creator and wearer. Hopefully your tasteful, modest way of dressing yourself and providing for your family reveals that you love God.

The clothing of the Proverbs 31 woman was a tapestry of beauty. It was appropriate to her position as a woman of dignity; it was appropriate for her profession as a weaver, making her a walking advertisement for her skill; and it was appropriate for her praiseworthy character, robing her in fabrics and colors that spoke of her excellence and high standards. I'm sure the clothing was also very appropriate for her family members.

What are your standards for attire? Are you following God's standards (1 Timothy 2:9; Titus 2:5)?

- *Modesty*—Observing the conventions of decency
- *Soberness*—Dressing in a proper and sensible manner
- *Moderation*—Wearing neither too much nor too little
- *Discretion*—Showing good judgment and taste
- *Chasteness*—Reflecting a relationship with a holy God

These words may sound old-fashioned, but the choice to dress in a way that reflects these qualities flows out of a heart intent on godliness.

## 201 *A Man of Influence*

***Her husband is known in the gates, when he sits among the elders of the land.***
PROVERBS 31:23

God's Word teaches that one of a wife's most important roles is to support her husband. The noble wife of Proverbs 31 poured her soul into helping her husband, who became a man of great influence. When he stepped out his front door every morning to serve in the city gates as a counselor and legislator, he was able to concentrate on his job in the community and not worry about his household. Because of his industrious and helpful wife, this man could be a godly and moral influence in the region.

Susannah Spurgeon, the wife of Charles Haddon Spurgeon, famed preacher at London's Metropolitan Tabernacle in the late 1800s, did the same. Pastor Spurgeon's ministry was thriving, but he became concerned that he might be neglecting his children. One night he returned home earlier than usual. Opening the door, he was surprised none of the children were in the hall. Ascending the stairs, he heard his wife's voice and knew she was praying with the children. One by one she lifted them before God's throne. When she finished her prayer and her nightly instructions to their little ones, Spurgeon thought, "I can go on with my work. My children are well cared for."[49] Because of her faithfulness and diligence, Mrs. Spurgeon enabled Charles to continue to stir and convict hearts for God. And Pastor Spurgeon's influence continues today through his writings.

What can you do to follow in the footsteps of these women of excellence? Support your husband in ways that will strengthen him and glorify God. Make a Proverbs 31:12 commitment to do your husband good all the days of your life by...

- helping him
- praising him
- encouraging him
- nurturing your marriage
- supporting his dreams
- praying for his success

## 202 Soaring to Excellence

*She makes linen garments and sells them,*
*and supplies sashes for the merchants.*
PROVERBS 31:24

Over the course of time, the contents of a woman's heart and the focus of her life's efforts are sure to be revealed. In the case of God's Proverbs 31 woman, her deep-seated dedication to excellence in all she did and her commitment to creativity showed.

Her commitment to excellence was born out of her desire to be the woman God wanted her to be, her decision to serve God, and the very grace of God. This noble woman loved God, desired what He wanted for her and from her, and expended her energies to strive for His goals. And she was richly blessed by Him.

Her commitment to creativity meant she actively and consciously cultivated her God-given abilities and talents. Fueled by her love for God and for her family, she sought ways to beautifully and uniquely express herself in the commonplace tasks of daily life. Clothes woven for her family became works of art. Food prepared in the kitchen became exceptional delights to sight and taste. Items made or purchased for the house turned it into a study in beauty.

Happy are the homes where God's creative servants reside. And happy is the woman who takes advantage of every task to grow in creativity and skills. What the Proverbs 31 woman faithfully did for her family with her signature flair soon became a sideline profession! How can you soar to creative excellence?

- *Be alert.* Notice how others express themselves and learn from them.
- *Plan.* Plan your projects and take steps to develop your skills.
- *Take initiative.* Act on your desires for a more creative lifestyle.
- *Work hard.* Work eagerly and diligently to achieve your heart desires and all God desires from and for you.

## 203 Three Wonderful Garments

*Strength and honor are her clothing; she shall rejoice in time to come.*
PROVERBS 31:25

In the same way that we put clothes on, God calls us to don the garment of godly character. Again the Proverbs 31 woman is an excellent model. What did she put on?

*Strength.* She faithfully builds economic strength and prepares for life changes even as she trusts the Lord, drawing on His strength for sorrows and cares. She's strong in wisdom and in knowledge of God. She possesses physical strength and enjoys the social strength that results from a life of virtue. Her powerful mind gives her inward vigor and resolution. Strength from the Lord is among the clothing of grace she wears.

*Dignity.* The spirit of the Proverbs 31 woman gave her an aura of respectability. We marvel at her virtuous character, her godly behavior, and her regal bearing. There was nothing common, low, or little in her wardrobe of character. Her greatness of soul—coupled with gracious conduct—spelled goodness to all. The beauty of dignity was hers.

*Hope.* Robed in such virtuous splendor, this woman rejoiced and laughed at the future. Rejoicing in the future requires clothing yourself today with the garment of strength, the ornament of dignity, and the robe of faith in your always-present God.

Give your life afresh to God and proceed full faith ahead into your beautiful day. Make the commitment to wake up every day and put on the virtues of strength, dignity, and hope, which are all rooted in your heavenly Father.

## 204 A Refreshing Fountain of Life-Giving Words

*She opens her mouth with wisdom, and on her tongue is the law of kindness.*
PROVERBS 31:26

Quenching thirst was a serious and everyday challenge for the people in arid Israel. The basic struggle to survive was—and remains—the rule of the day there. Against this harsh backdrop Proverbs 10:11 says, "The mouth of the righteous is a fountain of life" (NASB). Godly speech is likened to water, which is essential for sustaining life. And godly speech meets emotional needs just as water meets physical needs. Words of wisdom and kindness will be to people like finding a fountain of sparkling water in the desert.

God uses very few words to describe the Proverbs 31 woman's speech. Two basic comments seem to nicely describe her:

*Wise in speech*—"She opens her mouth with wisdom."

*Kind in heart*—"On her tongue is the law of kindness."

This godly woman was wise and kind in what she said and how she said it.

Think again about that fountain of life in the desert. Then switch to the hurting, stressed, struggling people you come into contact with or see in your daily world. While they may wear brave smiles, you know the truth behind every smile isn't always so pretty. Proverbs 14:10 and 13 (KJV) states, "The heart know[s] its own bitterness... Even in laughter the heart is sorrowful; and the end of that mirth is heaviness."

Won't you ask God to use you to refresh and encourage the people you encounter today? Ask Him to bless you with life-giving words that are wise and kind and uplifting. With His love in your heart and the careful choice of words you can help heal the downhearted and be as a refreshing fountain to them.

## 205 There's No Place like Home—Because of You!

*She watches over the ways of her household,*
*and does not eat the bread of idleness.*
Proverbs 31:27

Running a household is a responsibility God gives to all His women, married or single. Today's verse describes that task with the image of a watchman (watchwoman!). Women literally "watch over" their families and household affairs.

The image of a watchman conjures images of standing guard, eyes moving back and forth to note who's coming and going, overseeing the welfare and condition of family and property. Alert and energetic, the Proverbs 31 woman has her finger on the pulse of her household. Her job assignment from God was to maintain a watchful eye, to know what was going on under her roof as she went about her daily routine, and she accomplished that. Nothing escaped her oversight and care. Indeed, she sometimes seemed to have eyes in the back of her head!

How did the Proverbs 31 woman manage this huge assignment? She didn't eat the bread of idleness. This woman watched over herself too. How could she afford to be idle? How could she even find the time? Busy managing her house and watching over her flock, she had no time for laziness. The reverse was equally true: Because she wasn't idly wasting away the hours, she had the time she needed to carefully monitor and manage her home and its occupants.

Working (and watching!) at home may not sound very exciting, but your home is definitely worthy of diligent care. In fact, your home is the most important place in the world to spend your time and invest your energy. Why? Because the work you do for and with your family is important, significant, and eternal. It is your supreme service to God. Enjoy the beauty of serving there because...there's no place like home!

## 206 Essentials for Every Mom, Grandmother, and Aunt

*Her children rise up and call her blessed;*
*her husband also, and he praises her.*
PROVERBS 31:28

We finally meet the Proverbs 31 woman's children. And what are they doing? They're celebrating mom! They bless her. They praise her with words and actions. The Proverbs 31 woman received the highest accolades from those who mattered the most to her, those who knew her best, and those who received the firstfruits of her day-in, day-out love—her family. How did this praise come to be? Consider these mom essentials.

- *Essential 1: Mom cares.* She shows her care in daily and practical ways. She gives gifts of the basics (food, clothing, shelter, rest), of time, of love. And she gives these for the short haul *and* the long haul.
- *Essential 2: Mom focuses.* She uses her mothering energies and efforts to raise each child to love and serve the Lord.
- *Essential 3: Mom plans.* She sets the order for the daily operation of the home and trusts God with final outcomes.
- *Essential 4: Mom works.* She expends herself willingly, putting her love into action.

The mothering God calls you to requires constant attention, ongoing effort, a never-give-up attitude, and 100-percent commitment. God will give you the strength and joy to do this! Being God's kind of mother (and grandmother and aunt) touches generations of children with His love. Have you dedicated your children to the Lord? Committed to teaching them about Him? The impact you have on their lives lasts forever.

*Being a mother is worth fighting for,*
*worth calling a career,*
*worth the dignity of hard work.*[50]

## 207 *How Are You Doing?*

*Many daughters have done well,*
*but you excel them all.*
PROVERBS 31:29

Along with her children giving her praise, the Proverbs 31 woman's husband joins in. He proclaims, "You excel them all! You're the best of all!"

Now, how about you? Proverbs 31 reveals shining virtues you can use as a checklist for evaluating your character and life. Whether you're young or old, single or married, God wants your character to reflect His presence. So whisper a prayer and ask God to use the following questions to inspire you.

- *As a woman* are your deepest desires to know God, to represent Him in all you do, to reveal exemplary character in every situation?
- *As a homemaker* do you provide for the needs at home? Do you carefully and attentively look over the ways of your household? Do you take care of material possessions?
- *As a mother* are you raising your children to love and serve the Lord? Are you making your home a refuge for all who enter?
- *As a wife* does your behavior bring honor to your husband's reputation? Does your husband trust your faithfulness? Do your words encourage and build him up for the demands of life? Does he have peace about the household so he can be a positive influence in the community?
- *As a life partner and family member* do you contribute positively to the family's financial well-being through careful management of funds? Do you put the power of your mind and your body to work on behalf of your husband, your family, and your home?

## 208 *Growing in Jesus*

*Charm is deceitful and beauty is passing, but a woman who fears the LORD, she shall be praised.*
PROVERBS 31:30

Underneath all we admire in the Proverbs 31 woman is her deep reverence for God. Although our world values charm and beauty, God is concerned with our hearts. As you grow in your own love for Him, why not follow these time-honored practices?

*Commit to Christ.* In this New Testament age you have a personal relationship with God through His Son, Jesus Christ. When Jesus rules your heart and life, everything you do is an act of worship done for Him (Colossians 3:23).

*Schedule time with the Lord.* As a believer in Christ you're privileged to behold His awesomeness and worship Him in the beauty of His holiness (Psalm 29:2). Set aside a regular, daily time to be in His presence for praise, meditation, and study. Alone time with the Lord is so essential and valuable!

*Embrace God's plan and principles.* Proverbs 31 lays out God's plan and principles for your life. So love Him and embrace His wisdom. Delight in every aspect of His plan, live His principles, and follow Him more fully every day.

*Be sure.* If you don't have a personal relationship with Jesus Christ or are unsure, take care of that now. Talk to Jesus. You can use the following prayer if you'd like. Set your foot on God's path. You will never regret it!

> *Jesus, I'm a sinner. But I want to turn away from my sins and follow You. I believe You died for my sins and rose again victorious over sin and death. I accept You right now as my personal Savior. Come into my life and help me follow You from this day forward. Thank You!*

## 209 Beautiful and Honorable in God's Eyes

*Give her of the fruit of her hands,*
*and let her own works praise her in the gates.*
Proverbs 31:31

Voices—indeed, many voices!—are heard as we gaze in wonder and awe at God's portrait of all He finds worthy in His women. As Proverbs 31 comes to a close (and with it the book of Proverbs—God's book of wisdom), we see the fruit that is born over a lifetime of loving and serving God and people.

O what joy! What glory! What a wonderful harvest of praise! Every voice possible is praising this loving, industrious woman—

- the voices of her children sound her praise
- the voice of her husband issues forth praise in the gates
- the voice of God praises her
- even the voice of her works praise her

The beauty of the Proverbs 31 woman is seldom appreciated today. Satan and the fallen world we live in label her beauty old-fashioned and undesirable. How wrong they are! The Proverbs 31 woman lives out all that is wonderful and honorable in God's eyes.

Are you praising her? Are you recognizing the splendor of what God values? The richest kind of praise you can offer is to follow in her footsteps.

Won't you bow your head now and offer praise to God for His beautiful woman? She's indeed one of His precious gifts to you. She's presented in Proverbs 31 to inspire, instruct, and encourage you when you're discouraged, when you sense your priorities shifting, when you fail to be the woman you want to be. A visit with this woman who loves God will renew your vision, restore your strength, and rekindle your love and commitment to God and His plan for making you and your life beautiful.

## 210 A Song of Love, Commitment, and Passion

*The song of songs, which is Solomon's.*
Song of Solomon 1:1

"Song of Solomon," "Song of Songs," "Poem of Love," "Canticles"—these titles have been given to a tiny book tucked in the middle of your Bible. The Song of Solomon is a melody of love penned by King Solomon as he reflects on his wife, an unnamed maiden from Shunem. Note the stages of their deepening relationship...

*Knowing*—"Getting to know you" is the first step in any relationship. An individual's values, character, and personality are revealed over time. Time spent together also gives one person the opportunity to observe another's love for and commitment to God.

*Marrying*—A wedding marks the beginning of two lives becoming one and the blessing of sex and greater intimacy between partners.

*Cleaving*—Every marriage will be tested! As challenges and afflictions come, both partners must follow through on their commitment to the Lord and to the marriage. Properly handled with God's wisdom and grace, problems press a couple more closely to one another and to their heavenly Father.

*Journeying*—Hand in hand a husband and wife who love and honor God and one another can face the trials and tribulations of life with anticipation and joy.

Take ten minutes to curl up with your Bible and enjoy God's choicest love song. Consider the courtship, marriage, and maturing grace of this delightful couple. Listen for the spiritual music of a lifetime of marital harmony. This section of Scripture reveals God's intention for romance and loveliness in marriage, the most precious of human relations and "the grace of life" (1 Peter 3:7).[51]

## 211 *Blessed!*

*The book of the genealogy of Jesus Christ...*
*Mary, of whom was born Jesus who is called Christ.*
MATTHEW 1:1, 16

We're introduced to Mary, the mother of Jesus, at the very beginning of the book of Matthew. In Jesus' genealogy she is referred to as Joseph's wife. She will soon become known as the mother of our Lord and Savior!

Have you wondered why God chose Mary to be "blessed... among women," to carry within her womb God's Son, to love and cherish Him as her firstborn, to bring Him up in the knowledge of His heavenly Father? What do we know about Mary?

- *A chaste virgin*—The prophet Isaiah stated God's Son would be born of a virgin. Young Mary was unmarried and a pure, godly woman.
- *A humble maiden*—Hailing from the village of Nazareth, Mary was a small-town girl, not royalty or a sophisticated woman from high society.
- *A devoted follower*—Mary was a woman after God's own heart, a woman who would live according to His will.
- *A faithful Jew*—Of the tribe of Judah and the line of David, Mary worshiped the one true God and apparently did so in spirit and truth. Only such a woman would qualify for this important assignment from God.

What four phrases would you use to describe yourself? As you think about that, enjoy the relief that comes with knowing that no matter how humble, how simple, how poor, how ordinary, how intelligent, or how successful you are, God loves you! And like Mary, you can be blessed and used by Him to do great things. How? By loving Him...humbly, devotedly, faithfully, with all your heart, soul, strength, and mind.

## 212 Encouragement and Vision

*They saw the young Child with Mary His mother and fell down and worshiped Him.*
MATTHEW 2:11

Mary has given birth to Jesus and is now welcoming "wise men from the East." Perhaps there was confusion when these exotic foreigners arrived and tried to explain their presence. These Magi saw "His star" in the East and came to worship Him. First they went to King Herod, who was disturbed that someone besides him was deemed worthy of being called king. No one at court knew who this upstart was. But the Magi found out. At last the star that directed them for hundreds of miles led them to Mary, Joseph, and Jesus. Mary surely was encouraged by this visit from mysterious foreigners.

*Vision*—These men came to worship the Christ child, the King of the Jews. That they traveled several months from a faraway place probably gave Mary an even greater vision and clearer understanding of the future God had for her babe.

*Provision*—The wise men from the East paid homage with valuable gifts. These gifts may have financed Joseph and Mary's flight-for-life to Egypt. Their hasty journey was to protect Jesus from the jealousy of King Herod, who ordered Jewish baby boys in and around Bethlehem killed to eliminate potential rivals.

God knows His people's needs—including yours. Whether it's encouragement, a glimpse of what's to come, physical considerations, or something else, He's promised to "supply all your need according to His riches in glory by Christ Jesus" (Philippians 4:19). Look to Him. Lift up your needs to Him. The Lord is your shepherd; you shall not want! (See Psalm 23:1.)

## 213 *Faith and Following*

*[Joseph] took the young Child and His mother by night and departed for Egypt.*
MATTHEW 2:14

King Herod was angry, jealous, and fearful when he heard someone was being called "King of the Jews"—even though it was a child. He ordered the death of every Jewish boy under the age of two in the Bethlehem area to eliminate any potential rival.

We never know what marriage, motherhood, or even a given day will bring, do we? Mary—a woman who loved God, who was "highly favored" and "blessed…among women," who had found "honor with God"—nevertheless had lessons to learn about faith in God and following Him. God instructed Joseph—Jesus' earthly guardian—to take his family and flee to Egypt. What did this require from Mary?

*Following her husband's lead.* Can you imagine being awakened in the middle of the night to hear your husband declare you're leaving, you're moving right now?

> "But where are we going, Honey?"
> "To Egypt. It's only a 10- to 15-day journey."
> "But why?"
> "I had a dream, and God told me to go."

Imagine what would happen under most roofs with this announcement! But we know Mary loved God and lived His plan so she followed her husband…and saved their young son's life.

*Faith.* Faith in God enables you to follow God's plan. Adorn yourself with God's beautiful, gracious spirit and follow your husband or, if single, those God has in place to guide you.

Why not pray this prayer?

> *Father, help me be a strong woman of faith willing to follow my husband [or those in godly authority] as he leads me in Your good and acceptable and perfect will. Amen.*

## 214 *Joys and Sorrows Intertwine*

*[Joseph] took the young Child and His mother, and came into the land of Israel.*
Matthew 2:21

The book of Matthew is the only Gospel to record Mary, Joseph, and Jesus' flight to Egypt and their return to Israel. Both journeys were prompted when an angel of the Lord visited Joseph in a dream. This time the angel announced Herod's death and instructed Joseph to take his family back to Israel.

The small family settled down in Nazareth, Mary and Joseph's hometown. Looking over the past few years, they could thank God for how He'd guided them and protected them. But what about the future?

Mary would face many joys...and sorrows because "motherhood is a painful privilege."[52] What would Mary experience?

| *The Joys of...* | *The Sorrows of...* |
|---|---|
| Bearing and loving a child | Watching her child die |
| Raising a child | Not understanding Him |
| Knowing God through Jesus | Witnessing His death for her sins |

There were plenty of other joys for Mary! The happy sounds of a brood of children; joyous pilgrimages to worship God; family meals, cozy times gathered together; hearing her son—the Son of God—preach, observing His miracles, and witnessing His resurrection from the dead. But there were sorrows as well. The death of her husband, the townspeople's rejection of her son, letting go of her son as He started His ministry, the horrible events at the end of His life on earth.

Through the lows and highs, the pains and pleasures, the sorrows and joys, Mary loved God and looked to Him for strength that is made perfect in weakness (2 Corinthians 12:9). Mary shows you how to trust the Lord as you walk the unpredictable road of life God uses to conform you to the holy and perfect image of His Son.

## 215 A Mother's Request

*Then the mother of Zebedee's sons came to Him… kneeling down and asking something from Him.*
MATTHEW 20:20

Today we meet the mother of James and John, the sons of Zebedee and Jesus' disciples. In this brief scene we see a caring mother bringing the desires of her heart before her Savior.

*Person*—There is no doubt that the mother of Zebedee's sons sensed Jesus' authority.

*Posture*—As this devoted worshiper approached her sovereign Lord, the only fitting posture was one of humility. This mom knelt before Jesus.

*Petition*—A faithful follower of Jesus, the mother of James and John asked Jesus to "grant that these two sons of mine may sit, one on Your right hand and the other on the left, in Your kingdom." In other words, "Give them special positions."

This faithful mom wanted her sons to love and serve Jesus forever. She may have misunderstood Jesus' teachings, but she does show spiritual concern for her sons. How are you doing on the three P's?

*Person*—Is Jesus your personal Lord and Savior? Do you let Him reign as Lord over every aspect of your life?

*Posture*—Do you nurture a posture of humility that honors Jesus as Lord? Are you a reverent and true worshiper? A woman of prayer contrite in heart?

*Petition*—Do you bring every concern for your children to your heavenly Father? Do you ask, seek, and knock on behalf of your sons and daughters?

## 216 *A Bonfire of Faith?*

*While he was sitting on the judgment seat,*
*his wife sent to him [...a note].*
MATTHEW 27:19

Jesus was generating quite a stir. The Jews in the High Council feared His large following, so they plotted His arrest. Judas, one of Jesus' disciples, betrayed Jesus and He was arrested. Now Jesus was standing before the governor of Judea. A messenger suddenly appeared with a note for Pilate. It was a warning from his wife: "Have nothing to do with that just Man, for I have suffered many things today in a dream because of Him." Astounding! She had...

- *a brief dream*—We don't know the particulars of the dream, but it was troubling enough to prompt a warning to her powerful husband.
- *a brief insight*—Her dream either revealed or helped her conclude that Jesus was a "just Man."
- *a brief note*—Acting quickly, Pilate's wife dashed off a succinct message to him.

Flickers of knowledge led this woman to intercede on Jesus' behalf. Did she have faith in Jesus? Did the light of understanding or insight last? Don't you hope so? And what about your understanding? Do you know...

- renewing your commitment to living for God daily fans the flame of faith?
- studying the Bible fuels an accurate understanding of God's Word?
- obeying in faithfulness causes your light to shine brightly among people?
- praying with passion allows you to see the blaze of God's glory?

Are you building a bonfire of faith?

# 217 The Path to Jesus

*Behold, Jesus met them...[and] they came and held Him by the feet and worshiped Him.*
MATTHEW 28:9-10

Today we meet a small group of faithful women who witnessed Jesus' gruesome death. Three long, mournful days passed. Then they received the greatest blessing of all—they saw and spoke to the resurrected, glorified Jesus! Their story appears in all four Gospels, but only Matthew shares what Jesus said to these loyal ladies—words of reassurance ("Do not be afraid"), of instruction ("Go and tell My brethren"), and promise ("There they will see Me"). These women walked...

- *the path of faithfulness.* Most of Jesus' disciples deserted Him, but these women lingered at the cross to the end and then followed at a distance to see where He was buried. They returned to the tomb to tend to His body.
- *the path of learning.* At the tomb on Sunday morning, an angel instructed this little band of women to tell the disciples Jesus was alive.
- *the path of obedience.* Matthew tells us they departed quickly to carry out the angel's instructions. As they went in obedience to that divine order, Jesus met and spoke with them!

The women were awestruck, elated, and worshipful when they met their resurrected Savior—just like you would be in that situation! Can you picture it? The delightful shock, the smiles turning to grins, the laughter, the elation, the willingness to serve?

Does your relationship with Jesus inspire the same reactions? Do you need to reignite your faith through prayer, meditation, Bible study? Jesus was crucified for your sins, died, and was buried—then He rose from the grave, victorious over sin and death! And through Him you are too! Let Him know how thankful you are for His love and sacrifice.

## 218 Join Jesus' Family!

*Are not His sisters here with us?*
MARK 6:3

Mary was "blessed...among women" to be Jesus' mother. But at least two other women were also blessed—Jesus' sisters. Although their names aren't given, they spent their lives near Jesus. Imagine all they must have seen and experienced! They...

- heard Jesus teach.
- sought His wisdom and counsel.
- basked in His love...and learned how to love others.
- witnessed and maybe felt His healing touch.
- listened as He spoke to His (and their!) holy Father.
- marveled at His faith...that moved mountains.
- observed His miracles.
- learned from His actions, attitudes, and teachings.
- followed Him to the end of the age and on to heaven.

You too are privileged to be part of Jesus' family. "But as many as received Him, to them He gave the right to become children of God, to those who believe in His name (John 1:12). Through the Bible you can study His wisdom, learn His teachings, discover His principles. You can seek His counsel and know Him better by spending time with Him in prayer and meditation. Can you sing, say, and pray today, "I have decided to follow Jesus...no turning back, no turning back"?[53] If yes, "Hallelujah!" If not, why not pray now?

> *Jesus, I renounce my sins and dedicate my life to You. I believe You died for my sins and rose again victorious over sin and death. I accept You right now as my personal Savior. Come into my life as my Lord and Savior. Thank You!*

## 219 *Bold and Persistent*

*She kept asking Him to cast the demon out of her daughter.*
MARK 7:26

"Artists never depict Christ with His back turned," reports scholar Dr. Herbert Lockyer.[54] Yet today we meet an anguished mother Jesus refused to help. A Syro-Phoenician woman was heartbroken as she watched her daughter suffer from a demon. She'd probably tried many ways to "cure" her daughter...to no avail. Was her hope gone? And then Jesus arrived in her Baal-worshiping region. She'd heard of His kindness and powerful miracles. Did her heart leap as she thought, *Jesus can help!*

Humbly this dear woman sought out Jesus and fell at His feet. She asked Him politely and respectfully to cast the demon out of her daughter.

But Jesus refused!

Did she give up? No. She kept asking...and asking...and asking.

Jesus told her, "It is not good to take the children [of Israel's] bread and throw it to the little dogs [the Gentiles]."

With a flash of insight, this woman tried again. "Yes, Lord, yet even the little dogs under the table eat from the children's crumbs."

And then Jesus said, "For this saying go your way; the demon has gone out of your daughter." What relief and joy that woman felt! And when she arrived home, the demon had indeed left her daughter.

I pray this true story inspires you today. I encourage you to...

- place your faith completely in Jesus.
- have enough faith to boldly ask...and ask again...and again...and again...for what you need.
- know Jesus can and will help you.
- trust in the power and efficiency of God and His Word.

## 220 The Testimony of a Gentle, Quiet Spirit

*A woman came having an alabaster flask of very costly oil...[and] she broke the flask and poured it on His head.*
MARK 14:3

What is precious in God's sight when it comes to women? A gentle and quiet spirit (1 Peter 3:4). Such a spirit has been aptly described as "the silent preaching of a lovely life."[55] Let's see how this beautiful ornament glittered in the life of Mary of Bethany.

*Her emotion*—The heart of Mary, Lazarus and Martha's sister, overflowed with joy and love for the Savior who raised her brother from the dead. Imagine! Her beloved Lazarus, who was dead, was alive again! How could she demonstrate her love and gratitude to Jesus for this miracle?

*Her devotion*—Mary chose the most costly gift she could—precious spikenard oil in an alabaster flask. The fragrant oil was worth a year's wages. Mary was delighted as she broke the fancy bottle open and poured the ointment on her Master's head.

*A commotion*—Mary probably never dreamed her expression of thanksgiving and worship would be criticized. Yet censure came. As she continued to pour out her devotion and costly oil, she heard Jesus rebuke her accusers—

> Let her alone. Why do you trouble her? She has done a good work for Me. For you have the poor with you always, and whenever you wish you may do them good; but Me you do not have always (Mark 14:6-7).

Mary did nothing in her defense. She wasn't argumentative, combative, or defensive. We see only the beauty of her sincere devotion as she honored her Lord. Have you been criticized for your faith? Has your kindness been rewarded by harsh words? Let your gentleness speak in your defense and proclaim your love for God.

## 221 Overcoming Hardship and Pain

*His wife was of the daughters of Aaron, and her name was Elizabeth.*
LUKE 1:5

Meet Elizabeth, a woman from the priestly line of Aaron. She was married to a priest named Zacharias. In looking at their lives it's obvious they were both raised in families that feared the Lord and taught and practiced God's precepts.

Family devotion times are so wonderful and valuable. They'll bring your family together, encourage faith, teach God's principles, and equip members for handling life. The heritage of devotion to God helped Elizabeth walk bravely through a sometimes difficult and painful life. Today and in the next three devotions we'll look at some benefits for gathering as a family in worship and study.

> *Reason #1 for a Devotional Time*—"It will send you forth to your daily task with cheerful heart, stronger for the work and truer to duty, and determined in whatever is done therein to glorify God."[56]

Elizabeth was childless. In fact, she passed the age of childbearing without having kids. This means she endured decades of marriage under the dark cloud of barrenness in a culture that considered childlessness a calamity and possibly God's judgment for sin. How did this godly woman keep going? Perhaps her faithfulness of spending time with God fortified her for the day-in, day-out reality of not having children. Regular time with the Lord enabled her to have a cheerful heart, strength for her work, and the determination to glorify God regardless of her circumstances.

Do you have a daily devotional time? If not, begin today! Spend time each day being quiet before the Lord, studying His Word, and praying.

If you've been blessed with children, gather them every day to pray and hear God's Word. Encourage them to seek God in all they do.

## 222 Moment by Moment with God

*They were both righteous before God, walking in all the commandments and ordinances of the Lord blameless.*
LUKE 1:6

Elizabeth and Zacharias were blessed with a godly heritage, but they were ordained to walk down a difficult road. They had no children—no little ones to love, no grandchildren to cherish, no one to carry on the family name. Despite this, Luke tells us Elizabeth and Zacharias were followers of God. They were...

- *Righteous*—Elizabeth and her husband followed God's law in strict legal observance.
- *Obedient*—Elizabeth walked alongside her husband in all the Lord's commandments (moral obedience) and ordinances (ceremonial obedience).
- *Blameless*—Elizabeth and Zacharias lived lives pleasing to God. Outwardly obedient to the Law of Moses, they were also inwardly obedient to the Lord.

But still they suffered. Elizabeth shows us the way to love and follow God when life is difficult. What contributed to her faithfulness? Probably daily time with the Lord!

> *Reason #2 for a Devotional Time*—"It will make you conscious throughout the day of the attending presence of the unseen Divine One, who will bring you through more than [a] conqueror."[57]

Throughout the day, moment-by-moment awareness of God's unfailing presence with you helps you bear every cross and face every crucible in victory through Christ! You can endure difficult times and remain righteous, obedient, and blameless if you believe in Jesus as Savior and look to Him for strength and wisdom daily, diligently, and devoutly.

## 223 *Strength for Today*

***Elizabeth was barren, and they were both well advanced in years.***
LUKE 1:7

The childlessness Elizabeth and her husband knew may not sound too troublesome today, but in their time the Jewish rabbis believed and taught that seven kinds of people were to be excommunicated from God. Their list began with these searing words: "A Jew who has no wife, or a Jew who has a wife and who has no child." Besides being a great stigma in the Jewish culture, having no children was valid grounds for divorce!

But there was a heavier burden than the fear of divorce for childless women. Hebrew women hoped to bear the long-awaited Messiah. As a faithful, righteous, and obedient Jew, surely Elizabeth dreamed of being so privileged. Sadly the flame on Elizabeth's candle of hope died as her childbearing years flickered out.

How did Elizabeth handle this? Since her name means "God is my oath" or "a worshiper of God," I'm sure she looked to Him for strength for each day. And I encourage you to do so too.

> *Reason #3 for a Devotional Time*—"It will bring you strength to meet the discouragements, the disappointments, the unexpected adversities, and sometimes the blighted hopes that may fall to your lot."[58]

As you face your day, look to the power of God to assist you with problems that arise. Time with Him—worshiping, thanking, asking, listening—gives you strength to face whatever comes your way. The love and wisdom you receive from the Lord will fuel your love and keep the flame of hope burning. Cling to God's promise, "Be strong and of good courage; do not be afraid, nor be dismayed, for the LORD your God is with you wherever [and through whatever!] you go" (Joshua 1:9).

## 224 *Miracles and Blessings*

*Now after those days his wife Elizabeth conceived; and she hid herself five months.*
LUKE 1:24

A miracle! No, many miracles!

*First miracle*—An angel said, "Your prayer is heard and your wife Elizabeth will bear you a son…he will be great in the sight of the Lord."

*Second miracle*—Zacharias questioned the angel's glad tidings and lost his ability to speak…until his son's birth.

*Third miracle*—Elizabeth conceived in her old age.

How did Elizabeth respond to the miracle of pregnancy? Did she boast and tell everyone? No. She stayed home. Why?

- *She was joyful*—A baby was on the way! And this baby would be the forerunner of the Messiah.
- *She was grateful*—She probably spent much time at home bowed in thanksgiving before God.
- *She was realistic*—The expected child was to play a mighty part in the history of God's people, and the responsibility of training him in godliness demanded serious and prayerful preparation.

Do you go to the Lord with your sorrows *and* your joys, your gratitude and your responsibilities, your hopes for today and your dreams for tomorrow?

> *Reason #4 for a Devotional Life*—"It will sweeten home life and enrich home relationships as nothing else can do."[59]

God fills you with His love and hope, peace and strength when you spend time with Him. This blesses you and those you meet.

## 225 The Messiah Is Coming!

*The virgin's name was Mary.*
LUKE 1:27

The Messiah, the Savior of the world, was on His way! At long last, 400 years after the last prophecy concerning His arrival, the blessed event was about to happen. How would He arrive? Through a young woman named Mary. Little is known about this woman so richly blessed by God. Scripture reports she was a virgin from the city of Nazareth, of the tribe of Judah, of the royal line of David, and that she was engaged to a man named Joseph. Let's look at the culture of Mary's day to fill in some details.

*Parents*—Although Mary's parents aren't mentioned, based on Mary's character and knowledge of God's Word we can surmise she came from a home of devout Jews.

*Training*—As they grew up, girls were trained in household tasks and in the things of the Lord. This spiritual training is evident in the richness of Mary's praise-filled "Magnificat" (Luke 1:47-55). Mary knew the Scriptures well and had some memorized.

*Engagement*—Mary was engaged to Joseph. The engagement, made official by a signed, written document of marriage, came at least one year before the wedding.

*Age*—Most Israelite boys married by their late teens, but women wed earlier. The rabbis set the minimum age for marriage at 12 for girls.[60] Mary was most likely a young adolescent.

Although she was probably young and, from all appearances, poor, Mary had something priceless on the inside: She loved God deeply, obediently, and passionately.

With God, it's always the heart that matters. When He shines His holy light into your heart, what does He discover? Do you nurture a deep, obedient, passionate love for God? I hope so!

## 226 *Ordinary or Extraordinary?*

***Do not be afraid, Mary, for you have found favor with God.***
LUKE 1:30

So far we've discovered that Mary, who was blessed by God to be the mother of His Son Jesus, was...

- *young.* She was unseasoned, inexperienced, unaccomplished, and unmarried. She'd never been a mother.
- *poor.* She apparently had no wealth and no family inheritance.
- *unknown.* She was not famous or well known. Her father and mother aren't mentioned, and nothing is mentioned that indicates great beauty, intelligence, or talents.

From what we can see, no one would choose Mary as the mother of God's Son—except God! Despite what she lacked in the world's eyes, God chose this humble teenager. When God looked for a woman to bless as mother to His Son, He searched for a woman who loved Him, who honored Him, who followed His precepts. That woman was Mary!

Can you imagine the scene? Imagine what this angelic messenger from God looked like. Picture Mary receiving the startling announcements from the angel. This magnificent creature greeted her with "Rejoice, highly favored one, the Lord is with you; blessed are you among women!...You have found favor with God."

Do you sometimes feel ordinary...like no one special? Do you feel deficient—that maybe you need more education, better clothes, a better resumé, a better pedigree? Give that feeling and attitude up!

What's truly important in this life is loving and serving your omniscient, omnipotent, omnipresent, loving God. If you love Him—if you seek after Him with your whole heart—He'll bless you and use you to reach others with His love. Amazing! And isn't it exciting to contemplate what He might do in your life?

## 227 *Turning Points*

*Then Mary said to the angel,
"How can this be?"*
LUKE 1:34

The sun rose that morning just as it had risen every day. As she considered her list of chores, she had no hint that her life was about to be transformed from the mundane to the mysterious.

Seconds after it happened Mary's hopes for a quiet, peaceful life were gone. Gone also were the comfort and safety of predictable routine. What happened? The angel Gabriel appeared before young Mary and delivered an earth-shattering message. Nothing would ever be the same for Mary or the world. God chose her to be the mother of His Son. She would bring into the world its Savior, Lord, and King.

How did Mary handle this great turning point in her life? And what life lessons can we garner from her experiences?

We see in the Gospel of Luke that Mary humbly accepted the news that she would bear God's Son. Notice her initial response—"How can this be, since I am a virgin?" (NASB). This perfectly natural question received an answer that pointed to the supernatural: "The Holy Spirit will come upon you, and the power of the Highest will overshadow you; therefore, also, that Holy One who is to be born will be called the Son of God." The birth would be a miracle. And that was all the explanation Mary received.

Can you point to a day in your life that changed everything? Maybe a dark cloud hid the sun. Or the day was so bright you had to cover your eyes. Such turning points can shake us to the core. And they can send us to God, His Word, and His promises in praise for what He's brought or to the acceptance that sometimes the full understanding of the "how" and "whys" lies in the realm of God.[61]

## 228 Devoted, Alert Service

*Behold the maidservant of the Lord!*
Luke 1:38

Have you been inspired as you've gotten to know Mary, the mother of Jesus? Mary believed the angel when he said she would bear a son, and she worshiped God even as she wondered, "How can this be?" Two clues help us better understand how she was able to put total faith in God at this life-changing moment.

> *Clue 1: The heart of a handmaiden*—After God's messenger told Mary her part in God's glorious plan, her first words were "Behold the maidservant of the Lord!"

Biblically "maidservant" or "handmaid" refers to a female slave. A handmaiden sat near her master, watching for hand signals, which she would then obey instantly. Clearly Mary cultivated the heart of a handmaiden and gave devoted attentiveness to God. No longer regarding her will as her own, she was wholly committed to the one true God.

On that day in Nazareth when God moved His hand and signaled His will, His devoted young handmaiden noticed and responded positively. What a model for us! Mary gladly accepted God's will even though it wouldn't be a smooth ride.

Do you have the attitude Mary had? Do you have her understanding? Why not spend some time in prayer? Tell Him you want to let go of your daily concerns and totally embrace His good, acceptable, and perfect will for you. Then thank Him for what He is teaching you through the life of Mary. Ask Him to continue to grow your love and trust so you can serve Him wholeheartedly.

## 229 Ready to Step Out?

*Let it be to me according to your word.*
LUKE 1:38

Yesterday we marveled at Mary's remarkable servant heart. Today we note another amazing characteristic of this young woman.

> *Clue 2: An attitude of acceptance*—Having acknowledged herself as "the maidservant of the Lord," Mary said to God's representative, "Let it be to me according to your word."

When God told Mary she was chosen as the mother of His Son, she willingly accepted God's plan for her...and the life-altering changes that meant. Mary would be pregnant before she was married, meaning she'd be branded a fornicator (John 8:41). She would encounter trouble with her husband-to-be, trouble with her family, and trouble in Nazareth. And she had no idea what other radical changes might happen. Yet Mary's acceptance of God's plan was clear: "Let it be to me according to your word."

Why was Mary so willing to instantly accept God's amazing plan? She knew her heavenly Father well enough to trust Him, to rest in His love, and to accept what He ordained.

What about you? Do you accept what God has planned? Are you excited and eager to step forward even if you don't know what's around the bend? Consider the following questions.

- How do you handle shocking news or unfair circumstances?
- Is your response to God, "Let it be to me according to your word"? If not, why?
- What can you do to increase your trust in God?
- What step toward that goal will you take today?

## 230 The Give-and-Take of Blessing and Encouragement

*And [Mary] entered the house of Zacharias and greeted Elizabeth.*
LUKE 1:40

An exciting and blessed meeting occurred between two very special women. Mary, the mother-to-be of Jesus, journeyed to her cousin Elizabeth's house for a time of fellowship and support. This is the same Elizabeth who was pregnant in her old age with the child who would be known as John the Baptist! Truly the women's friendship illustrates God's design that older women encourage younger ones (Titus 2:3-5)!

Two women who loved God. Two pregnancies. Two miracles! And what sweet fellowship these two enjoyed in Elizabeth's home. Going back to our discussion on spending time regularly with the Lord, here's another benefit:

> *Reason #5 for a Devotional Time*—"It will exert a helpful, hallowed influence over guests in your home."[62]

Certainly "a helpful, hallowed influence" greeted young Mary as she crossed the threshold into Elizabeth's warm and welcoming home. As Mary entered, the give-and-take of blessing and encouragement, of assurance and edification, of praying and sharing, of godly fellowship began immediately.

Are you a young woman whose love for God is growing? Ask God to lead you to someone older who will help fan the flame of your growing love. Are you a woman who has loving guidance and experience to offer? Seek out those who need your influence and wisdom.

## 231 Spending Time with God

*And it happened, when Elizabeth heard the greeting of Mary... Elizabeth was filled with the Holy Spirit.*
LUKE 1:41

What a joyous scene is painted in the opening chapter of Luke! Elizabeth, a woman well past the age of childbearing, is expecting a baby. She's chosen to remain at home to ponder and meditate and enjoy this wonder and the role God said her babe would play heralding the arrival of the Messiah. Can you picture her joyfully exalting the Giver of all good gifts and the Source of every blessing? Elizabeth exemplified another reason for solitary time with the Lord.

> *Reason #6 for a Devotional Time*—"We honor Him who is the giver of all good and the source of all blessings."[63]

Elizabeth sought the Lord, privately praising Him for her babe and for the Messiah who was coming. This is the godly environment the expectant Mary entered. I imagine she was in a bit of shock over all that was happening...and maybe a bit unsure of what she'd experienced. But God provided any reassurance and support she may have needed. As Mary entered her cousin's home, Elizabeth greeted Mary with joy and not a hint of skepticism about the workings of the Lord. As the babe in her womb leaped for joy in response to the Holy One in Mary's, Elizabeth understood and acknowledged the great importance of the child Mary carried.

The illuminating work of God's Spirit in Elizabeth's carefully prepared heart led to discernment, insight, and understanding. Her regular quiet times with God enabled her to believe in His amazing plan, rejoice wholeheartedly, and support Mary.

Do you desire to love God more deeply? Seek alone time with Him. Ask Him to open your eyes so you behold the wondrous things from His Word and His impact in your life.

## 232 Strength for Today and Hope for Tomorrow

*"Blessed are you among women, and blessed is the fruit of your womb!"*
LUKE 1:42

Let's take a closer look at the Spirit-empowered encounter between Mary and her cousin Elizabeth. What an electrically charged moment! When these two women came together they were filled with the Spirit of God. Each woman's baby was central to God's eternal plan for humanity. In the shelter of Elizabeth's home, these cousins and sisters in the Lord communed with God, drawing much-needed strength for their today and bright hope for their tomorrows from God as well as from one another.

Imagine the joy as they shared their adoration of the omnipotent, true God. Consider the rich sisterhood in the Lord they exhibited and how that was enhanced by God's visible work in their lives. Note too the sweet ministry they offered to one another in the quiet of Elizabeth's peaceful household.

Sounds like a lovely moment, a sweet relationship, a tender time, doesn't it? But remember what awaited each of these lovely women. Church tradition suggests that Elizabeth soon saw the death of her husband, and she soon followed, enjoying only a brief taste of motherhood. And we know Mary's soul was pierced with sorrow as her precious Jesus walked the path to Calvary's rugged cross.

Do you have a friend such as Mary or Elizabeth? Someone who knows Christ and serves Him with wholehearted devotion? One who encourages you to grow spiritually? More importantly, are you such a friend to others? Christian encouragement is both a command to be obeyed and a gift God graciously gives His people. As you walk through treacherous valleys and clouded byways, as you climb mountains and rest in meadows, you are to strengthen others and be strengthened by others in the Lord.

## 233 Join the Chorus of Praise!

*Mary said: "My soul magnifies the Lord."*
LUKE 1:46

The surest test of a heart is the caliber of its speech—the quality of the words that issue forth. Through Mary's words we see her pure heart. As she arrived at Elizabeth's, this young woman opened her mouth and offered rich words of praise, a song now known as Mary's "Magnificat." Mary began, "My soul magnifies the Lord," and the inspired words that follow contain 15 quotations from the Old Testament (Luke 1:45-55). As one author observed, the number of Scriptures quoted in the "Magnificat" shows that "Mary knew God, through the books of Moses, the Psalms and the writings of the prophets. She had a deep reverence for the Lord God in her heart because she knew what He had done in the history of her people."[64]

Clearly Mary's heartstrings were tuned to the heart of God! Her heart was saturated with His Word! Knowing God and His mercy, provision, and faithfulness, Mary sang...

- a song of joy, of gladness, of celebration.
- a song of substance based on the Scriptures.
- a song reflecting the love and devotion of Hannah, a saint from the past (1 Samuel 2).
- a song for today since God is the same yesterday and today.
- a song for eternity because God's Word stands forever.

Join Mary in her chorus of praise! Because you know God and recognize His infinite power and love, make Mary's solo a duet. Read her beautiful and joyful words and add your voice to her sweet melody, "My soul magnifies the Lord!"

## 234 *Jesus, Your Precious Savior*

*My spirit has rejoiced in God my Savior.*
LUKE 1:47

In the richness of Mary's "Magnificat," notice she began where every testimony begins—in praise to God for salvation. Mary's baby Jesus was the long-awaited Savior. He would take away the sins of the world—including Mary's. Her song begins, "My spirit has rejoiced in God my Savior." Mary freely acknowledged she needed a Savior. She recognized salvation was through the divine grace of God revealed in His Son, her Messiah.

Are you wondering if you need a Savior? Consider what Jesus Christ, the Savior God sent, offers you and me. He...

**S**ubstitutes His sinless life for our sinful one (2 Corinthians 5:21).

**A**ssures us of eternal life (John 10:28-29).

**V**anquishes Satan's hold on our lives (2 Timothy 2:26).

**I**nitiates us into the family of God (Galatians 4:4-6).

**O**verthrows the power of sin (Romans 6:1-10).

**R**econciles us to a holy God (2 Corinthians 5:19).

Do you enjoy in Jesus Christ all the word "Savior" represents—the forgiveness of sin, the assurance of heaven, freedom from Satan's power, fellowship with fellow believers, and a personal relationship with God? If not, accept Jesus' offer right now! Pray,

*Jesus, please forgive my sins.*
*Come into my heart today and forever.*

Whether you've belonged to the Savior for a minute or years, sing and shout, "Hallelujah! What a Savior!"

## 235 Gifts You Can Give to God

*For He who is mighty has done great things for me.*
Luke 1:49

"Worship...is as old as humanity...a necessity of the human soul as native to it as the consciousness of God itself, which impels it to testify by word and act its love and gratitude to the Author of life and the Giver of all good."[65] Worship was exactly what Mary was doing when she spoke her famous "Magnificat." Her heart gave shared love and gratitude to the Author of life and Giver of all good things for the great works He had done and was doing for His people and for her.

How do you express your appreciation to your Savior? He loves you. You were lost, and He found you. You were spiritually blind, but now you see. You were dead in your sins, and He made you alive. He called you out of darkness and into His marvelous light. He provides everything you need, blessing you with abundant life in Him (2 Corinthians 9:8; Ephesians 1:3; John 10:10).

I encourage you to praise and worship Jesus often. Name specifically the awesome things He has done for you and give thanks for the many things He will do. What acts of worship can you offer Him today and every day—acts that befit such a mighty, protecting, saving, and loving Lord? Consider these gifts...

- *time* in His Word, in service, in prayer.
- *money* given out of love for Him.
- *faith* for the future and what He will enable you to give and do.
- *witness* to people who don't know Him, sharing His love.
- *praise* to Him when you're alone and when others can hear.

Worship now. Extravagantly...loudly...sincerely. He who is mighty has done great things for you!

## 236 Building a Firm Foundation of Faith

*Holy is His name.*
LUKE 1:49

Do you long to be a woman of great faith? Fill your heart and mind with the Word of God. Mary, Jesus' mother, obviously had great faith because her words reveal a heart overflowing with Old Testament law, psalms of praise, wisdom from the prophets, and prayers of believers...

- *God's holiness*—"Holy is His name!" God is wholly pure in total contrast to sinful, self-centered humans. In Jesus, God revealed His holiness (Luke 1:49).
- *God's mercy*—"His mercy is on those who fear Him from generation to generation." In Jesus God extended His mercy by providing for our salvation (verse 50).
- *God's power*—"He has shown strength with His arm; He has scattered the proud in the imagination of their hearts. He has put down the mighty from their thrones, and exalted the lowly" (verses 51-52). Stand in awe of God's power!
- *God's goodness*—"He has filled the hungry with good things, and the rich He has sent away empty." God is good, and Jesus' life and teachings reflect His desire to reach out to everyone (Luke 1:53; 6:35).
- *God's faithfulness*—"He has helped His servant Israel, in remembrance of His mercy, as He spoke to our fathers, to Abraham and to his seed forever." God is eternally faithful to His Word and to His chosen people. In Jesus, God sent the Redeemer He promised to Abraham and to us as Abraham's seed (Luke 1:54-55).

## 237 Darkness Swept Away in an Instant!

*Elizabeth's full time came…*
*and she brought forth a son.*
Luke 1:57

God, who is mighty, performs great things for those who love Him! Elizabeth's "great things" included a miraculous pregnancy in her old age and the birth of her son, John the Baptist. "When her neighbors and relatives heard how the Lord had shown great mercy to her, they rejoiced with her."

Imagine Elizabeth's complete and utter joy at God's goodness to her. She'd been so long without a child and then, miracle of miracles, God chose her to bear John, the forerunner for the Lord. Elizabeth's little baby would be great in the sight of the Lord, filled with the Holy Spirit, turn the hearts of many to the Lord, and herald the coming of the Messiah. The blazing light of God's goodness made decades of darkness fade into a distant memory.

- Do you think about the great things God's done for you? Elizabeth hid herself for five months to contemplate God's goodness.
- If you're a mother, do you consider that one of life's greatest blessings? Do your children bring you great joy? When John was born, his mother's heart was filled with overflowing joy.
- Do you rejoice with others over the great things God does in their lives? Elizabeth's neighbors rejoiced with her.
- Are you faithful to God and trust in His goodness even when you can't see obvious signs of His love? Do you "walk by faith, not by sight," choosing to trust in God's redemptive goodness and unfailing love?

## 238 Walking the Path of Faith

*She brought forth her firstborn Son, and wrapped Him in swaddling cloths, and laid Him in a manger.*
LUKE 2:7

The most wonderful thing happened to Mary. She was chosen by God to bring Jesus, His only Son and best gift to mankind, into the world. But consider what she encountered on the road to Jesus' birth.

- Her fiancé wanted to divorce her because she was pregnant.
- The timing of the Roman census meant Mary had to make a treacherous trip during her final weeks of pregnancy.
- Mary was away from her family and friends when it was time to deliver her first child.
- There was no room in the town's inn so Mary's baby was born in an animal stall—a manger.

These aren't ideal circumstances! But God transformed these potential stumbling blocks into stepping-stones for Mary's faith.

- Obeying God, Joseph stayed by Mary's side.
- Mary was in exactly the right place when Jesus was born. The prophecy that Jesus (Immanuel) would be born in Bethlehem was fulfilled (Micah 5:2).
- Mary's family and friends weren't there, but God was… and He is all-sufficient. He stands in as Father and also as a Friend who sticks closer than any relative or friend.
- God was Mary's refuge, and He provided her with His power when she needed it.

What difficulties do you face? Turn to God and lean on Him. Just as He took care of Mary, your faithful, loving heavenly Father will take care of you as you walk in faith.

## 239 True Treasure

*But Mary kept all these things and pondered them in her heart.*
LUKE 2:19

Great news! Christ the Savior is born! God wanted this message spread, and He chose a divine means to proclaim the news and an unlikely group to receive it and share it. On the night of Jesus' birth, God's angels appeared to a group of lowly shepherds. The radiant messengers lighted up the sky with their presence and praise as they heralded the birth of Christ the Lord. Wasting no time, the shepherds went to Bethlehem to verify the angels' message. Once they'd done so, they broadcast the glad tidings for all to hear. Some who heard the good news merely wondered about it, but Mary, Jesus' mother, quietly treasured everything in her heart.

Do you know what it means to treasure something in your heart? It means to guard that thing so surely and faithfully that it's secure in your mind. You marvel at its truth and ponder its meaning and impact. Again and again Mary thought through the words and events, considering how they fit together, comparing them to prophecy, weighing them against what she knew of God, carrying their message in her heart.

We noted earlier that Mary may have been a woman of few words. Here we see her keeping the many wonders she saw and heard within her heart, treasuring them because they came from God.

I encourage you to read the full account of the birth of Jesus in Luke 2. This was probably told to Luke by Mary herself! Treasure in your heart the details and truths revealed, and then praise the Lord for coming to ensure your salvation and eternal life.

## 240 *Are You Walking in God's Ways?*

*They brought Him to Jerusalem to present Him to the Lord...and to offer a sacrifice according to...the law.*
LUKE 2:22,24

God never makes a mistake, and He certainly didn't make one when He chose Mary as the mother of His Son. The responsibility of raising Jesus called for parents who followed God's law in spirit as well as in word. As Luke 2 shows, Mary and Joseph clearly met that criterion. Four verses address the law and its fulfillment.

- Jesus was circumcised exactly eight days after His birth, just as God's law required.
- Mary's purification after childbirth took place exactly 40 days after the birth of her male child, and the sacrificial offering of two turtledoves was made as God's law required.
- Mary presented Jesus to the Lord exactly as required by God's law.

In Mary we see the kind of woman God delights in—a woman after His own heart, a woman willing to do His will. Through Jesus Christ's perfect fulfillment of God's law we live in the age of God's marvelous grace, but obedience and wholehearted commitment to walking in His ways are still essential. How are you doing?

- Do you love others? All of God's law is fulfilled in one word—"love."
- Do you confess sin instantly and sincerely? Fellowship with God is sweeter when sin is confessed and turned away from.
- Are you training your children in the nurture and admonition of the Lord? That's God's command to parents.

## 241 *Being Blessed Doesn't Mean a Carefree Life*

*Yes, a sword will pierce through
your own soul also.*
LUKE 2:35

None of us knows what the future holds, but God gave Mary a hint about what awaited her—"a sword would pierce her soul." Mary was highly favored by God and greatly blessed to be the mother of His Son, but this privilege also meant real trials.

When Mary and Joseph took Jesus to the temple to dedicate Him to God surely their hopes and dreams soared as they considered His bright future. Affirming their thoughts, an old man named Simeon—a devout man of God who worshiped regularly and waited expectantly to see the coming of the Lord—took Jesus in his arms and prophesied concerning His ministry to the world. But as Simeon finished his blessing, he turned to Mary and said, "A sword will pierce through your own soul also." Mary must have wondered what that meant. What was going to happen that would cause her so much pain?

We'll never fully know the depth of Mary's anguish, but Simeon's words paint a gruesome picture. The word for "sword" is the same one used in the Old Testament to describe Goliath's large weapon (1 Samuel 17:51).

God's great blessings so often come at the cost of our personal comfort. But the more we listen and follow Him, the more He can transform us and those around us so His messages of love and salvation are known. Perhaps this cost is why the Bible encourages you and me to highly regard those we may be tempted to envy. We're to...

- rejoice with those who rejoice.
- esteem those who rule over us in the Lord.
- pray for those who rule and obey them.

We don't always know the price of God's favor, but we do know His love and favor are worth the cost.

## 242 Bringing Light into the Darkness

*Now there was one, Anna, a prophetess.*
LUKE 2:36

Prophetesses were empowered to speak God's Word, bringing light into darkness—

> *Miriam* led the Israelite women in praise when God defeated the Egyptian Pharaoh and his army (Exodus 15:20).
>
> *Deborah* served as a judge in Israel and gave Barak instructions from God that led to victory against Sisera (Judges 4:4-7).
>
> *Huldah* counseled King Josiah regarding the book of the law (2 Kings 22:14).

Today, even as our minds may still be reeling from yesterday's look at the prophet Simeon's words to Mary, God once again sends light into the darkness. When Simeon made his somber pronouncement, Anna, a prophetess, "gave thanks to the Lord, and spoke of Him to all those who looked for redemption in Jerusalem." Perhaps her words momentarily lifted the dark cloud that crossed Mary's happy heart with Simeon's dark warning.

Anna's life was touched by darkness. Her dear husband died young and for many, many years she daily lifted her eyes to the hills and looked for the coming of the Messiah. On this particular day the Light of the world entered the temple! Mary arrived, carrying the long-awaited Christ child in her arms—the One who would dispel the world's darkness. No wonder Anna praised and thanked God!

And how gracious of God to use Anna to remind Mary that her dear son—her Savior, her Lord, and her Master—would bring the brilliance of His light to her needy heart. Everyone needs light—the light of God's Word, the light of His promises, and the light of joyful trust in Him. Won't you share that light with someone today?

## 243 A Refreshing Balm of Encouraging Words

*[She] did not depart from the temple, but served God with fastings and prayers night and day.*
LUKE 2:37

In just a few verses God gives us all we know about Anna, a godly woman who loved God into her sunset years.

> *Anna was a widow.* Having lost her husband after only seven years of marriage, this woman knew sorrow. But she apparently allowed her suffering to soften her fiber and strengthen her faith. Anna spent her long life in faithful service to the Lord night and day.
>
> *Anna was a senior citizen.* At age 84 Anna still looked for "the deliverance of Jerusalem," for the Messiah, for the Savior, for Jesus! How truly blessed she was when God rewarded her many years of faith by allowing her to see—in the flesh—the Hope of Israel!

The life of Anna offers us two important lessons. First, we see the fruit of long-term faith, of faith that "is the substance of things hoped for" (Hebrews 11:1). Is your faith ever-burning? Never dimming, never cooling, never faltering as you look to God for the hope of Jesus' Second Coming?

Second, we learn about encouraging one another. How Anna's joyous outpouring of faith must have sunk deeply into Mary's confused soul after Simeon's pronouncement that she would encounter sorrow. Anna's words of encouragement were a balm of refreshment that soothed her bruised spirit.

I encourage you to lift up and restore someone who is cast down today. Speak timely words of ever-burning faith in God to those who are weary.

## 244 Renewed Day by Day

*[She] did not depart from the temple, but served God with fastings and prayers night and day.*
LUKE 2:37

The apostle Paul spoke for all of us when he declared that "our outward man is perishing" (2 Corinthians 4:16). We all feel it, sense it, and know it. The body gives way day by day. But in his next breath Paul offers the secret of enduring: "Yet the inward man is renewed day by day." William Barclay noted:

> All through life it must happen that a man's bodily strength fades away, but all through life it ought to happen that a man's soul keeps growing. The sufferings which leave a man with a weakened body may be the very things which strengthen the sinews of his soul. It was the prayer of the poet, "Let me grow lovely growing old." From the physical point of view life may be a slow but inevitable slipping down the slope that leads to death. But from the spiritual point of view life is a climbing up the hill that leads to the presence of God. No man need fear the years, for they bring him nearer, not to death, but to God.[66]

Certainly the prophetess Anna must have grown more lovely as she aged. Undoubtedly enduring the ailments old age delivers, this dear saint renewed her mind and inner person day by day through prayer accompanied and enhanced by fasting. This continual, faithful contact with God, the Source of all strength, enabled her to mount the hill that leads to His active presence. Indeed, Anna's faithfulness was rewarded as she saw God-in-flesh. Maybe she even held baby Jesus in her arms!

Follow in Anna's footsteps and look to the Lord for His renewing strength and grace minute by minute, hour by hour, day by day.

## 245 *Celebrating Your Faith as a Family*

*His parents went to Jerusalem every year at the Feast of the Passover.*
LUKE 2:41

Hasn't it been inspiring to see how faithfully Mary and Joseph followed God's law? Today we fast-forward 12 years and find more evidence of their commitment and obedience to God's law. One thing they did was celebrate their faith as a family.

*Worship*—God calls believers to come together on the first day of the week for worship. He tells us to be careful not to forsake such assembling together (Acts 20:7; Hebrews 10:25). So wise and godly moms and dads ensure the family worships together. They do what Mary and Joseph did—take the young ones to church (the Temple, in Mary and Joseph's case).

*Observe the traditions God gives through the Bible*—Just as Jesus' parents made sure He observed the Jewish rites and feasts according to God's instructions, we need to follow the Lord's instructions for worship, baptism, and communion (Matthew 28:19; 1 Corinthians 11:23-25).

*Celebrate*—Does your church mark special seasons of worship such as Advent and Lent? Does it celebrate ministry dedications; revival meetings, praise and prayer meetings, baby dedications, baptisms, worship services on special holidays, special Easter celebrations? Whatever your church celebrates, be there! These special times further your family's dedication to God and His church. It also cements your family's ties with the body of Christ and creates rich soil for fellowship, spiritual growth, and the seeds of sacred memories.

Many mothers you meet will tell you they wish they'd done more during their children's formative years to impress upon their moldable hearts the importance and joy of family life in the church. So establish this delightful and foundational family practice today.

## 246 Did Mary Forget?

*When they saw Him, they were amazed.*
LUKE 2:48

When Jesus was 12, now a man according to Jewish tradition, He accompanied His parents to Jerusalem to celebrate Passover. Nine verses describe the journey to this city, and I'm sure they barely touch on the emotions and insights that happened on the trip!

The worship at this annual Jewish festival was glorious and meaningful for Jesus, especially since this was the first time He participated as an adult.

Then, on the way home, in the evening of the first day's journey, Mary and Joseph realized Jesus was missing from the crowd of people returning to Nazareth. I shudder as I imagine the fear and consternation Mary and Joseph felt. Their young son was alone in a crowded, bustling city!

Mary and Joseph hurried back to Jerusalem. They spent three frantic days in the city searching for Jesus. At last they found Him in the temple sitting among the teachers, calmly interacting with them.

As any other mother would, Mary exclaimed, "Son, why have You done this to us? Look, Your father and I have sought You anxiously."

Now we hear the first of Jesus' words preserved for us! "Why did you seek Me? Did you not know that I must be about My Father's business?"

How that must have given Mary pause. She was amazed and didn't understand. In her worry did she forget what the angel Gabriel said about her son? Did she forget what Elizabeth said about her unborn child? What the shepherds told her, what Simeon prophesied, what Anna announced? Did she forget who Jesus was?

Do you know who Jesus is? He isn't merely a baby in a manger, a wise teacher, a good man. He was and is God in the flesh, the Savior of the world! Believe today and worship Him.

## 247 The Gifts of Life, Home, and Training

*Then He went down with them...*
*and was subject to them.*
LUKE 2:51

Even though the young Jesus obviously felt "at home" in His Father's house, and even though He was gaining a more complete understanding of His calling and purpose as the Son of God, the Holy child still needed a mother and a home. As someone marveled, "Not even to the angels fell such an honor as to the parents of Jesus!"[67] Instead, the high calling of mothering the Master fell to sweet Mary.

So after leaving the religious teachers in the temple area, Jesus returned to Nazareth with His earthly parents. The Scriptures say He "was subject to them." He was obedient while He lived under their authority. So Mary and Joseph continued raising Jesus, the Son of God. What exactly did they give Jesus?

- *Mary gave Jesus life, humanly speaking.* Hers was the body that brought God's precious Son into this world.
- *Mary and Joseph gave Jesus a home.* The Man of Sorrows—who all too soon would have no place to lay His head—received from the heart and hands of His folks the gift of a home.
- *Mary and Joseph gave Jesus training in godliness.* God had carefully selected them for the special job of mothering the Master. Surely they who found such favor with the Almighty would model godly virtues and guide those in their care toward a life devoted to God.

We who have children give them these same gifts of life, home, and training in godliness. Even those who don't have children can model godly character to others, reach out to children at church and elsewhere, and offer hospitality to all who enter our homes.

## 248 Loving Your Mother-in-Law

*But Simon's wife's mother was sick with a high fever.*
LUKE 4:38

- The penalty for bigamy is two mothers-in-law.
- The husband isn't always boss—sometimes it's his mom.
- To wives the "blessed event" is when his mother goes home.
- "Double trouble" is a mother-in-law with a twin sister.

These one-liners make gentle fun of mothers-in-law, but they don't reflect most people's experiences. Consider, for instance, the apostle Peter. He opened his home to his mother-in-law, and when she needed help, he was there for her. One Sabbath Peter told Jesus his wife's mother was extremely ill. Jesus "rebuked the fever, and it left her. And immediately she arose and served them."

This scene highlights at least three situations.

- *Do you have a mother-in-law?* Are you showing the kind of generous and gracious spirit Peter had toward his wife's mother? Ask God to give you a sincere concern for your mother-in-law's well-being. You may even want to review the beautiful relationship Ruth and Naomi enjoyed (see the book of Ruth).
- *Are you a mother-in-law?* Peter's mother-in-law was obviously accustomed to loving those in her son-in-law's home by serving them. She immediately arose and looked to their needs. Are you a generous and gracious giver, seeking to make life easier for your family? Ask God to reveal greater ways for you to express your love for your family and your gratitude for the blessing they are to you.
- *Do you or those you love have needs?* If so, go to Jesus! He's loving and compassionate and powerful enough to do something about human weakness and pain.

## 249 *For God, to Know Is to Provide!*

*A dead man was being carried out, the only son of his mother; and she was a widow.*
LUKE 7:12

Today we meet yet another woman in sorrow. "The widow of Nain" lost her husband, and today we read that she lost her only son. Jesus noticed this weeping woman as she followed her son's funeral procession. What would a person in that day and age do without a husband or son to provide for her and protect her?

Jesus—whose own mother was probably a widow by this time—was deeply moved by this woman's painful predicament. So He reached out and touched the coffin of her dear son…and literally gave him back to his mother! We can only imagine the joy mother and son experienced as God graciously gave each of them new life. Jesus overcame the power of death and revealed His awesome power!

We too can know the awesome power of God. Consider this truth and promise: "The LORD is my shepherd; I shall not want" (Psalm 23:1). Did you know that the English words "I shall not want" are the translation of the great name of God "Jehovah-jireh"? Consider its wondrous meaning!

- God foresees the needs of His children.
- God meets the needs of His children.
- God's faithful and loving character demands that He provide for His children.
- God knows and sees what we need, and He provides for these needs. One is connected to the other. God cannot know of a need and not provide. For God, to know is to provide!

If you feel you lack in any area of life, take heart! God knows your plight. He acts on your behalf to meet all your *real* needs. Glorify Him now as the people who witnessed His miraculous provision for the widow of Nain did.

## 250 A Guide for Prayer and Life

*And behold, a woman...who was a sinner...began to wash His feet with her tears... and anointed them with the fragrant oil.*
LUKE 7:37-38

Do you know this simple acrostic that guides prayer? It also guides godly life!

**A**doration of God
**C**onfession of sin
**T**hanksgiving for blessings
**S**upplication for concerns

Today we meet a woman who isn't identified by name, but her love for the Lord is recorded for eternity in the Bible. At a dinner for Jesus, this woman was scorned by the host for her many sins. Yet she washed Jesus' feet with her tears, wiped them with her hair, kissed His feet, and anointed them with fragrant oil.

- She *adored* Jesus.
- Probably a prostitute, she *acknowledged and confessed her sins.*
- She *poured out her thanks* to the One who could—and did—forgive, cleanse, and change her.
- Perhaps she put her *request for forgiveness into words* since she clearly received that gift. Jesus said, "Your sins are forgiven."

How can you follow this acrostic?

***Adore*** the One who opens the life gates to heaven.

***Confess*** any sin that blocks your relationship with God.

***Thank*** Jesus for His gift of salvation and eternal life.

***Start asking*** God humbly for what you need.

## 251 *A Special Ministry*

*Certain women...provided for Him from their substance.*
LUKE 8:2-3

When our Lord Jesus walked this earth "certain women" enjoyed a role "absolutely unique in the gospels," explains theologian Charles Ryrie.[68] They ministered to the Lord—a role that His male followers and disciples didn't have. We more fully appreciate the specialness of this role when we realize the Greek word used here for serving appears in the four Gospels only when the ministry is being rendered directly to Jesus. And in those cases it is administered by either angels or women! What a wondrous honor to serve the Savior this way.

Who comprised this honored band of faithful followers? Mary Magdalene, Joanna, Susanna, and "many others." These women, whom Jesus healed and delivered, chose to follow Him and support His ministry, giving of their substance and their service.

*Substance.* By funding Jesus' ministry and supporting Him and His disciples as they preached, these women met a very practical need.

*Service.* Graciously and unobtrusively, these dear women also saw to Jesus' personal comfort and well-being.

Today we serve the Lord by serving His people. As one godly person noted regarding our service to those who labor for the Lord, "It is not always the person in the foreground who is doing the greatest work. Many a man who occupies a public position could not sustain it for one week without the help of [others]. There is no gift that cannot be used in the service of Christ. Many of His greatest servants are in the background, unseen but essential to His cause."[69]

Think of three specific ways you can advance Christ's cause through your substance and service. Write them down and commit to doing them. Jesus said, "Inasmuch as you [helped] one of the least of these My brethren, you did it to Me" (Matthew 25:40).

# 252 *Following in the Lord's Shadow*

*Mary called Magdalene, out of whom had come seven demons.*
LUKE 8:2

Have you heard the saying "the worst first"? Well, on Luke's roster of women who served Jesus and were healed and delivered by Him, "the worst" is the first to be named. Mary Magdalene was delivered from seven demons. Can you imagine the pain, the torment, the destruction Mary suffered?

Jesus—the God of compassion and power—delivered this desperate woman. The details "out of whom had come seven demons" and that she was from the town Magdala on the Sea of Galilee are the specifics we're told. But from the moment of her release she appears to have followed Jesus. She who was delivered from much loved much.

How blessed that the past has no hold on our present or our future! Consider these truths:

- "Therefore, if anyone is in Christ, he is a new creation; old things have passed away; behold, all things have become new" (2 Corinthians 5:17).
- "It is no longer I who live, but Christ lives in me" (Galatians 2:20).
- "I press on…forgetting those things which are behind and reaching forward to those things which are ahead" (Philippians 3:12-13).
- "Set your mind on things above, not on things on the earth. For you died, and your life is hidden with Christ in God" (Colossians 3:1-3).

Choose one of these passages and memorize its freeing truth. Like Mary Magdalene, you can—in God's power—rise up from your past and press on. Follow Jesus!

## 253 *Principles for Giving*

***Certain women who had been healed of evil spirits and infirmities...Joanna...and Susanna.***
LUKE 8:2-3

How refreshing to marvel over the goodness of the Lord who freed Mary Magdalene from the dark power of seven demons! And now we are privileged to meet two other women whom Jesus touched with His healing hand. They are:

| *Joanna* | *Susanna* |
|---|---|
| Her name means Jehovah has shown favor. | Her name means a white lily. |
| She was the wife of Chuza, the house steward of Herod the Tetrarch. | No husband's name is given. |

How does someone thank God for the miracle of healing? These two women gave money to Jesus. Evidently they had funds at their disposal and delighted in supporting Jesus' ministry. Ponder these principles for giving.

- *Give freely.* "Freely you have received, freely give" (Matthew 10:8).
- *Give bountifully.* "He who sows bountifully will also reap bountifully" (2 Corinthians 9:6).
- *Give cheerfully.* "Let each one give as he purposes in his heart, not grudgingly or of necessity; for God loves a cheerful giver" (2 Corinthians 9:7).

Oswald Smith said, "I would not like to meet God [and have] a large bank account. That would be a terrible calamity. He expects me to invest it somehow before I die, for Him."[70] Consider your giving to the Lord's work. Pray about what you're doing and ask if it's what God wants. Are you giving freely...bountifully...cheerfully?

## 254 Faith in the Darkness

*He had an only daughter about twelve years of age, and she was dying.*
LUKE 8:42

Many people were blessed by gracious miracles Jesus worked. Today we meet a young girl who desperately needed His healing touch. This girl is identified only as Jairus' daughter.

The girl's father, Jairus, was "president" of the synagogue. He was powerless over his daughter's illness.

- The young girl stood at death's door.
- People surrounded Jesus, and Jairus worried he wouldn't get to the Healer in time.
- As Jairus led the Healer to his house, a crowd pressed in. As Jesus stopped to heal a woman, a messenger rushed up to announce the girl died.
- Jesus continued to Jairus' house where wailing women had been hired (as was the custom) and were mourning the girl's death.
- Jesus brought the young girl back to life!

Imagine the desperate father's emotions—the fear, the impatience, the fading hope as he watched Jesus' progress slowed by people who needed healing. The mass of people caused Jairus and his family twice the pain and twice the tragedy because Jesus didn't make it to their house in time. But these circumstances gave the Lord the glorious opportunity to double the miracle!

Jesus' miraculous raising of Jairus' daughter from death is about faith—faith when time seems short, faith when circumstances turn ugly, faith when Jesus seems slow to respond, faith when time is gone, faith in the darkness.

When every trace of light is extinguished, do you still believe in the power of God? As Jesus told Jairus, "Only believe."

## 255 *A Simple Touch...and a Miracle!*

*Now a woman...came from behind and touched the border of His garment.*
LUKE 8:43-44

*Why not?* she may have thought, spotting Jesus in the throng of people. *Jairus seems distraught and in a hurry, so I shouldn't interrupt. But a simple touch of the Miracle Worker's robe won't slow Him down.*

So as Jesus passed on the way to the home of Jairus, the ruler of the synagogue, this diseased, full-of-hope-in-Jesus woman summoned her courage and faith and reached her trembling fingers out until she felt the garment of God flutter through them.

Instantly two things happened. First this dear woman felt the healing power. After suffering a dozen years from incurable hemorrhaging and spending all she had on doctors who didn't help, she was cured! Second, Jesus instantly turned around and asked, "Who touched Me?"

*How could He have possibly noticed?* she wondered.

The disciples wondered too. "Master, the multitudes crowd around You, yet You say, 'Who touched Me?'"

But Jesus perceived His healing power going out, and He wanted the person healed to speak up.

Perhaps our sister-in-suffering thought she could quietly return home healed. How much more comfortable she'd be if this situation stayed low-key. But she couldn't let Jesus' question go unanswered. Shaking, she stepped forth, fell before His feet, and shared her affliction for all to hear, telling why she'd touched the Master's robe and noting she'd been healed.

What a model for us! This dear woman gave her testimony before many witnesses. She gave God the glory He so richly deserved and received Jesus' benediction—"Daughter, be of good cheer; your faith has made you well. Go in peace."

What wondrous thing has God done for you? Have you publicly given Him the glory? Have you told others of His goodness to you and His power in your life?

## 256 When Hope Is Gone, Walk by Faith

*He permitted no one to go in except...*
*the father and mother of the girl.*
LUKE 8:51

The multitude of people surrounding Jesus had so many needs. Among them were Jairus, the ruler of the synagogue, whose 12-year-old daughter was dying, and a woman who had a continual issue of blood. Only God could meet such needs, so Jesus, God-in-the-flesh, healed the dear woman who now worshiped at His feet. Her 12-year-long hemorrhage ended. A messenger arrived and told Jairus his daughter died. But Jesus assured Jairus that his daughter would be restored...if he would "only believe." But what about Jairus' wife, the little girl's mother?

When Jairus went to get Jesus, the anxious mother tended to their dying daughter, doing all she could—hoping...praying...waiting. The minutes dragged by agonizingly. Where was Jesus? Her hope died when she witnessed her beloved daughter's final breath. Perhaps this devastated mother sent the messenger to her husband to let him know it was too late. Perhaps she also called in the mourners to begin their vigil.

Despite the message, in strode the Healer, filled with strength and power and honor and glory and majesty. Jesus dismissed everyone but the girl's parents and His three closest disciples. He took the dead child's hand and spoke: "Little girl, arise." Her spirit returned, and she arose immediately!

Have you known the power of the Word of God in your life? Have you clung to it as you've hoped and prayed and waited? Oh, believe God's Word regardless of life's events, regardless of hopeless circumstances, regardless of what appears to be, regardless of timing and events that go wrong. Don't look at what you can see, but look to the things that are not seen, "for we walk by faith, not by sight" (2 Corinthians 4:18; 5:7).

## 257 *Peace or Panic?*

*Martha welcomed Him into her house.*
*And she had a sister called Mary.*
LUKE 10:38-39

We face so much stress and pressure today. We never seem to have enough time—pressure. We want to do well as a wife and a parent—pressure. We are called to be good stewards of finances—pressure. We strive to be effective managers of our homes—pressure. How do you handle all the pressures of life? Do you experience peace or panic?

In sisters Mary and Martha, God gives us a classic study in opposites. Jesus went to their home for dinner. Martha welcomed Him in, but then she became distracted by all the preparations. Busy in the kitchen, lots of details on her mind, anxious that everything go well, Martha was a whirlwind of activity. Was she at peace? No!

How did her stress show? Martha was stirring the pot in the kitchen, but she was also in the family room. There she accused Christ ("Don't you care?") and accused Mary ("She's left me to serve alone"), complaining about the burden of dinner. Martha is bossy, blaming, distracted. She's "yarping"—which, you'll notice, is "praying" spelled backward!

In contrast to this hurricane of hyperactivity, we find Mary...

- resting at the Lord's feet while Martha is restless
- worshiping while Martha worries
- remaining at peace while Martha's panic level rises
- sitting while Martha is stewing
- listening while Martha is lashing out

What was Jesus' response? He commended Mary for doing what is most important—spending time with Him.

Would an outside observer see Martha or Mary in you as you deal with schedules, commitments, and pressures? Do you need to make any changes?

## 258 Living the Spirit of God's Law

*And behold, there was a woman who had a spirit of infirmity eighteen years, and was bent over and could in no way raise herself up.*
LUKE 13:11

Jesus was teaching in a synagogue when he noticed a solitary woman bent over and in pain. What a scene ensued when He approached her!

- *Malady*—For 18 years this woman was a prisoner of a disease that deformed her body.
- *Mercy*—Our great and compassionate Savior didn't let such a tragedy go unaddressed. After announcing she was released from her infirmity, Jesus laid His healing hands tenderly and powerfully on her back.
- *Murmuring*—Can you believe that the ruler of the synagogue spoke up indignantly? He thought the miracle was wrong because it was done on the Sabbath day.
- *Masterful defense*—"Hypocrite!" Jesus exclaimed. "Does not each one of you on the Sabbath loose his ox or his donkey from the stall, and lead it away to water it? So ought not this woman, being a daughter of Abraham, whom Satan has bound—think of it—for eighteen years, be loosed from this bond on the Sabbath?"
- *Merriment*—Jesus' adversaries hung their heads, but the crowd of people who witnessed this scene rejoiced for the glorious things He was doing among them.

Oh, the wisdom and grace in the spirit of God's love behind the letter of His law! Surely a handicapped woman deserves to be released from physical bondage no matter what day of the week it is! Ask God to grace you with His wisdom, discernment, and mercy as you daily go about your life and share Him with others.

## 259 The Truth About Giving

*He saw also a certain poor widow putting in two mites.*
Luke 21:2

I surrender all...
All to Thee I freely give...
I surrender all![71]

These simple words from a well-known song touch a chord deep within my heart. We're called by God and privileged to relinquish our all to Him, to fully accept His perfect will, and to live "the surrendered life." Today we come face to face with a woman who truly did just that.

As Jesus sat in the temple area, He watched many people deposit money into the collection boxes. These gifts were for the day-in, day-out operation and upkeep of God's temple. The rich were openly putting in their large gifts. But what caught Christ's eye was a poor widow quietly putting in two small coins. In His omniscience Jesus knew how many and how much. Her gift was two lepta, two of the smallest coins in existence, two of "the thin ones."

But Jesus knew something else as well. Perhaps clearing His throat before He spoke, He stated to those around Him, "Truly I say to you that this poor widow has put in more than all; for all these out of their abundance have put in offerings for God, but she out of her poverty has put in all the livelihood that she had."

What praise for this dear widow's sacrificial giving then and forever preserved in God's Word. This woman of poverty—this woman with few resources—gave all she had.

What might be written about your giving pattern and purposes? Do you give regularly, freely, and sacrificially? How much you give of what you have and how you give those gifts—these are true measures of your love for God. As Jesus said, "Where your treasure is, there your heart will be also" (Matthew 6:21). Where is your heart?

## 260 Being Faithful Even When It Hurts

*All His acquaintances, and the women who followed Him from Galilee, stood at a distance, watching these things.*
LUKE 23:49

What was the worst day of your life? Perhaps your dark experience will help you relate to the faithful women who followed Jesus. They were with Him to the end and witnessed the worst day the world has known.

- Jesus was arrested in the garden of Gethsemane.
- Jesus' disciples fled, leaving Him to fend for Himself.
- Jesus was tried unjustly, whipped, beaten, spit upon, scoffed at, and sentenced to death.
- Beaten up, bleeding, in agony, He was forced to walk through the crowded streets to the site of crucifixions.
- He was nailed to a cross.
- As Jesus hung dying, soldiers gambled for His cloak. Jesus was mocked, sneered at, ridiculed, and given vinegar to drink.
- The noonday sky became as dark as night for three hours. The ground shook, rocks split, and the graves of the dead opened.
- After Jesus died, His body was pierced with a sword.
- His body was laid in a tomb without burial preparation.

It's one thing to quietly sit and listen to Jesus' wonderful words of life. To give goods to sustain His ministry. To benefit from His miracles. To fix Him a meal. To enjoy His company. It's quite another thing to love Him and follow Him faithfully when times are hard. Pray for strength and dedication to Jesus in good times, bad times, and terrible times.

## 261 Little Things Are Important Too

***And the women who had come with Him from Galilee followed after, and they observed the tomb and how His body was laid.***

LUKE 23:55

How is true love measured? In the case of the faithful women who loved and followed Jesus, their great devotion was evident in little things. On history's darkest day their devotion shone brilliantly.

*Love stayed.* Although Jesus' disciples fled in fright, these dear women stayed with Him through His crucifixion, never wavering, ever watching, modeling a to-the-end devotion.

*Love followed.* We don't know how many people followed the crucified Jesus to His tomb (were there church officials, government representatives, the curious, professional mourners?), but we do know this loyal company of ladies walked behind those who carried His body. And they went for one reason—to learn the way to Jesus' tomb.

*Love cared.* These caring women realized no one prepared Jesus' body for burial. It was a little thing, perhaps, yet they decided to see to their Master's final earthly need.

*Love worked.* These dedicated followers of Jesus returned home after a long, gruesome, agonizing day at the crucifixion and prepared spices and ointments for the embalming of Jesus' body.

Little things. Yet they revealed hearts that loved God. Can you think of something you can do today for your Friend and Savior? Can you stay a little longer in prayer, follow a little closer in obedience, care a little more for His people, work a little harder for His kingdom? Ask for His guidance.

## 262 *No Excuses!*

*Very early in the morning, they, and certain other women with them, came to the tomb.*
LUKE 24:1

Sunrise sent forth its signal. The Sabbath was over. And so was the most dreadful day in the history of the world—the day Jesus was murdered. Now it was time for the faithful, devoted women—those who had stayed through the crucifixion, witnessed every vile abuse, and followed Jesus' body to the tomb—to carry out the last offices of love by embalming His body. It was early—very early—when this little fellowship of faithful followers went to the tomb.

Why didn't others go along? What might have been their reasons... or excuses?

*Excuse 1: Someone else will do it.* "I'm sure someone else noticed that Jesus' body wasn't properly prepared for burial. Surely someone is already planning on doing it."

*Excuse 2: We're tired.* "Oh, wasn't it awful? That horrible sight of Jesus hanging on the cross. I thought the day would never end. My feet are killing me, and I have a headache from crying."

*Excuse 3: Jesus' disciples should do it.* "Can you believe it? His 12 main disciples left Him to die alone! They ought to at least show up today and take care of things."

*Excuse 4: It can't be done!* "Didn't you see that giant stone they rolled across the opening of Jesus' tomb? There's no way we could push that massive thing aside."

Such reasons seem legitimate, yet for the women who followed Jesus, no obstacle, discomfort, or inconvenience would keep them from doing what they could for their Lord. Are you serving your Savior with diligence, faithfulness, follow-through? Do you need to make any changes? And how are you serving your family, Christians, and others?

## 263 Faithfully Following Jesus

*Then they returned from the tomb and told all these things to the eleven and to all the rest.*
LUKE 24:9

We talk about, we desire, and we pray for a life spent faithfully walking with Jesus. As we say farewell to the circle of women who loved Jesus and faithfully followed Him to the end, we see more of what it means to truly follow Him.

- *They followed Him in life.* As Jesus ministered throughout Jerusalem, Judea, and Samaria, these women ministered to Him (Luke 8:2-3).
- *They followed Him after He died.* They waited at the foot of the cross, watched as His body was removed, and walked to the tomb.
- *They followed through in duty.* These dear women realized that Jesus' body was not properly prepared for burial. The next morning, as they followed through on this final duty to their departed Friend, they were blessed to be the first to witness His resurrection from the dead and to talk with the risen Lord (John 20:11-18)!
- *They followed His instructions.* When they spoke with Jesus, He said to tell His brethren these things (John 20:17). These women rushed to do just that!

I'm sure you desire to truly follow Jesus. What does such discipleship require? That you follow Him in life, in death, in duty, and in obedience. Make the words of this old familiar hymn, "He Leadeth Me," the prayer of your heart.

> He leadeth me, He leadeth me,
> By His own hand He leadeth me.
> His faithful follower I would be,
> For by His hand He leadeth me.[72]

## 264 *Look to the Eternal*

*When they ran out of wine, the mother of Jesus said to Him, "They have no wine."*
John 2:3

"The mother of Jesus." The phrase sounds glorious, doesn't it? But as we might imagine, being Jesus' mom did have its challenges. Consider today's scripture. When the wine ran out at this wedding in Cana, Mary must have wondered, *What can I do to help? I know, I'll tell Jesus!* We don't know exactly what she expected, but Jesus' response reminded her that He was more—much more!—than her firstborn son. He reminded her of His position and duties as Deity: "Woman, what does your concern have to do with Me? My hour has not yet come." Mary said, in hope, to the servants, "Whatever He says to you, do it." What can we learn from this exchange?

*God's purposes.* God doesn't exist to serve mankind, mankind exists to serve God. Although Jesus provided the wine, He performed this miracle to serve His divine purposes, not merely to please His mother. Jesus' purpose was to manifest His glory and deity so others might believe. Mary was concerned with the temporal, while Jesus was primarily concerned with the eternal.

Do you worry about unimportant details? Are you concerned with the minutiae of daily life? Receive with grace Jesus' gentle rebuke of Mary's earthly preoccupation and set your affection on things above—on the eternal, more significant issues of life.

*God's timing.* God's timing is governed by His great wisdom and knowledge. Mary may have feared that no one noticed the lack of drink and felt the need to point it out to Jesus. But Jesus, in his omniscience, knew and—in His time, on His divine schedule—acted.

Are there things you need? Are there matters you fear have gone unnoticed? Wait on the Lord. Trust in His timing.

# 265 A Visit with God

*A woman of Samaria came to draw water.*
JOHN 4:7

Today we meet a woman known simply as "a woman of Samaria." As Jesus traveled through her region, He stopped to rest by a well where she came to draw water. What do we know about this exchange?

| *Message to the Samaritan Woman* | *Message to Us* |
| --- | --- |
| She'd sinned. She'd been wed five times, and the man she lived with now wasn't her husband. | We have sinned. That's the clear message of Romans 3:23—"For all have sinned." |
| She was saved. After talking with Jesus, the woman drank of the water Jesus offered, living water springing up into everlasting life. | We can be saved. Jesus extends the same living water to us. He promises, "I give them eternal life, and they shall never perish" (John 10:28). |
| She shared the good news. Rushing into the city, this woman spread the news of Jesus' presence and His message. | We must share the good news. The Bible asks, "How shall they believe in Him of whom they have not heard?" (Romans 10:14). |

When the Savior visited with this woman, she was saved—and others were saved as well! Talk with the Savior. Speak with Him about everlasting life, about yourself, about the sin that mars your life, about your loved ones who don't know Him. Drink deeply from His Word. Then tell others the good news of Jesus Christ.

## 266 *Forgiveness*

*Then the scribes and Pharisees brought to Him a woman caught in adultery.*
JOHN 8:3

The scribes and Pharisees, hoping to catch Jesus breaking the law, dragged a woman to Him. "Teacher, this woman was caught in adultery...Now Moses, in the law, commanded us that such should be stoned. But what do you say?" Jesus said, "He who is without sin among you, let him throw a stone at her first." After the accusers departed, Jesus forgave the woman.

Let's consider the components of forgiveness.

**F**orget the offense. Jeremiah 31:34—"I will forgive their iniquity, and their sin I will remember no more." This doesn't mean you get into the same situation again.

**O**ur forgiveness is in Christ. "We have redemption through His blood, the forgiveness of sins" (Colossians 1:14).

**R**epentance refuses to sin again. The forgiven sinner repents of his sin, goes his way, and purposes to not sin again.

**G**o on. All have sinned. Those who are forgiven go forward, leaving behind their sinful ways (Romans 3:23; Philippians 3:13-14).

**I**nfinite forgiveness. Forgiveness covers offenses again and again. When Peter asked, "Lord, how often shall my brother sin against me, and I forgive him? Up to seven times?" Jesus answered, "Up to seventy times seven" (Matthew 18:21, 22).

**V**alue the sinner as God does. "While we were still sinners, Christ died for us" (Romans 5:8).

**E**mulate God. We are to forgive one another just as God in Christ also forgave us (Ephesians 4:32).

## 267 *When Crises Come...*

*Now a certain man was sick, Lazarus of Bethany, the town of Mary and her sister Martha.*
JOHN 11:1

What do you do when trouble comes your way?

- Call a counselor?
- Eat something?
- Fall apart?
- Get a new hairstyle?
- Go shopping?
- Hide in a novel?
- Join a group?
- Take a pill?
- Tell a friend?
- Watch a movie?

We've seen Mary and Martha before as they welcomed Jesus and His disciples into their home for a meal, but now they faced a crisis. Their beloved brother, Lazarus, was sick. Besides being dear to them, he was probably their sole means of support. (The Bible never mentions Mary and Martha having husbands or children.) Their brother's serious illness meant great sadness and an unknown future. These two women knew of Jesus' miracles and His deep love for their brother. So they sent for Him.

O that we would follow in this wise pair's footsteps! Why do we turn to a friend, a counselor, or a support group when we have Jesus, the Friend who sticks closer than a brother? As a simple message from an eloquent psalm reminds us:

> I will lift up my eyes to the hills—
> From whence comes my help?
> My help comes from the LORD,
> Who made heaven and earth
> (Psalm 121:1).

May we call on Jesus when problems and crises come!

## 268 "He Who Believes in Me"

*Then Martha, as soon as she heard that Jesus was coming, went and met Him.*
JOHN 11:20

An "odd couple" consists of two people who handle life in contrasting ways. Sisters Mary and Martha certainly qualify! When Jesus visited, Martha bustled with unbridled energy while Mary was content to worship at His feet. Today we see this "odd couple" in another situation. Their brother, Lazarus, was seriously ill. The sisters sent for Jesus, but He didn't come. Their brother died. Then the sisters heard Jesus was approaching their village. How did Martha respond? True to form, she leaped up, rushed out the door, and ran down the road to meet Him.

*Martha's statement of faith.* Martha may have been abrupt and hurried, but her heart was right. She believed in Jesus and trusted in His power to heal. "Lord," she ventured when she met Him, "if You had been here, my brother would not have died."

*Martha's lesson in faith.* Martha was right to go to Jesus, but she missed a central truth about Him. When she volunteered, "I know that whatever You ask of God, God will give You," Jesus corrected her by stating, "I *am* the resurrection and the life. He who believes in Me, though he may die, he shall live." He was saying, "Martha, I don't have to ask of God. *I am God!* And life is in Me. He who believes in Me shall live."

Who do you believe Jesus is? Martha recognized His power, but her understanding of His deity was incomplete until He corrected her. Do you believe Jesus is God—God-in-the-flesh—and that belief in Him, though you die physically, gives you eternal life? That is the message Martha heard from the lips of Jesus, and it is His message to us too. Jesus asked Martha, "Do you believe this?" Do *you?*

## 269 *Heavenly Fruit*

*But Mary was sitting in the house.*
JOHN 11:20

Yesterday we saw how Martha, one member of the "odd couple" of sisters Mary and Martha, responded to Jesus after her brother's death. Almost on cue, the energetic, do-it-yourself Martha leaped up and bolted out of the house to meet Him.

But how did the ever-pensive Mary respond? She stayed in the house, waiting for the Savior. Soon word arrived, "The Teacher has come and is calling for you."

Joining Jesus, Mary fell at His feet and declared: "Lord, if You had been here, my brother would not have died."

These sisters show us two ways of managing life, and each way has its benefits. Martha definitely gets things done and makes things happen, but don't miss the importance of going into "Mary mode"—spending time waiting on the Lord. When we choose to spend time close to Jesus, important things can happen:

- We read and study God's Word.
- We linger in sweet prayer.
- We commit to memory favorite scriptures.
- We meditate on things of the Lord.

In our busy world it's tempting to think that time alone with God, time spent waiting on Him, doesn't accomplish much. Waiting is difficult. There is no action, no recognition, no glory, no splash. Consider these thought-provoking words of nineteenth-century Scottish lecturer Henry Drummond: "Talent develops itself in solitude; the talent of prayer, of faith, of meditation, of seeing the unseen."[73]

Do you want to bear this heavenly fruit that grows only in the shade of God's presence? Then today and every day seek time alone with God.

## 270 *Service and Worship*

***There they made Him a supper; and Martha served [and] Mary...anointed the feet of Jesus, and wiped His feet with her hair.***

JOHN 12:2-3

Before we bid Mary and Martha Godspeed, let's peek through a window. The whole family is at home: Mary, Martha, and Lazarus, whom Jesus raised from the dead. We see a truly joyous celebration as these grateful folks prepare another meal for their beloved Jesus. The scene is both priceless and instructive.

*Service.* As usual, Martha served. Are we surprised? Service is Martha's way of expressing love. She was a practical woman. She delighted in actively meeting the needs of Jesus and the other people she loved.

And you? Are you faithful to serve where God places you, remembering that whatever you do, you are to do it heartily "as to the Lord and not to man" (Colossians 3:23)? Do you regard the practical tasks at home—meals to prepare, floors to sweep, clothes to wash—as expressions of your love for God? While these daily duties may seem mundane, God knows the sacrifice involved and is pleased when we serve as unto Him!

*Worship.* As usual, Mary worshiped. Again, are we surprised? This evening she poured her expensive oil over Jesus' feet in an act of extravagant love and then wiped His feet with her hair.

Are you an uninhibited worshiper of God? Do you seek new ways to show your love for Him? Have you done "outrageous" things that pleased Him? Oh, your acts of adoration may be scoffed at, as were Mary's. People may consider your worship unwise, your sacrifice of finances and time wasteful, your activities for Him foolish. But God welcomes the gifts of worship you bring!

## 271 *Love Triumphs over Pain*

*Now there stood by the cross of Jesus His mother.*
John 19:25

"Yes, a sword will pierce through your own soul also." Remember when Simeon shared these words with Mary? (See Luke 2:35.) My, how they must have echoed in Mary's mind for almost 30 or so years.

And now Mary stood at the foot of Jesus' cross, watching her firstborn son die a criminal's agonizing, torturous death. Her heart and soul were indeed pierced. Then, in the horrible quiet, Mary heard the clear voice of Jesus speaking to His disciple John. And He was speaking about her! "Behold your mother!" Even in this terrible moment of pain, her son was thinking of her…the Son of God was thinking of her and still taking care of her.

Consider two principles from Mary's difficult life we can take with us along our own sometimes painful paths.

*Principle 1:* We should never allow pain of any kind to interfere with caring for our loved ones. Jesus shows us that. Despite the agonizing pain He felt as He hung dying on the cross, He was thinking of Mary and His disciple John, and how they could help each other.

*Principle 2:* Life's pain should never cause us to doubt God's care for us. The Almighty is with us always, even to the end of the age (Matthew 28:20). He will not fail to provide for us (Psalm 23:1). He will always love us…here on earth and when we're in His presence in eternity!

Today thank God for His unfailing love and care for you. Follow His example by caring for your loved ones, even if your world isn't going as well as you'd like.

## 272 A Beautiful Portrait of Love

*These all continued...in prayer and supplication, with the women and Mary the mother of Jesus, and with His brothers.*

Acts 1:14

Today we say farewell to Mary. Let's examine carefully the details of her final appearance.

*Fact 1: Mary is in the upper room.* Perhaps the very spot where Jesus shared His last meal with His disciples, this room became the meeting place for His followers after His glorious resurrection.

*Fact 2: Mary is among Jesus' faithful followers.* No single believer in Christ is more important than another. Mary and others stand on equal ground.

*Fact 3: Mary is praying.* Kneeling shoulder to shoulder with the other saints, Mary joins with the group, persisting in prayer for strength and grace.

*Fact 4: Mary is with other women.* Among Jesus' followers were the wives of some of the disciples and other women who supported His ministry.

*Fact 5: Mary's other sons are present.* How Mary must have rejoiced when her other sons joined her. They didn't believe in Jesus before His death, but they were brought to faith by His death and resurrection (John 7:5; Acts 1:14). Finally her sons were united in faith.

What a beautiful portrait of love we find in the life of Mary. She worshiped and fellowshipped with believers, prayed often, and valued her family's faith. How about you?

P.S. Aren't you glad you can visit these women anytime by simply opening your Bible? And you'll meet them in paradise!

# 273 Making Your Life Count for Christ

*At Joppa there was a certain disciple named...Dorcas. This woman was full of good works and charitable deeds which she did.*

Acts 9:36

Come to Joppa, a city on the Mediterranean Sea. Let's look in at a local church.

*The people.* Serving in the congregation at Joppa was a woman named Dorcas. Her name, meaning "gazelle," suggested her loveliness and beauty. This dear woman spent hours and energy making coats and garments for widows, who were among the most needy persons in her day and culture. Dorcas didn't merely dream, make grand plans, or passionately desire to better the lives of her suffering sisters—she acted! And she was adored by the Christians in the area for her love, good works, and charity.

*The problem.* When Dorcas died, the church mourned and grieved. A gracious, giving saint was taken from them.

But a special thing happened in this little town. And we'll look at that tomorrow. For now, let's pause and ponder Dorcas' ministry. Did you notice we don't see her teaching, evangelizing, or counseling? Instead, we see her working quietly, doing some hands-on labors of love, putting forth practical efforts to help people. Hers was not a "sowing" ministry, but a literal "sewing" ministry.

Do you want your life to count? Do you yearn to make a difference for God's kingdom? Do you long to influence others for the Lord and touch them with His love? Put on a heart of compassion and kindness (Colossians 3:12). Look at people and their situations through Jesus' eyes of love and consider the afflictions and hardships you see. Then ask God, "What would ease the lives of the unfortunate? What would help them?" When you work to meet the needs of others, your life counts for Christ.

## 274 A Heart of Goodness

*Then [Peter]...presented her alive.*
Acts 9:41

Wasn't it delightful yesterday to meet Dorcas? She cared for people through the very practical acts of making coats and garments. It's easy to understand why the people in her church mourned her death. So what did they do?

*The petition.* As the people contemplated the loss of Dorcas, two of Christ's disciples from her hometown went to talk to the apostle Peter. Hadn't Peter just healed a paralyzed man in Lydda? Perhaps he could use divine power on behalf of Dorcas!

*The presentation.* Peter followed these men back to the crowded house of dear Dorcas. The widows showed him the many clothes this thoughtful woman had made for them. Asking everyone to leave the room where Dorcas lay, Peter knelt, prayed, and commanded the corpse, "Arise." Peter helped Dorcas up and then presented her to the saints and widows. Dorcas was alive again!

What an amazing chain of events! And beyond bringing the good and godly Dorcas back to life, what else happened as a result of Peter's prayer and the Lord's goodness?

- *God was glorified.* No person but God has the power to raise someone from the dead. Oh, how He must have been praised!
- *Faith was generated.* Many believed as a result of Peter's miracle. May God be praised for that too!
- *The people were gladdened.* Joy rippled through the church at Joppa: Dorcas was back!

Is your heart continually filled with God's love and goodness? Do you see the needs of people at church and then help? Oh, how I pray your love for Jesus results in good works and Him being glorified!

# 275 Risking Everything for Jesus

*So...[Peter] came to the house of Mary...*
*where many were gathered together praying.*
Acts 12:12

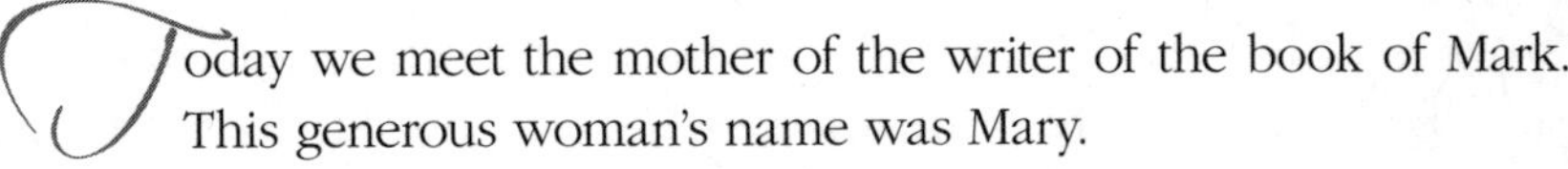

Today we meet the mother of the writer of the book of Mark. This generous woman's name was Mary.

- *Mary was the sister of Barnabas.* Barnabas was "a good man, full of the Holy Spirit and of faith" (Acts 11:24). He gladly sold the property he owned and gave the funds to benefit the body of Christ (Acts 4:36-37). Barnabas was generous in spirit and deed.
- *Mary was the devoted mother of John Mark.* John was an evangelist who accompanied the apostle Paul on his travels and later wrote the Gospel of Mark. He gave all he was and had for the cause of Christ.

At a time when Christians were being relentlessly persecuted and murdered, Mary risked her life and possessions by opening her home so Christians had a place to worship. In today's verse the believers have gathered at her house to pray for Peter, who was in prison awaiting execution by King Herod.

Would you willingly risk everything and generously sacrifice your time, effort, and money to serve the Lord? Have you considered what serving God requires? *Time.* You have to say no to lesser things, make time for projects, prepare for ministry, be with people, extend yourself beyond your comfort level. *Effort.* For hospitality you have to clean your house, prepare meals. *Money and resources.* It costs to purchase groceries, provide shelter, give to the church, support pastors and missionaries.

*But the rewards outweigh the costs!* You please Jesus! Ask Him to help you nurture a loving heart and generous spirit.

## 276 An Answer to Prayer

*And as Peter knocked at the door of the gate,*
*a girl named Rhoda came to answer.*
Acts 12:13

Mary, the mother of John Mark, was hosting a late prayer meeting. The believers were gathered to ask God to deliver Peter from prison and certain execution. Suddenly someone knocked at the gate. Mary's maid, Rhoda, went to see who was there. (Note that she was on duty late at night as others—and maybe she—prayed!) Peter was there! Rhoda was so excited that instead of opening the door she ran back inside to share the good news. Imagine her shrieks of joy as she burst into the room filled with pray-ers. "Peter's here! It's Peter! Hallelujah! Our prayers have been answered! He's here!"

And what reaction did Rhoda get? As faithful and effervescent as she was, this dear woman, whose name means "rose," was called Manias by the others. They basically said, "You're a maniac! You're crazy!" Then they conceded, "Maybe it's Peter's ghost?" Finally they went to the door...and there stood Peter in the flesh!

Do you wonder how Rhoda handled the name-calling, the put-downs, and the unjust criticism she received? We're not told, but we know how godly women respond in such circumstances...

- Put on a gentle and quiet spirit, which is very precious in the sight of God (1 Peter 3:4).
- A servant of the Lord must not quarrel, but be gentle to all and patient (2 Timothy 2:24).
- Love suffers long, is kind, does not behave rudely, and is not provoked (1 Corinthians 13:4-5).
- The fruit of the Spirit is love, joy, peace, longsuffering, kindness, goodness, faithfulness, gentleness, and self-control (Galatians 5:22-23).

The next time you're misunderstood or unjustly criticized, look to the Lord's good Word for His guidance and to His Spirit for the ability to exhibit a gracious spirit.

## 277 What If My Husband Doesn't Believe in Jesus?

*And behold, a certain disciple was there, named Timothy, the son of a certain Jewish woman who believed, but his father was Greek.*
ACTS 16:1

Nike is the Greek goddess of victory, and the name means "conquering well." Today we meet Eunice, and her name derives from Nike. What victory do we see in her life?

Eunice was the mother of Timothy, one of the apostle Paul's most trusted companions and disciples. She was married to a Greek, a Gentile, an unbeliever. What instruction does the Bible give to those married to unbelievers?

- Demonstrate your affection and respect for your mate (Ephesians 5:33).
- Pray for your husband and marriage (James 5:16).
- Praise, encourage, build up, and communicate your love to your man (Colossians 4:6).
- Put on a gentle and quiet spirit (1 Peter 3:4), which is priceless to the Lord and helpful in marriage.
- When trouble arises hold your tongue, breathe a prayer, and find in the Lord the wisdom and grace you need to give a soft, appropriate answer (Proverbs 15:1, 28).
- Draw encouragement from the women in the Bible who loved God and were married to men who weren't believers. Esther (the book of Esther) and Abigail (1 Samuel 25) stand out as victors in this special role.
- Stay with your husband (1 Corinthians 7:10).
- Respond to negatives with good (Romans 12:21).

Your faith in Jesus can and will sustain you in your marriage—and may even soften the heart of your spouse.

## 278 The Power of a Woman

*Lydia heard us...The Lord opened her heart to heed the things spoken by Paul.*
Acts 16:14

Lydia was a very influential and take-charge woman. Into her heart were sown the seeds from which the church at Philippi grew. Consider some of the threads that make up the tapestry of her life.

- *She was a woman.* This obvious fact is important. You see, ten *men* were required to organize a synagogue, and apparently this quorum was missing in Philippi. Not having a synagogue in which to gather, the women met outside the town to pray.
- *She was a worshiper.* Lydia believed in the God of Israel, but she hadn't yet become a follower of Jesus Christ.
- *She was attentive.* One day down by the river the apostle Paul showed up at the women's prayer meeting, sat down, and began talking about Jesus. Lydia listened.
- *She was baptized.* As the truth about Jesus Christ penetrated Lydia's open heart, she accepted God's gracious gift of salvation. The *first* thing she did as a Christian was to get baptized.
- *She was influential.* Lydia wasn't baptized alone. Evidently she was instrumental in her entire household—relatives and servants alike—becoming believers.
- *She was hospitable.* Not only did she open her heart, but she also opened her home. Paul's message had helped her, and now she wanted to help him and his friends by providing a home-away-from-home for them.

In what ways is your life similar to Lydia's? Are you worshiping regularly with other believers? Are you attentive and open to the teachings of God's Word? Have you been baptized according to the Lord's command? Are you sharing Christ with other people?

# 279 Success & Wealth

*So they went out of the prison and entered the house of Lydia.*
ACTS 16:40

Yesterday we began noticing the intricacies of the beautiful tapestry of Lydia's life. Let's look at a few more strands.

- *She was a businesswoman.* Lydia lived in Thyatira, a city famous for expensive purple dye. Now living in Philippi, she sold clothes made from her deep-purple fabrics. These goods were very expensive. As a dealer of these highly prized garments, Lydia prospered.
- *She was generous.* Lydia cared for her relatives and servants. She also opened her home for the cause of Christ. Immediately after her conversion and baptism, she insisted Paul and his companions stay with her. Evidently her house was spacious because the budding church in Philippi met there.

God blessed Lydia with ability, creativity, and a strong work ethic, just as He's blessed you and me. He expects us to live out our priorities, to work willingly with our hands, and to do what we do heartily for Him. With the blessings of ability and prosperity comes responsibility. We must remember...

- *the source of our wealth.* We're not to think, "My power and the might of my hand have gained me this wealth." We're to "remember the LORD your God, for it is He who gives you power to get wealth" (Deuteronomy 8:17-18).
- *the purpose of wealth.* We're "not to be haughty, nor to trust in uncertain riches." We're to trust in "the living God, who gives us richly all things to enjoy...[and to] do good, that [we may] be rich in good works, ready to give, willing to share" (1 Timothy 6:17-18).

## 280 A Magnificent Team for the Lord

*And [Paul] found a certain Jew named Aquila... with his wife Priscilla...and he came to them.*
Acts 18:2

Bookends. That image comes to mind when I think of Priscilla and her husband, Aquila. This woman and her husband were a magnificent team as they served God's kingdom.

- *Servants*—Always mentioned together, Priscilla and Aquila stand as a team in marriage and ministry.
- *Itinerants*—Each time this couple is mentioned, they're in a different location. Each city was a key site for ministry.
- *Industrious*—They were tent-makers and leather workers.
- *Hospitable*—They opened their hearts and homes. They took in Paul, and the church in Ephesus met in their home (1 Corinthians 16:19).
- *Persevering*—Expelled from Rome, they knew persecution, yet they remained faithful to the Lord.
- *Knowledgeable*—Priscilla and Aquila listened attentively to Paul as he taught Jews and Greeks alike, gaining the knowledge they needed to serve Jesus.
- *Willing*—This husband-wife duo would do anything, go anywhere, do whatever for the cause of Christ.

*If you're married,* you're to support your husband's dreams, hold up your end of the responsibility for family and home, and shoulder your part of the load of life.

*If you're single,* the pursuit of these godly qualities is important too!

## 281 *The Blessings of Being Single*

*Now this man had four virgin daughters who prophesied.*
ACTS 21:9

Meet four single women who loved and served God. Although only one verse in the Holy Scriptures speaks about these women, we know they served God in a very special way. What made their service unique?

*Their father*—The first men selected to serve in the church after Jesus ascended into heaven were described as "men of good reputation, full of the Holy Spirit and wisdom" and "full of faith" (Acts 6:3, 5). Philip was among the seven men who met these standards, and he was the father of these four single women. What a blessing for them to have such a godly heritage and spiritual model at home.

*Their ministry*—As we've noted, only a handful of women are mentioned that God empowered to prophesy to His people. These four beloved sisters are in that category along with Miriam, Deborah, Huldah, and Anna.

*Their singleness*—Scripture sets forth singleness as a sacred calling: "There is a difference between a wife and a virgin. The unmarried woman cares about the things of the Lord, that she may be holy both in body and in spirit. But she who is married cares about the things of the world—how she may please her husband" (1 Corinthians 7:34). A single woman can be wholly dedicated to the Lord and His work.

Being single allows you to serve Jesus in a special and unique way. Don't succumb to pressure to marry. The Lord completes each woman's life, whether she's married or single. Embrace your special opportunity—a high calling and high privilege—and serve Christ wholeheartedly.

## 282 Radiant Servanthood

*I commend to you Phoebe our sister,*
*who is a servant of the church in Cenchrea.*
ROMANS 16:1

Everyone needs help. There is so much to do and so many responsibilities to juggle, not to mention sorrows to bear and ailments to cope with. And the apostle Paul was no different. Second Corinthians 11 lists the many trials he faced. In the face of those trials Paul had Phoebe to help him. Phoebe, meaning "bright and radiant," definitely stands as a shining example of the faithful servanthood God desires in each of us. Three special titles describe her.

- *A sister*—Paul calls Phoebe "our sister." A devoted and committed member of the family of God, Phoebe was a Christian sister to Paul and the other saints.
- *A servant*—The apostle commends Phoebe as "a servant of the church." The honored title "servant," from which we derive "deacon" and "deaconess," denotes one who serves any and all in the church.
- *A helper*—Paul praises Phoebe, "She has been a helper of many and of myself also." In Greek, "helper" refers to a trainer in the Olympic games who stood by the athletes to see they were properly trained and girded for competition. "Helper" means "one who stands by in case of need."

God's message to us is clear. As sisters who love God, we're to be in faithful attendance at church, to be ready in case a need arises, and to willingly meet any needs. Such dedicated, selfless service shimmers in our dark world.

P.S. Like Paul, you too can thank God for Phoebe because she most likely delivered the incredible book of Romans to Rome for Paul. As one scholar aptly wrote, "Phoebe carried under the folds of her robe the whole future of Christian theology."[74]

## 283 Developing the Heart of a Servant

*I commend to you Phoebe our sister,*
*who...has been a helper of many and of myself also.*
ROMANS 16:1-2

As Robert Cunningham quipped, "Some folks are poor spellers. They think service is spelled serve us!" But that's not the Bible's picture! God's Word gives us Phoebe as an example. She was described by the apostle Paul as a sister, servant, and helper. Before we leave her shining life of ministry, take to heart these thoughts about helping others.

*Serve all*—Phoebe served the famous apostle Paul and those in her small-town home church at Cenchrea. *Check:* Do you offer the same heartfelt service to everyone, regardless of their stature?

*Serve humbly*—In the early church a servant and helper cared for the sick and the poor, ministered to martyrs and prisoners, and quietly assisted the people and ministry of the church whenever help was needed. *Check:* Are you happy to serve in the shadows—satisfied that the work of Christ is furthered, glad to be assisting those efforts, and joyfully meeting the needs of others without recognition? Do you serve faithfully and quietly?

*Serve always*—Dear Phoebe's service seems constant. Probably a widow, she "has been a helper," so she continues to do in the present what she'd done in the past. Hers was a distance runner's track record of faithfulness. Having served faithfully in the past, she was still serving as she carried Paul's precious letter from Corinth to Rome. *Check:* Are you a servant in the present and brimming with plans for serving in the future?

## 284 The Truth About Suffering

*Greet Priscilla and Aquila...who risked their own necks for my life.*
Romans 16:3-4

Throughout his ministry Louis B. Talbot, the founder of Talbot Theological Seminary, kept *Foxe's Book of Martyrs* on his bed stand. Each night before turning out the light he read about the persecution and suffering of one of God's saints.

Today we visit Priscilla again, a believer who probably came close to death as a martyr. She and her husband, Aquila, somehow, at some time, intervened to save the apostle Paul's life. We have no details other than Paul's acknowledgment that they put their lives in harm's way on his account. While we may shudder at the thought of persecution, the Bible isn't shy about addressing the fact we'll suffer.

*Expect suffering.* We must expect persecution and suffering in this dark and fallen world as we reflect the light of Christ. "All who desire to live godly in Christ Jesus will suffer persecution" (2 Timothy 3:12). "For to you it has been granted on behalf of Christ, not only to believe in Him, but also to suffer for His sake" (Philippians 1:29).

*Rejoice in suffering.* Overflowing joy in Christ regardless of circumstances is the reward for those who suffer for righteousness in this life. "Beloved, do not think it strange concerning the fiery trial which is to try you, as though some strange thing happened to you; but rejoice to the extent that you partake of Christ's sufferings, that when His glory is revealed, you may also be glad with exceeding joy" (1 Peter 4:12-13).

What awaits those of us who might meet a martyr's death like Priscilla faced? As Dr. Talbot loved to say, "It would be wonderful for a martyr to die with tears in his eyes, only to open his eyes and find the hand of the Lord Jesus wiping those tears away."[75]

# 285 Dedicated Service Without Recognition

*Greet Mary...Junia...Tryphena and Tryphosa...Persis... Rufus['s mother]...Julia...Nereus['s sister].*
ROMANS 16:6-15

"Lesser lights" was coined by writer and preacher Chuck Swindoll to identify those saints in Scripture who, although in God's economy are no less important than others, are not as well-known to us because very little is written about them. The roll call of "lesser lights" includes eight women Paul greeted in his letter to the Christians in Rome.

- *Mary*—Paul declares that Mary worked hard for the Roman church, toiling to the point of weariness and exhaustion.
- *Junia*—Paul greeted her as a kinsman.
- *Tryphena and Tryphosa*—These two sisters in Christ may have been twins. Although their names mean delicate and dainty, they labored strenuously for the Lord.
- *Persis*—Beloved by all who knew her, this woman worked hard for the cause of Christ.
- *Rufus' mother*—This dear woman cared for Paul as if he were her own son.
- *Julia and Nereus' sister*—These two women were outstanding members of and leaders in the church at Rome.[76]

What does it take to stand tall among Paul's friends and colaborers? The bottom-line quality seems to be hard work for God's kingdom. These women labored to the point of weariness and fatigue. They tirelessly served the Lord and His people. Have you lately considered the intensity of your labor for Christ's church and for His sheep? Pray about it and ask God if your work intensity needs to be turned up a notch or two.

If you ever feel like a "lesser light," remember that the Lord knows all your efforts! Your name is known in heaven. Indeed, it is written in the Lamb's Book of Life (Revelation 21:27).

## 286 A Dynamic Duo

*Euodia and...Syntyche...these women who labored with me in the gospel.*
PHILIPPIANS 4:2-3

They were heroes in the church. Euodia and Syntyche were prominent members of the Philippi church and apparently accomplished many great deeds for God. What else do we know?

- They were probably among the women who met to pray with Lydia by the river outside Philippi when the apostle Paul arrived and preached the gospel (Acts 16:13). Quite possibly that was the day of their salvation.
- They were probably deaconesses in the church founded in Philippi. In that position, they would have been involved in serving the body and teaching other women.
- They toiled side by side with Paul. He reports that Euodia and Syntyche labored and strove as fellow athletes in the arena with him.

We too can make a meaningful contribution to the Lord's causes. We are gifted by God to profit other believers (1 Corinthians 12:7). While our work may not be alongside someone like the apostle Paul, our efforts are important and count greatly in God's kingdom (1 Corinthians 15:58). When we do our part, when we labor selflessly for God, the gospel is shared, people are introduced to Jesus, members of the body of Christ are edified, and the world sees the reality of Jesus Christ.

*A warning.* The efforts of this ministry team for Christ were tarnished by their problems with one another, with their inability "to agree with each other." After all they did for the cause of Christ and for Paul, and after all the energy they valiantly expended in the arena for Christ, the final word on these women points to their contentiousness and the disruption of the Lord's work. As you serve, pray that this kind of closing statement will never be made about you or your ministry.

## 287 *A Godly Heritage*

***The genuine faith that is in you, which dwelt first in your grandmother Lois and your mother Eunice.***
2 Timothy 1:5

Today's Scripture passage pairs the portraits of two outstanding women who loved God—the mother/daughter team of Lois and Eunice. Let's get to know Lois today and then meet her daughter tomorrow.

- *Her name.* Lois' name most likely means "agreeable," and we know the apostle Paul found that to be true.
- *Her background.* A devout Jewess, Lois apparently instructed her daughter, Eunice, and her grandson, Timothy, in the Old Testament scriptures, thus preparing their hearts to hear the words about eternal life through Jesus Christ, which Paul preached when he passed through their hometown of Lystra (Acts 16:1).
- *Her faith.* Commendations by others show respect and honor. Paul lauds Lois' faith as genuine and sincere.
- *Her legacy.* Have you heard of Timothy? He's the young Christian who accompanied Paul as he preached the gospel of Jesus and helped establish churches throughout the Mediterranean. This young man became Paul's true son in the faith and someone Paul could point to as "like-minded" with himself (Philippians 2:20).
- *Her title.* Many grandmothers are mentioned in the Bible, but Lois is the only one referred to by the honored and revered label "grandmother."

Mothers and grandmothers are on assignment to teach God's Word to our children and to our children's children.

## 288 Truth Always Shines

*The genuine faith that is in you, which dwelt first in your grandmother Lois and your mother Eunice.*
2 Timothy 1:5

Yesterday we met Lois, a godly mother and grandmother. Now let's look at the picture of Eunice, Lois' daughter. As we consider her portrait, are you surprised by one of the brush strokes that make up the details of Eunice's daily life? She had an unbelieving husband (Acts 16:1). Eunice was a believing Jewess who shared her faith with her son Timothy, inspiring him to believe in Jesus Christ.

Are you married to a nonbeliever? Do you know women in that position? Be encouraged! If you've worried that your children will not discern the truth about Jesus when another belief system and another set of values are represented by their father daily, be assured through Eunice that truth always shines brighter. Also remember your children are "holy," set apart to the Lord by the presence of Christ in you (1 Corinthians 7:14). And because Christ lives in you, Christ lives in your home! That means your children are exposed to a godly witness, whether they want it or not and regardless if they're aware of it. They have divine blessing and protection because of you, their believing mother.[77]

So take heart! Be faithful to sow the seeds of love and divine truth. Be diligent to share the Scriptures with your little ones. Take every opportunity to pray with them and for them. Share the wonderful stories about Jesus and the specifics about how He can become their Savior. Be steadfast in your faith...and in your faith for your children's spiritual development. Above all, live out God's love in your life. And when you're discouraged and it seems your godly efforts for your children are failing, press on remembering that "He who is in you is greater than he who is in the world" (1 John 4:4).

## 289 *A Portrait in the Great Hall of Faith*

*By faith Sarah herself also received strength to conceive seed, and she bore a child when she was past the age, because she judged Him faithful who had promised.*
HEBREWS 11:11

Shhh! Today we tiptoe into the hallowed Hall of Faith (Hebrews 11). This is God's portrait gallery of great men and women who have loved Him through the ages. There are the larger-than-life pictures of Noah, Abraham, Isaac, Jacob, Joseph, Moses, and Joshua. But just as grand is the portrait of Sarah, wife of Abraham, who possessed a strong-as-steel faith (1 Peter 3:1-6). What merited her inclusion?

*Motherhood*—This blessing came late to the long-barren Sarah. At age 90 she gave birth to Isaac. Sarah was a fierce, loyal mother (see Genesis 21).

*Mother of a nation*—Sarah has been esteemed as a mother figure to God's chosen nation of Israel. From Sarah and her husband, Abraham, through their son, Isaac, come—through faith—all true believers (Romans 4:16).

*Mother of faith*—What was Sarah's outstanding act of faith? Although there were a few "hiccups," Sarah steadfastly considered God faithful and able to follow through on His promise of a son in her old age.

"With God nothing will be impossible" (Luke 1:37). Are you facing trials? Does difficulty or affliction affect every moment? Identify your greatest challenge, and then look to the Lord with faith. Remind yourself what the angel of the Lord asked Sarah—"Is anything too hard for the LORD?" (Genesis 18:14). The answer is no!

## 290 The Quiet Strength of Unwavering Faith

*By faith Moses, when he was born, was hidden three months by his parents, because...they were not afraid of the king's command.*
HEBREWS 11:23

As we continue walking through God's Hall of faith we next pause before the portrait of Jochebed. Behold her quiet strength that comes with unwavering faith.

- *Faith of her fathers*—Her father, Levi, and her brother Kohath were priests. This suggests much about Jochebed's heritage and upbringing. Hers was a family set apart to serve the Lord.
- *Faith as a wife*—When Jochebed became the wife of Amram, a priest, her faith joined with his and another family of faith was born.
- *Faith as a mother*—Defying Pharaoh's command that every son born to the Hebrew people be killed, Jochebed hid baby Moses. She wasn't afraid of the king and his power. Then she trusted God to protect her babe as she placed Moses in a basket in the Nile River. Jochebed loved God, and that love dispelled all fear and enabled her to act in faith and courage. Jochebed passed her godly heritage on to all three of her children. Aaron and Moses became priests, and Miriam served alongside them (Micah 6:4).

I encourage you to look for ways to live out your faith. Even seemingly small choices can require faith and courage, and those situations help perfect faith. As you focus on God's all-sufficient power and grace, problems will dim and obstacles diminish as He demonstrates His faithfulness and your faith in Him grows.

## 291 *A Before-and-After Masterpiece*

*By faith the harlot Rahab did not perish with those who did not believe, when she had received the spies with peace.*

Hebrews 11:31

It's been a long-time practice of artists to paint over their less impressive works. Sometimes they create a grand masterpiece on a canvas that once held a less-than-remarkable picture. Today, we see just such a canvas—the before-and-after portrait of Rahab.

- *A prostitute*—Rahab was referred to as "Rahab the harlot."
- *A heroine*—Rahab hid Joshua's spies from her king, saved their lives by sending them out of town a secret way, declared her faith in their God, marked out her home with a scarlet cord, and trusted the Israelites to honor their word. She waited for his army and counted on Joshua's mercy.
- *A hallowed vessel*—Believing in the holy and mighty God of Israel transformed Rahab into a woman fit for God's use. What the prophet promised became true of Rahab, "Though your sins are like scarlet, they shall be as white as snow; though they are red like crimson, they shall be as wool" (Isaiah 1:18).

Do you consider your life permanently tainted by past failures, poor decisions, and sickening sin? You don't have to! Welcome the cleansing that is yours through faith in Jesus Christ, the only One who can wash away your sins. Declare along with Rahab that "the Lord...God, He is God in heaven above and on earth beneath" and allow Him to wash your crimson sins as white as snow (Joshua 2:11; Isaiah 1:18). Let the Lord transform your life, your "before" picture, into something lovely and worthy to hang in the halls of heaven.

## 292 Joining God's Hall of Faith

*For God so loved the world that He gave His only begotten Son, that whoever believes in Him should not perish but have everlasting life. For God did not send His Son into the world to condemn the world, but that the world through Him might be saved.*
JOHN 3:16-17

How can you gain a place in God's great hall of faith? John 1:12 says, "As many as received Him, to them He gave the right to become children of God, to those who *believe in His name*." You need to do two important things.

*Receive*—To become a child of God, you must receive Jesus Christ as your personal Savior and acknowledge His death and resurrection on your behalf for your sins and to give you eternal life with Him.

*Believe*—Jesus Christ is the living Word of God, and God calls you to acknowledge Him as God-in-flesh and place your faith in Him as Savior and Lord.

Have you yielded your life to Jesus Christ? Have you received God's grace gift of salvation and eternal life through Jesus? Believing in Jesus as God-in-flesh and receiving Him into your heart and life by faith qualifies you for a place in the portrait halls of heaven. If you want to take this step of faith now, pray this simple prayer:

*Jesus, I'm a sinner. But today I'm turning away from my sins and following You. I believe You died for my sins and rose again victorious over sin and death. I accept You right now as my personal Savior. Come into my life and help me follow You from this day forward. Thank You!*

I encourage you to daily stroll through the pages of the Bible for encouragement, excitement, and comfort.

# Notes

1. John Milton, *Eve.*
2. Herbert Lockyer, *All the Promises of the Bible.*
3. Donald Grey Barnhouse, *Let Me Illustrate* (Grand Rapids, MI: Fleming H. Revell, 1967), pp. 253-54.
4. Proverbs 11:14.
5. Herbert Lockyer, *The Women of the Bible* (Grand Rapids, MI: Zondervan Publishing House, 1975), p. 111.
6. Neil S. Wilson, ed., *The Handbook of Bible Application* (Wheaton, IL: Tyndale House Publishers, Inc., 1992), p. 485.
7. Philip Melancthon.
8. Elizabeth George, *A Woman After God's Own Heart* (Eugene, OR: Harvest House Publishers, 1997), p. 29.
9. Mrs. Charles E. Cowman, *Streams in the Desert,* vol. 1 (Grand Rapids, MI: Zondervan Publishing House, 1965), p. 331.
10. Ben Patterson, *Waiting* (Downers Grove, IL: InterVarsity Press, 1989), p. i.
11. Anne Ortlund, *Building a Great Marriage* (Old Tappan, NJ: Fleming H. Revell Company, 1984), p. 146.
12. Adapted from 1 Corinthians 13:7-8.
13. V. Raymond Edman.
14. Merrill F. Unger, *Unger's Bible Dictionary* (Chicago: Moody Press, 1972), p. 348.
15. Lord Dewar.
16. Horace Bushnell.
17. Phil Whisenhunt.
18. Stephen G. Green.
19. Ruth Vaughn.
20. See Judges 4:4; 2 Kings 22:14; Luke 2:36; Acts 21:9.
21. Adapted from principles found in J. Oswald Sanders, *Spiritual Leadership* (Chicago: Moody Press, 1967).
22. Charles W. Landon.
23. *The Zondervan Pictorial Encyclopedia of the Bible*, vol. 5, p. 575.
24. See Exodus 7–12; 11–12; 14; 14:30-31.
25. Adapted from Herbert Lockyer, *The Women of the Bible* (Grand Rapids, MI: Zondervan Publishing House, 1975), p. 180.
26. Adapted from *The Zondervan Pictorial Encyclopedia,* vol. 5, pp. 890-91.
27. John Oxenham.
28. Exodus 12:41; 7–12; 14:9; 14:22; 14:27; Deuteronomy 1:3.
29. Elizabeth George, *Beautiful in God's Eyes* (Eugene, OR: Harvest House Publishers, 1998), pp. 13-16.
30. Julie Nixon Eisenhower, *Special People* (New York: Ballantine Books, 1977), pp. 3-37.
31. Psalm 99:5.
32. J.H. Morrison.
33. Matthew Henry, *Matthew Henry Commentary,* vol. 2, pp. 204-05.
34. Information from Kenneth W. Osbeck, *Amazing Grace* (Grand Rapids, MI: Kregel Publications, 1990), p. 216.
35. John MacArthur, *The MacArthur Study Bible* (Nashville: Word Publishing, 1997), p. 373.

36. Lockyer, *Women of the Bible,* pp. 144-49.
37. William Temple, Archbishop of Canterbury.
38. James Strong, *Strong's Exhaustive Concordance of the Bible* (Nashville: Abingdon Press, 1973), p. 95.
39. Lockyer, *Women of the Bible,* p. 36.
40. Adapted from Herbert Lockyer, *All the Kings and Queens of the Bible* (Grand Rapids, MI: Zondervan Publishing House, 1971), p. 212.
41. Adapted from Bill Gothard Ministries material.
42. Adapted from Russell Kelso Carter's hymn "Standing on the Promises," 1886.
43. Reverend E.H. Hamilton, China Inland Mission missionary, cited in Kathleen White, *John and Betty Stam: The Story of the Young American Missionaries Who Gave Their Lives for Christ and China* (Minneapolis: Bethany House, 1989), p. 120.
44. Richard C. Halverson, "Perspective" newsletter, Oct. 26, 1977. (Gender changed.)
45. Proverbs 31 woman material is drawn from Elizabeth George, *Beautiful in God's Eyes: The Treasures of the Proverbs 31 Woman* (Eugene, OR: Harvest House Publishers, 1998). For further insights into the Proverbs 31 woman, read this practical and inspirational verse-by-verse summary.
46. Cheryl Julia Dunn, "A Study of Proverbs," master thesis (Biola University, 1993), p. 25.
47. Douglas Malloch, "A Woman's Love."
48. Stanley High, *Billy Graham.*
49. John MacArthur, "God's High Calling for Women," part 4 (Panorama City, CA: Word of Grace, #GC-54-17, 1986).
50. Edith Schaeffer, *What Is a Family?*
51. MacArthur, *MacArthur Study Bible,* p. 941.
52. *Life Application Bible* (Wheaton, IL: Tyndale House Publishers, Inc. and Youth for Christ, 1988), p. 1471.
53. "I Have Decided to Follow Jesus," praise chorus.
54. Lockyer, *Women of the Bible,* p. 225.
55. William Barclay, *The Letters of James and Peter,* rev. ed. (Philadelphia: The Westminster Press, 1976), p. 217.
56. Walter B. Knight, *Knight's Master Book of New Illustrations* (Grand Rapids, MI: Wm. B. Eerdmans Publishing Company, 1979), pp. 204-05.
57. Ibid.
58. Ibid.
59. Ibid.
60. J.A. Thompson, *Handbook of Life in Bible Times* (Downers Grove, IL: InterVarsity Press, 1986), pp. 83-85.
61. The contents of this devotion drawn from Elizabeth George, *Loving God with All Your Mind* (Eugene, OR: Harvest House Publishers, 1994), p. 183.
62. Knight, *Knight's Master Book,* pp. 204-05.
63. Ibid.
64. Gien Karssen, *Her Name Is Woman* (Colorado Springs: NavPress, 1975), p. 131.
65. Merrill F. Unger, *Unger's Bible Dictionary,* quoting Keil (Chicago: Moody Press, 1972), p. 1172.
66. William Barclay, *The Letters to the Corinthians,* rev. ed. (Philadelphia: The Westminster Press, 1975), p. 201.
67. German scholar Johann Albrecht Bengel.

68. Charles Caldwell Ryrie, *The Role of Women in the Church,* quoted material by Walter F. Adeney (Chicago: Moody Press, 1970), p. 34.
69. William Barclay, *The Gospel of Luke,* rev. ed. (Philadelphia: The Westminster Press, 1975), p. 97.
70. Oswald J. Smith, *The Man God Uses* (London: Marshall, Morgan, and Scott, 1932), pp. 52-57.
71. Judson W. Van Deventer, "I Surrender All," hymn, 1896.
72. Joseph H Gilmore, "He Leadeth Me," hymn, 1862.
73. Henry Drummond, *The Greatest Thing in the World.*
74. Marvin R. Vincent, *Word Studies in the New Testament,* vol. III, "The Epistles of Paul," quoting Renan (Grand Rapids, MI: Wm. B. Eerdmans Publishing Co., 1973), p. 177.
75. Quoted in Carol Talbot, *For This I Was Born* (Chicago: Moody Press, 1977), p. 208.
76. Adapted from John MacArthur, Jr., *The MacArthur New Testament Commentary,* Romans 9–6 (Chicago: Moody Press, 1994), pp. 364-69.
77. Elyse Fitzpatrick and Carol Cornish, *Women Helping Women* (Eugene, OR: Harvest House Publishers, 1997), pp. 207-19.